CONCISE DICTIONARY OF INFORMATION TECHNOLOGY & COMPUTER SCIENCE

A Perfect Reference tool for Computer & IT Professionals, Students, Technical writers & Other Readers

Editorial Board

V&S PUBLISHERS

Published by:

V&S PUBLISHERS

F-2/16, Ansari road, Daryaganj, New Delhi-110002
☎ 23240026, 23240027 •Fax: 011-23240028
Email: info@vspublishers.com

Regional Office : Hyderabad
5-1-707/1, Brij Bhawan (Beside Central Bank of India Lane)
Bank Street, Koti, Hyderabad - 500 095
☎ 040-24737290
E-mail: vspublishershyd@gmail.com

Branch : Mumbai
Flat No. 1Ground Floor, Sonmegh Building
No. 51, Karel Wadi, Thakurdwar, Mumbai - 400 002
☎ 022-22098268
E-mail: vspublishersmum@gmail.com

Follow us on:   

For any assistance sms **VSPUB** to **56161**

All books available at **www.vspublishers.com**

ISBN 978-93-505712-2-4

Edition: 2014

Printed at: Param Offsetters, Okhla, New Delhi

Publisher's Note

A fairly good response received from the market to eight dictionaries published last year on science and commerce subjects encouraged us to take up yet another dictionary witnessing a rapid growth in demand - **Concise Dictionary of Information Technology & Computer Science**. Like previous ones this again is a concise version. This edition is expected to fulfil the requirements of students, educationists, researchers, scholars, and writers.

Innumerable dictionaries are available in the market for use as a reference manual. Quite a number of these dictionaries come replete with jargon-filled *terms*; and as such don't quite connect to readers' curiosity level. On top of that, many of them fail to include new computer *terms* that keep finding their way into regular usage every other day. Absence of freshly coined *terms* contributes to difficulty in keeping up to date with definitions and explanations of new words.

Unlike other reference dictionaries that take readers' understanding of scientific *terms* for granted; and make short passing references while alluding to another *term* in the text, we have tried to be more specific and to-the-point. This dictionary has been written with the belief that an average reader is interested only in knowing what specific *terms* mean without getting burdened with heavy sounding inputs.

For easy reference *terms* have been arranged alphabetically. *Terms* that have come into the reckoning lately have been incorporated; and suitably explained such that a secondary and senior secondary student can grasp them easily. Illustrations and examples, where appropriate, have been added. Even an average reader, who has not made a special study of any science subject, explanations of computer terms will be found to be reasonably comprehensible.

This computer dictionary includes important scientific charts, tables, constants, conversion tables as appendices. A glossary of Nobel Prize winners and their contributions is an added attraction

We would be happy to have your views and comments for improving the content and quality of the book.

Contents

08/10BLocal Fibre

8-byte/10-byte local fibre. Fibre channel physical media that supports speeds up to 149.76 Mbps over multimode fibre.

10Base2

10-Mbps baseband Ethernet specification using 50-ohm thin coaxial cable. 10Base2, which is part of the IEEE 802.3 specification, has a distance limit of 185 metres per segment.

10Base5

10-Mbps baseband Ethernet specification using standard (thick) 50-ohm baseband coaxial cable. 10Base5, which is part of the IEEE 802.3 baseband physical layer specification, has a distance limit of 500 metres per segment.

10BaseF

10-Mbps baseband Ethernet specification that refers to the 10BaseFB, 10BaseFL, and 10BaseFP standards for Ethernet over fibre-optic cabling.

10BasefB

10-Mbps baseband Ethernet specification using fibre-optic cabling. 10BaseFB is part of the IEEE 10BaseF specification. It is not used to connect user stations, but instead provides a synchronous signalling backbone that allows additional segments and repeaters to be connected to the network. 10BaseFB segments can be up to 2,000 metres long.

10BasefP

10-Mbps fiber-passive baseband Ethernet specification using fiber-optic cabling. 10BaseFP ispart of the IEEE 10BaseF specification. It organizes a number of computers into a star topology without the use of repeaters. 10Base FP segments can be up to 500 metres long.

10BaseT

A specification of the IEEE 802.3 committee for the implementation of 10 Mbit Ethernet on unshielded twisted pair wiring.

10Broad36

10-Mbps broadband Ethernet specification using broadband coaxial cable. 10Broad36, which is part of the IEEE 802.3 specification, has a distance limit of 3,600 metres per segment.

100BaseFX

100-Mbps baseband Fast Ethernet specification using two strands of multimode fiber-optic cable per link. To guarantee proper signal timing, a 100BaseFX link exceed 400 meters in length. Based on the IEEE 802.3 standard.

100BaseT

A 100MB Ethernet specification using Level 5 UTP.

100BaseT4

100-Mbps baseband Fast Ethernet specification using four pairs of Category 3, 4, or 5UTP wiring. To guarantee proper signal timing, a 100BaseT4 segment cannot exceed 100 meters in length. Based on the IEEE 802.3 standard.

100BaseTX

100-Mbps baseband Fast Ethernet specification using two pairs of either UTP or STP wiring. The first pair of wires is used to receive data, the second is used to transmit. To guarantee proper signal timing a 100BaseTX segment cannot exceed 100 meters in length. Based on the IEEE 802.3 standard.

100BaseX

100-Mbps baseband Fast Ethernet specification that refers to the 100BaseFX and 100BaseTX standards for Fast Ethernet over fiber-optic cabling. Based on the IEEE 802.3 standard.

100VG-AnyLAN

100-Mbps Fast Ethernet and Token Ring media technology using four pairs of Category 3, 4, or 5 UTP cabling. This high-speed transport technology, developed by Hewlett-Packard, can be made to operate on existing 10BaseT Ethernet networks. Based on the IEEE 802.12 standard.

10BaseFL

10-Mbps baseband Ethernet specification using fiber-optic cabling. 10BaseFL is part of the IEEE10BaseF specification and, while able to interoperate with FOIRL, is designed to replace the FOIRL specification. 10BaseFL segments can be up to 1,000 meters long if used with FOIRL, and up to 2,000 meters if 10BaseFL is used exclusively.

4B/5B local fibre

4-byte/5-byte loc 100 Mbps over multimode fibre.

A&B bit signaling

Procedure used in T1 transmission facilities in which each of the 24 T1 subchannels devotes one bit of every sixth frame to the carrying of supervisory signaling information. Also called 24th channel signaling.

AA#

Altered Assembly number is the part number for a motherboard and all its attached components

AAL

ATM adaptation layer. Service-dependent sublayer of the data link layer. The AAL accepts data from different applications and presents it to the ATM layer in the form of 48-byte ATM payload segments. AALs consist of two sublayers, CS and SAR, AALs differ on the basis of the source-destination timing used, whether they use DBR or VBR, and whether they are used for connection-oriented or connectionless mode data transfer. At present, the four types of AAL recommended by the ITU-T are AAL1, AAL2, AAL3/4, and AAL5.

AAL1

ATM adaptation layer 1. One of four AALs recommended by the ITU-T. AAL1 is used for connection-oriented, delay-sensitive services requiring constant bit rates, such as uncompressed video and other isochronous traffic.

AAL2

ATM adaptation layer 2. One of four AALs recommended by the ITU-T. AAL2 is used for connection-oriented services that support a variable bit rate, such as some isochronous video and voice traffic.

AAL3/4

ATM adaptation layer 3/4. One of four AALs (merger from two initially distinct adaptation layers) recommended by the ITU-T. AAL 3/4 supports both connectionless and connection oriented links, but is primarily used for the transmission of SMDS packets over ATM networks.

AAL5

ATM adaptation layer 5. One of four AALs recommended by the ITU-T. AAL5 supports connection-oriented, VBR services, and is used predominantly for the transfer of classic IP over ATM and LANE traffic. AAL5 uses SEAL and is the least complex of the current AAL recommendations. It offers low bandwidth over head and simpler processing requirements in exchange for reduced bandwidth capacity and error-recovery capability.

AARP

AppleTalk Address Resolution Protocol. Protocol in the AppleTalk protocol stack that maps a data-link address to a network address.

AARP probe packets

Packets transmitted by AARP that determine whether a randomly selected node ID is being used by another node in a nonextended AppleTalk network. If the node ID is not being used, the sending node uses that node ID. If the node ID is being used, the sending node chooses a different ID and sends more AARP probe packets.

AB switch

A device used to switch an incoming cable to either an 'A' output or 'B' output. Before the wide-spread introduction of dual output video cards, AB Switches were in common use with VGA outputs to switch from one monitor to another. However AB switches were produced to switch many types of cable interfaces, as in switching from one RS232 output to another, or switching between TV antennas as shown in the graphic to the right.

ABM

Asynchronous Balanced Mode. An HDLC (and derivative protocol) communication mode supporting peer-oriented, point-to- point communications between two stations, where either station can initiate transmission.

ABR

1. Available bit rate. QOS class defined by the ATM Forum for ATM networks. ABR is used for connections that do not require timing relationships between source and destination. ABR provides no guarantees in terms of cell loss or delays, providing only best-effort service. Traffic sources adjust their transmission rate in response to information they receive describing the statue of the network and its capability to successfully deliver data.
2. Area border router. Router located on the border of one or more OSPF areas that connects those areas to the backbone network. ABRs are considered members of both the OSPF backbone and the attached areas. They therefore

maintain routing tables describing both the backbone topology and the topology of the other areas.

ABS plastic

A type of plastic formed by Acrylonitrile Butadiene Styrene and other chemicals.

Absolute address

The location of a storage element.

Absolute gain

The ratio of the signal level at the output of the device to that of its input under a specified set of operating conditions.

Absolute maximum rating

The electrical rating at or above which damage to the device will occur, to include supply voltage, input/ and output voltages and junction temperature. Stress ratings that do not imply functional operation.

Absolute positioning

Using pixel coordinates to position GUI components.

Absolute reference

A cell or range reference in a formula whose location remains the same (absolute) when copied.

Absorption

Dissipation of radio or sound waves as they interact with matter. The absorbing of light waves without reflection or refraction.

Absorption wavemeter

An instrument used to measure audio frequencies.

Absorption, law

In Boolean algebra, the law which states that the odd term will be absorbed when a term is combined by logical multiplication with the logical sum of that term and another term, or when a term is combined by logical addition with the logical product of one term and another term (for example, A(A + B) = A + AB = A).

Abstract class

A class that cannot have direct instances but whose descendents can have instances; a class that has declared one or more methods for which it does not provide definitions (i.e. abstract methods).

Abstract data type (ADT)

A data declaration packaged together with the functions that operate on it.

Abstraction

A mental facility that permits humans to view real-world problems with varying degrees of detail depending on the current context of the problem; the process of focusing on the essential, inherent aspects of an entity and ignoring its accidental properties; the selective examination of certain aspects of a problem.

AC

Alternating Current. An electrical power transmission system in which the direction of current flow alternates on a periodic basis.

AC coupled amplifier

An amplifier circuit that uses AC Coupling to block DC between amplifier stages. In the circuit to the right, C3 blocks the DC component of Q1 from effecting the operation of Q2. This circuit style is also called RC coupling, with the resistors also affecting the signal between stages. Same as DC Blocking.

AC coupling

The interconnection between two circuits through a capacitor, transformer or other device which passes AC voltage but blocks any DC component. C3 in the circuit to the right is a DC blocking capacitor.

AC generator

[Alternator] A rotating machine that converts mechanical energy into alternating current.

AC power plug

A male connector designed to carry 120v or 240 volts. .

AC resistance

The opposition to the flow of current without regard to phase shift or complex impedance.

AC/DC power adapter

A device that converts AC power (electrical outlet power) to DC power (battery power).

AC'97

Audio Codec '97 is a specification for a high quality, 16- or 20-bit audio architecture used in many desktop systems.

Accelerated life testing

A test used to subject a component, device or system to extreme conditions to determine the useful life of the device under test [DUT], which includes operating at elevated temperatures to simulate long term operation.

Accelerating anode

An electrode charged several thousand volts positive and used to accelerate electrons toward the front of a Cathode-Ray Tube.

Acceleration servosystem

A servo-system that controls the acceleration (rate of change in velocity) of a load.

Accelerator

A hardware addition to an existing computing device that increases the computer's processing speed and capabilities.

Accelerometer

A device that measures the acceleration to which it is subjected and develops a signal proportional to it.

Acceptor impurity

An impurity which, when added to a semiconductor, accepts one electron from a neighboring atom and creates a hole in the lattice structure of the crystal. Also called Trivalent Impurity.

Access

The reading or writing of data; as a verb, to gain entry to data. Most commonly used in connection with information access, via a user ID, and qualified by an indication as to the kinds of access that are permitted. For example, read-only access means that the contents of the file may be read but not altered or erased.

Access bus

Is a low speed 4-wire serial bus once used on Personal Computers. Access.Bus uses the I2C [IIC] bus as the electrical hardware interface. The Access bus has a maximum speed is 100kbps over a maximum cable distance of 10 meters, however a repeater may be used. The 4 wires of the interface bus are power/ground, Send Data [SDA] and Serial Clock [SCL].

Access control list

A list of the services available on a server, each with a list of the hosts permitted to use the service.

Access list

List kept by routers to control access to or from the router for a number of services. For example, the list can prevent packets with a certain IP address from leaving a particular interface on the router.

Access method

The type of Media Access Control method that a node uses to gain control of a network.

Access point

Stand-alone Wi-Fi hub that allows any computer that has a Wi-Fi network adapter to communicate with another computer and to connect to the Internet. This device is typically used in an enterprise or corporate environment with a large number of users.

Access time

The difference in time between when data is requested and when data is delivered. The time lapsed between a given command and when the function is performed. The time for the [disk drive] access arm to reach the desired track and the delay for the rotation of the disk to bring the required sector under the read-write mechanism.

Access transparency

A type of transparency that enables local and remote information objects to be accessed using identical operations.

Accessory

An assembly of a group of parts or a unit which is not always required for the operation of a set or unit as originally designed but serves to extend the functions or capabilities of the set, such as headphones for a radio set supplied with a loudspeaker, a separate power unit for use with a set having a built-in power supply, or a remote control unit for use with a set having integral controls.

Accident report

A document that should be filled out by anyone involved in workplace accidents/injuries, regardless of however minor they might be.

Account

Your subscription to a networked computer system.

Account name

Same as your login ID or user ID. The word you type at the "Login:" prompt; your electronic name.

Accumulator

A register that both stores a number and adds to other numbers loaded into the register.

Accuracy

Referring to how closely a test instrument's measurements compare to a standard value, usually expressed as a percentage of the value measured.

ACF

Advanced Communications Function. A group of SNA products that provides distributed processing and resource sharing.

ACF/NCP

Advanced Communications Function/ Network Control Program. The primary SNA NCP. ACF/NCP resides in the communications controller and interfaces with the SNA access method in the host processor to control network communications.

Acknowledge character

A transmission control character transmitted by the receiving station.

Acknowledgment
Notification sent from one network device to another to acknowledge that some event (for example, receipt of a message) has occurred. Sometimes abbreviated ACK.

Acorn tube
A small tube, used in low power uhf circuits, with closely spaced electrodes and no base. The tube is connected to its circuits by short wire pins that are sealed in a glass or ceramic envelope.

Acoustic noise
The unintended sound a component produces while operating. Some fields apply this to mean an audible sound, while other fields take it to mean any sound.

Acoustic wave
A sound wave.

Acoustics
The science of sound.

ACPI
Advanced Configuration and Power Interface is a specification for power management.

Acquisition
The process of acquiring synchronism.

Acquisition number
A unique number given to an item of inventory

Acquisition time
In a communications system, the time interval required to attain [clock] synchronism.

ACR
Allows cell rate. Parameter defined by the ATM Forum for ATM traffic management. ACR varies between the MCR and the PCR, and is dynamically controlled using congestion control mechanisms.

ACSE
Association control service element. An OSI convention used to establish, maintain or terminate a connection between two applications.

Action
An instantaneous operation. Actions are associated with events and are usually formal in nature.

Active component
A component that draws current or some type of gain.

Active filter
A filter that uses an amplifier in addition to passive components. For example an Active Low Pass Filter Circuit.

Active high
Refers to a non-inverted output, the output is true when high and false when low. When the Sum-of-Products expression is true the output is high.

Active hub
Multiported device that amplifies LAN transmission signals.

Active listening
Responding to what you hear, indicating you are listening.

Active low
Refers to an inverted output, the output is true when low and false when high. When the Sum-of-Products expression is true the output is low.

Active monitor
Device responsible for managing a Token Ring. A network node is selected to be the active monitor if it has the highest MAC address on the

ring. The active monitor is responsible for management tasks such as ensuring that tokens are not lost or that frames do not circulate indefinitely.

Active pullup

A transistor or FET used to pull a line high instead of a resistor. Active Pull-ups are common within ICs, but they are not designed to sink much current [weak pull-up].

Active rendering

A technique often used in animation where an application manages its own visual updates rather than relying on the operating system's rendering thread.

Active serial interface

A term used with programming an FPGA. In the Active Serial [AS] configuration scheme, Altera FPGAs are configured with serial configuration devices. Also called Active Serial Mode, or Active Serial Scheme; where Active Serial may be Abbreviated as AS.

Activex

A Windows technology which allows programmers to do various things on your computer. The early versions had security issues which hackers could exploit.

Activity

An operation that takes time to complete. Activities are associated with states and represent real-world accomplishments.

Activity diagram

A UML diagram that models the activity (workflow) of a portion of a software system.

Actor object

An active object that drives a data flow graph by producing or consuming values.

Actuating force

The force applied to the actuator to operate the contacts. The force required to operate a mechanical switch.

Actuator

The part of a switch that is acted upon to cause the switch to change contact connections; for example, toggle, pushbutton, and rocker. The mechanism of the switch or housing which, when moved as intended, will operate the contacts.

Ad hoc network

A communication configuration in which every computer has the same capabilities, and any computer can initiate a communication session. Also known as a peer-to-peer or computer-to-computer network.

Adapter

A device used to connect two different components by matching the physical or electrical characteristics of each component

Adapter class

A class in the java.awt.event package that provides empty implementations of event listener methods so that the programmer can write code for only relavant events.

ADCCP

Advanced Data Communications Control Protocol.

Address

A character or group of characters that identify a register, a location or some other data source or destination.

A numerical designation that uniquely refers to a specific communication entity.

Address mapping

Technique that allows different protocols to interoperate by translating addresses from one format to another. For example, when routing IP over X.25, the IP addresses must be mapped to the X.25 addresses so that the IP packets can be transmitted by the X.25 network.

Address mask

Bit combination used to describe which portion of anaddress refers to the network or subnet and which partrefers to the host. Sometimes referred to simply as mask.also subnet mask.

Address resolution

When two addressing systems refer to the same entity, the process of translating or expressing the address of an entity on one system to the equivalent address of the same entity in the second system. For instance, translating an IP address to its given DNS name.

Address space

A collection of ranges of virtual memory locations with specific memory access rights.

Adjacency

Relationship formed between selected neighboring routers and end nodes for the propose of exchangingrouting information. Adjacency is based upon the useof a common media segment.

Adjacent nodes

1. In SNA, nodes that are connected to a given node with no intervening nodes.
2. In DECnet and OSI, nodes that share a common network segment (in Ethernet, FDDI, or Token Ring networks).

Administrative distance

A rate of the trustworthiness of a routing information source. The higher the value, the lower the trustworthiness rating.

ADPCM

Adaptive differential pulse code modulation. Process by which analog voice samples are encoded into high-quality digital signals.

ADSL

Asymmetric Digital Subscriber Line is a technology for transmitting digital information at a high bandwidth on existing phone lines to homes and businesses. ADSL is asymmetric in the sense that it uses most of the channel to transmit downstream to the user and only a small part to receive information from the user. This means, high download rates and slower upload rates. Generally if you see 2Mb ADSL broadband, it refers to 2 Mbit/s Max d/load rate. The upload rate will probably be around 256 kbit/s Max.

ADSU

ATM DSU. Terminal adapter used to access an ATM network via an HSSI-compatible device.

Advertising

Router process in which routing or service updates are sent at specified intervals so that other routers on the network can maintain lists of usable routes.

Adware

Software which displays advertisements on your computer. Sometimes installed as part of a "free" application, sometimes by stealth.

AEP

AppleTalk Echo Protocol. Used to test connectivity between two AppleTalk nodes. One node sends a packet to another node and receives a duplicate, or echo, of that packet.

AES

Advanced Encryption Standard

AFP

AppleTalk Filing Protocol. The Apple proprietary specification for a network file system.

Agent

1. An active process in a computer that is responsible for a certain type of activity when demanded by an outside entity.
2. In SNMP, the active process in a computing device that is responsible for determining the parameters defined in the MIB (Management Information Base) and reporting them on demand to a Console.

Aggregate

A total created from smaller units. For instance, the population of a county is an aggregate of the populations of the cities, rural areas, etc. that comprise the county.

Aggregate data

Data that have been aggregated.

Aggregation

A tightly coupled form of association, between a whole and its parts, in which the whole is composed of the parts.

Aggressive

To put others down, only see your point of view, pushy and abusive at times.

AGP

(Advanced Graphics Port) A special slot on the PC **motherboard**for graphics cards, and the format of the cards themselves. Standard on new PCs from 1998. "AGP x 2" runs at twice the speed of the original AGP, AGP x 4 at four times the speed etc. Now being replaced by **PCI Express**.

AHCI

Advanced Host Controller Interface is a specification that defines communication between a storage controller and Serial ATA hard drives

AI (Artificial Intelligence)

A program designed to respond "intelligently" to various situations, for example the computer opponent(s) in a game.

AIS

Alarm indication signal. In a T1 transmission, an all-ones signal transmitted in lieu of the normal signal to maintain transmission continuity and to indicate to the receiving terminal that there is a transmission fault that is located either at, or upstream from, the transmitting terminal.

AIUI

(As I Understand It) Internet slang.

AIX

IBM's implementation of Unix.

Alarm

Message notifying an operator or administrator of a network problem.

Algorithm

A finite sequence of unambiguous instructions which, when given the required input, produces the correct output and then stops; A procedure for solving a problem in terms of the steps to be taken and the order in which the steps are to be carried out.

Alias

A file whose sole purpose is to represent another file.

Alignment error

In IEEE 802.3 networks, an error that occurs when the total number of bits of a received frame is not divisible by eight. Alignment errors are usually caused by frame damage due to collisions.

All-routes explorer

Explorer packet that traverses an entire SRB network, following all possible paths to a specific destination. Sometimes called all-rings explorer packet.

Aloe

Archaic. AppleTalk Low Overhead Encapsulation. A vendor-developed alternative to AURP, ALOE provides a mechanism to tunnel AppleTalk protocols inside IP packets, typically in WAN links.

Alpha blending

A graphics term where the material property of transparency or opacity is added to an object.

Alpha stippling

A graphics term that gives a screen door effect by allowing only partial pixels from the source surface to appear over the destination surface.

Alphanumeric

Referring to a group of printable characters that includes the letters of the alphabet in both upper and lower case, the numerals plus a limited group of additional symbols and punctuation marks.

ALU

Arithmetic/Logic Unit — the part of the CPU responsible for performing arithmetic and Boolean operations.

Always-on

An internet connection which remains on 24/7 such as **ADSL** or**cable**, rather than only connecting on demand like a dialup.

AM

Amplitude Modulation. Modulation technique whereby information is conveyed through the amplitude of the carrier signal.

Ambient I

When referring to temperature, ambient refers to the temperature of the surrounding air

Ambient II

Referring to a set of conditions that exist independently of the system of interest.

AMI

Alternate mark inversion. Line-code type used on T1 and E1 circuits. In AMI, zeros are represented by 01 during each bit cell, and ones are represented by 11 or 00, alternately, during each bit cell. AMI requires that the sending device maintain ones density. Ones density is not maintained independent of the data stream. Sometimes called binary coded alternate mark inversion.

Amp

Ampere. A standard unit of measurement for electrical current flow.

Amplitude

In the terminology of wave motion, the height of the wave. Amplitude is usually measured from a reference point of 0. In electrical waves, amplitude is typically expressed in volts.

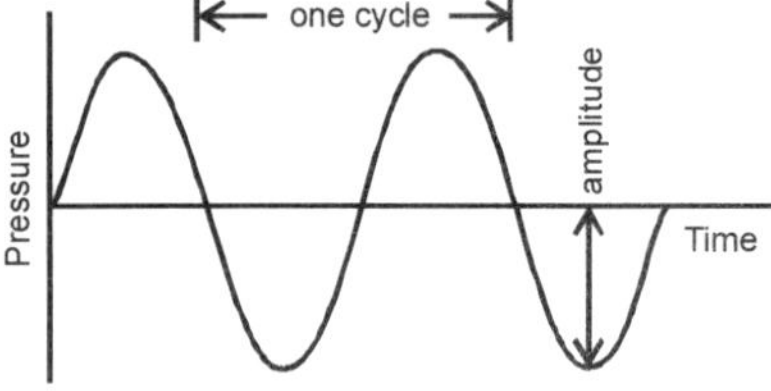

AMT

Intel® Active Management Technology is a feature of specific Intel processors that allows IT to locate, protect, and heal the computer systems on their network

Analog

A method of storing information, used by most audiotapes, videotapes and laserdiscs. An analog device uses a physical quantity, such as length or voltage, to represent the value of a number. By contrast, digital storage relies on a coding system of numeric units.

Analog transmission

Signal transmission over wires or through the air in which information is conveyed through variation of some combination of signal amplitude, frequency, and phase.

Analysis

A stage in the development cycle in which a real-world problem is examined to understand its requirements without planning the implementation.

Android

A popular operating system for **smartphones** and **tablets**, owned by Google.

Anomaly

An unusual instance or circumstance.

Anonymous class

A local class that is declared and instantiated in a single statement, often as a parameter to a method.

Anonymous FTP site

Sites that offer files that are open to the general public for downloading.

ANSI

American National Standards Institute. The principle group in the US. for defining standards.

Answering machine

A machine that records messages when the telephone is unanswered. The recipient can play these messages back.

Antispam

An antispam program is used to filter out email spam.

Antivirus

Software which protects computers from viruses and suchlike. Has to be updated frequently to keep up with the latest threats, so is usually sold with a subscription which enables you to download updates from the internet.

AOCE

Apple Open Collaboration Environment. A system of higher- level protocols used for the transmission of data and authentication between applications.

AOL

(America On Line) An Internet Service Provider, or ISP. AOL were in business as a large commercial bulletin board before the internet really took off. Now they are an ISP specialising in family-friendly internet access.

AP

Access Point, a device that connects wireless devices to another network. For example, a wireless LAN, Internet modem or others.

Apart

Automated packet recognition/ translation. Technology that allows a server to be attached to CDDI or FDDI without requiring the reconfiguration of applications or network protocols. APaRT recognizes specific data link layer encapsulation packet types and, when these packet types are transferred from one medium to another, translates them into the native format of the destination device.

API

Application Programming Interface is an interface that allows two independent computer programs to communicate with each other

APM

Advanced Power Management is an API that enables an operating system to work with the BIOS to achieve power management

Apollo domain

Proprietary network protocol suite developed by Apollo Computer for communication on proprietary Apollo networks.

App

(APPlication) Any software used to carry out a particular task, such as office programs or games, particularly on smartphones. Usually downloaded to the device from an online store. Essentially another word for program.

Appc

Advanced Program-to-Program Communication. IBM SNA system software that allows high-speed communication between programs on different computers in a distributed computing environment. APPC establishes and tears down connections between communicating programs, and consists of two interfaces, a programming interface and a data-exchange interface. The former replies to requests from programs requiring communication; the latter establishes sessions between programs. APPC runs on LU 6.2 devices.

Apple

The Apple Corporation makes the only successful mass-market personal computer which doesn't use Microsoft Windows, the Mac, and the phenomenally successful iPhone (smartphone), iPod (music player) and iPad (tablet).

Appleevent

Apple's primary mechanism for interprocess communication.

Applescript

A programming language that can call tasks within Macintosh applications.

Appleshare

An application published by Apple that allows a Macintosh to be a file server using the AFP protocol.

Applet

A small program used to carry out a particular task, often on a web page.

Appletalk

1. Apple's proprietary network architecture.
2. The protocols, applications, networks and services included in Apple's network architecture.

Application
The use to which a data processing system is put within a given discipline, such as a payroll application, an airline reservation application or a network application.

Application layer
Layer 7 of the OSI reference model. This layer provides services to application processes (such as electronic mail, file transfer, and terminal emulation) that are outside of the OSI model. The application layer identifies and establishes the availability of intended communication partners (and the resources required to connect with them), synchronizes cooperating applications, and agreement on procedures for error recovery and control of data integrity. Corresponds roughly with the transaction services layer in the SNA model.

Application program
A program that is written for or by a user that applies to the users discipline.

Application server
Application Server is a specialized server that is based on client/server architecture. Its sole responsibility is to run specific applications within the network.

Application software
A group of programs designed to perform tasks that can be tailored to a users specific needs.

Appn
Advanced Peer-to-Peer Networking. Enhancement to the original IBM SNA architecture. APPN handles session establishment between peer nodes, dynamic transparent route calculation, and traffic prioritization for APPC traffic.

Appn+
Next-generation APPN that replaces the label-swapping routing algorithm with source routing. Also called high-performance routing.

Ara
AppleTalk Remote Access. Protocol that provides Macintosh users direct access to information and resources at a remote AppleTalk site.

Archie
A search engine for anonymous FTP sites.

Architecture
The basic design of a computer's hardware. Computers with different architecture, such as the PC and the Mac, cannot run each others' programs.

Archive
To copy programs and data onto an auxiliary storage medium (disk, tape,etc.) for long-term retention, such as when disk space has become full. A file with a structure that allows storage of multiple files within it in such a way that the names of the files can be listed and files can be individually added and deleted. The terminology is typically associated with microcomputers. On a mainframe, such a file is typically called a library.

Arcnet
Attached Resource Computer Network. A 2.5-Mbps token-bus LAN developed in the late 1970s and early 1980s by Datapoint Corporation.

Area
Logical set of network segments (either CLNS-, DECnet-, OSPF-based) and their attached devices. Areas are usually connected to other

areas via routers, making up a single autonomous system.

Argument

A value supplied to a procedure, macro, subroutine, or command that is required in order to evaluate that procedure, macro, subroutine, or command. Synonymous with parameter.

ARM

Asynchronous response mode, HDLC communication mode involving one primary station and at least one secondary station, where either the primary or one of the secondary stations can initiate transmissions.

ARP

Address Resolution Protocol. The protocol for mapping IP addresses to physical addresses such as Ethernet or Token Ring.

ARPA

Advanced Research Projects Agency, Research and development organization that is part of DoD. ARPA is responsible for numerous technological advances in communications and networking. ARPA evolved in DARPA, and then back into ARPA again (in 1994).

Arpanet

Advanced Research Projects Agency Network. Landmark packet-switching network established in 1969. ARPANET was developed in the 1970s by BBN and funded by ARPA (and later DARPA). It eventually evolved into the Internet. The term ARPANET was officially retired in 1990.

Arq

Automatic repeat request. Communication technique in which the receiving device detects errors and requests retransmission.

Array

An array is similar data saved on a computer system in a sequential form.

ASBR

Autonomous system boundary router. ABR located between an OSPF autonomous system and a non-OSPF network. ASBRs run both OSPF and another routing protocol, such as RIP, ASBRs must reside on a nonstub OSPF area.

ASCII

American Standard Code for Information Interchange (pronounced ask-ee). The form in which text characters are handled in most computer systems and networks. ASCII text has no special characters for formatting such as underlined or bold characters, font changes, etc., thus can be viewed on any personal computer or terminal.

ASDSP

AppleTalk Secure Data Stream Protocol. An encrypted version of ADSP used by AOCE.

ASF

Alert Standards Format is a specification for technologies that are used to allow a computer system to be remotely managed and controlled even if an operating system is not present

ASIC

Application-Specific Integrated Circuit is an integrated circuit that has been customized for a particular use

ASLM

Apple Shared Library Manager.

ASN.1

Abstract Syntax Notation One. In SNMP, the language used to describe data managed by the MIB.

Assembler

A program that converts symbolically-coded programs into object level, machine code. In an assembler program, unlike a compiler, there is a one-to-one correspondence between human-readable instructions and the machine-language code.

Assertive

To be clear and honest when speaking about your feelings and respect the rights and needs of others without making judgements.

Asset

An item having some value.

Assignment

An operation that places a value in a variable.

Association

A relationship between objects and classes that describes a group of links with common structure and common semantics.

Associative memory

Memory that is accessed based on its contents, not on its memory address. Sometimes called content addressable memory (CAM).

AST

Automatic spanning tree. Function that supports the automatic resolution of spanning trees in SRB networks, providing a single path for spanning explorer frames to traverse from a given node in the network to another. AST is based on the IEEE 802.1 standard.

ASTA

Advanced Software Technology and Algorithms. Component of the HPCC program intended to develop software and algorithms for implementation on high-performance computer and communications systems.

Asymmetric mode

This mode is used when only one DIMM is installed or the memory capacities are unequal. Also known as single-channel mode.

Asymmetry

In networking, a system in which the relationship between two entities is inherently unequal, with each entity restricted to a set of operations and prerogatives defined by its role in the relationship.

Asynchronous

Term describing digital signals that are transmitted without precise clocking. Such signals generally have different frequencies and phase relationships. Asynchronous transmissions usually encapsulate individual characters in control bits (called start and stop bits) that designate the beginning and end of each character.

Asynchronous communication

communication in which the sending process can proceed as soon as the message has been sent out to a buffer.

AT (form factor)

The AT form factor referred to the dimensions and layout (form factor) of the motherboard for the IBM AT.

AT commands transmission

A set of commands that control a modem or alter its characteristics.

ATA

Advanced Technology Attachment is an interface between storage devices such as hard drives and a computer.

ATAPI

(At achment Packet Interface) An upgrade to EIDE which allows the hard disk controller to control CD drives as well. Almost all CD and DVD drives are controlled this way.

ATB

(All The Best) Internet slang.

ATDM

Asynchronous time-division multiplexing. Method of sending information that resembles normal TDM, except that time slots are allocated as needed rather than preassigned to specific transmitters.

At-least-once call semantics

RPC semantics in which a caller sends a request message several times until a reply is received.

ATM

Asynchronous Transfer Mode. A standard for cell relay that uses fixed length cells of 53 bytes, 5 bytes of which are headers. Can support multiple services including voice, video and data.

Atm

(At The Moment) Internet slang.

Atm forum

An industry-wide effort that is now an international consortium of more than 400 companies who define ATM interoperability specifications and promote industry-wide cooperation to help proliferate ATM and thus drive implementation costs down.

At-most-once call semantics

RPC semantics in which duplicate messages are filtered out and replies are retransmitted without re-executing operations so that the remote procedure is executed once or not at all.

Atomic multicast

A multicast message that is either received by all intended recipients or none of them.

ATP

AppleTalk Transaction Protocol. Transport-level protocol that allows reliable request-response exchanges between two socket clients.

Attachment

A file sent by email is "attached" to the email. An attachment can be a picture, a document, a program or any other type of file. You should never open an attachment if you are not sure what it is, because someviruses propagate as email attachments; but they can't infect your machine if you don't open the attachment.

Attenuation

A loss in the amplitude or strength of a signal due to an interaction with the signal's media. Generally expressed in decibels.

Attribute

Configuration data that defines the characteristics of database objects such as the chassis, cards, ports, or virtual circuits of a particular device. Attributes might be preset or user-configurable. On a LightStream 2020 ATM switch, attributes are set using the configuration program or CLI commands.

ATX

Advanced Technology Extended is a motherboard form factor where the motherboard is typically 9.6x12 inches

Audit

A personal or computerized review process that accounts for the adequacy, effectiveness, security and overall functionality of a data activity.

AUI

Attachment unit interface. IEEE 802.3 interface between an MAU and a NIC (network interface card). Also called transceiver cable.

AUP

(Acceptable Use Policy) A document setting out what an Internet Service Provider deems an acceptable use of their services, usually published on their website. Typically it will forbid the publication of obscene or defamatory material, and sending email or newsgroupspam. If you violate your ISP's AUP, they will usually close your account down immediately.

AURP

AppleTalk Update-Based Routing Protocol. Apple's WAN protocol.

AURP tunnel

Connection created in an AURP WAN that functions as a single, virtual data link between AppleTalk internetworks physically separated by a foreign network (a TCP/IP network, for example).

Authentication

Verifies the identity of a user logging onto a network. Passwords, digital certificates, smart cards and biometrics are used to prove the identity of the client to the network. Passwords and digital certificates are also used to identify the network to the client.

Authentication server

A server that provides a secure way for pairs of processes to obtain secret keys for secure encryption.

Authority zone

Associated with DNS, an authority zone is a section of the domain-name tree for which one name server is the authority.

Authorization

Permission to access non-public information or use equipment that is either fully or partially restricted. Process of establishing what you can do.

Auto correct

Automatically corrects common typing and spelling errors as your type

Auto text

Offers a way to store and quickly insert text, graphics, fields, tables, bookmarks, and other items that you use frequently.

Autocorrect

A feature in many programs which automatically corrects your spelling, and even your grammar, as you type. Better switched off if you use obscure technical terms, or prefer your own interpretation of the rules of grammar, or else you are likely to find that it's "corrected" your text to something you didn't intend.

Automatic call reconnect

Feature permitting automatic call rerouting away from a failedtrunk line.

Automatic data processing (ADP) system

An organized assembly of resources and methods used to collect, process, and distribute messages largely by automatic means.

Automatic variable

A local variable.

Autonomous confederation

Group of autonomous systems that rely on their own networkreachability and routing information more than they rely on that received from other autonomous systems or confederations.

Autonomous system

Collection of networks under a common administration sharing a common routing strategy. Autonomous systems are subdivided by areas. An autonomous system must be assigned a unique 16-bit number by the IANA.

Auto reconfiguration

Process performed by nodes within the failure domain of a Token Ring network. Nodes automatically perform diagnostics in an attempt to reconfigure the network around the failed areas.

Auxiliary carry flag (AC)

A carry flag used by instructions that perform binary coded decimal (BCD) arithmetic; the second bit in the PSW register.

Availability

A measure of a proportion of time that something can be used.

Avatar

A picture or figure representing a person in an online environment.

Average rate

The average rate, in kilobits per second (kbps), at which a given virtual circuit will transmit.

B

B channel

Bearer channel. In ISDN, a full-duplex, 64-kbps channel used to send user data.

B8zs

Binary 8-zero substitution. Line-code type, used on T1 and E1 circuits, in which a special code is substituted whenever 8 consecutive zeros are sent through the link. This code is then interpreted at the remote end of the connection. This technique guarantees ones density independent of the data stream. Sometimes called bipolar 8-zero substitution.

Back end

Node or software program that provides services to a front end.

Back end processor

A computer running an application that supplies data to other computers on demand, but has no user interface.

Back pressure

Propagation of network congestion information upstream through an internetwork.

Back resistance

The larger resistance value observed when you are checking the resistance of a semiconductor.

Back shell

The rear portion of a connector.

Backbone

A high traffic connectivity portion of any communications network. In packet-switched networks, a primary forward direction path traced sequentially through two or more major relay or switching stations. In packet-switched networks, a backbone consists primarily of switches and inter-switch trunks.

Background noise

The total system noise in the absence of a signal.

Background processing

Users may use a terminal for one project and concurrently submit a job that is placed in a background queue that the computer will run as resources become available. Also refers to any processing in which a job runs without being connected to a terminal.

Background task

A computing task that is executing while another task or application is displaying its user interface.

Backoff

The (usually random) retransmission delay enforced by contentious MAC protocols after a network node with data to transmit determines that the physical medium is already in use.

Backplane

A circuit card that contains two or more connectors of the same type which are connected together via discrete wires or copper traces on the circuit board to form an interface bus, which allows the boards to communicate with each other.

19 Slot VME Backplane

Backspace

A keyboard operation that moves the cursor one place to the left. A destructive backspace erases characters as it goes, thus allowing users to modify what has been typed (distinguished from the left- arrow key).

Backup

A backup is an extra copy of your work, eg documents, pictures etc, saved onto a removable storage medium such as CD, DVD or magnetic tape, so that if your computer is stolen or breaks down you don't lose everything. Backup is a noun, back up is a verb.

Backward compatible

An upgraded component of a computing system that can be used interchangeably with its previous version.

Backward learning

Algorithmic process used for routing traffic that surmises information by assuming symmetrical network conditions. For example, if node A receives a packet from node B through intermediate node C, the backward-learning routing algorithm will assume that A can optimally reach B through C.

Bad block / bad sector

An area on a hard disk drive that is damaged or detected as unreliable.

Balance

In electrical circuits and networks, to adjust the impedance to achieve specific objectives, such as to reach specified return loss objectives at a hybrid junction of two-wire and four-wire circuits.

Balanced amplifier

An amplifier with two identical branches connected to operate in opposite phase, with their input and outputs connections balanced to ground. A Push-Pull Amplifier. An amplifier having one output is considered balanced when the quiescent DC output voltage is reduced to zero or a specified level. An amplifier having two outputs is considered balanced when the difference between the quiescent DC output voltages is reduced to zero or a specified level.

Balanced attenuator

An attenuator which uses resistance elements in both sides of the line. Refer to the Resistor Attenuator page for a schematic of many of the different types of balanced attenuators.

Balanced bridge

A bridge circuit adjusted to produce a zero output.

Balanced code

In PCM systems, a code constructed so that the frequency spectrum resulting from the transmission of any code word has no DC component. A code that has a finite digital sum variation. A number of additional terms are related, use the search bar, below right, to find the correct definition.

Balanced configuration

In HDLC, a point-to-point network configuration with two combined stations.

Balanced line

A cable or circuit having two identical conductors with the same electromagnetic characteristics in relation to other conductors and to ground, as in a pair of conductors. A twisted pair line. A transmission line consisting of two conductors in the presence of ground, capable of being operated so that when the voltages of the two conductors at all transverse planes are equal in magnitude and opposite in polarity with respect to ground, the currents in the two conductors are equal in magnitude and opposite in direction. .

Balanced mixer

A circuit or device that generates the sum and difference frequencies of two input signals.

Balanced phase detector

A circuit that controls the oscillator frequency.

Ballast

A device or component used to stabilize current flow, as in a Ballast Resistor.

Ballast resistor

A resistor used to compensate for fluctuations in an AC power line. A resistor connected in series to absorb small changes in applied voltage to stabilize the current.

Balun

An acronym for Balanced/ Unbalanced. A device used to couple a balanced system to an un-balanced system.

Balun

Balanced/Unbalanced. A device that links together dissimilar wire types and attempts to minimize any negative effects to the signal that would normally result from the dissimilarity.

Banana jack

A type of female connector or receptacle that accepts a Banana plug. The Banana Jack may be a male on one end and a female on the other end, or a completely different style connector.

• **BNC to Banana Plug**

Banana plug

A connector with the male-end using a Banana shaped, spring metal tip, providing a compression fit into a banana jack.

Band

In analog communications, the range of frequencies over which a communication system operates.

Band-elimination filter

Same meaning as a Band-Reject Filter.

Bandgap reference

A type of voltage reference.

Bandpass amplifier

An amplifier stage design to pass a range of frequencies. .

Bandpass filter

A filter that allows a narrow band of frequencies to pass through the circuit. Rejects or attenuates frequencies that are either higher or lower than the desired band of frequencies. A filter that ideally passes all frequencies between two non-zero finite limits and bars all frequencies not within the limits. The cutoff frequencies are normally taken to be the 3-dB points.

Band-reject filter

A tuned circuit that does not pass a specified band of frequencies. Refer to the entry on Passive Filters. A filter that attenuates, usually to very low levels, all frequencies between two nonzero, finite limits and passes all frequencies not within the limits.

Band-stop filter

Same as a Band-reject Filter.

Bandwidth

The width of a communication channel, measured as frequency. The difference between the highest usable frequency of a device (upper frequency limit) and the lowest usable frequency of the device (lower frequency limit) - measured at the half-power points. The difference between the limiting frequencies within which performance of a device, in respect to some characteristic, falls within specified limits. The difference between the limiting frequencies of a continuous frequency band. The capacity of a telecom line to carry signals. The necessary bandwidth is the amount of spectrum required to transmit the signal without distortion or loss of information.

Bandwidth reservation

Process of assigning bandwidth to users and applications served by a network. Involves assigning priority to different flows of traffic based on how critical and delay-sensitive they are. This makes the best use of available bandwidth, and if the network becomes congested, lower-priority traffic can be dropped. Sometimes called bandwidth allocation.

Bank

A number of devices of the same kind.

Bar chart

A type of graphic in which data items are shown as rectangular bars. The bars may be displayed either vertically or horizontally and may be distinguished from one another by color or by some type of shading or patter Positive and negative values may be shown in relation to a zero baseline. Two types of bar charts are common: a standard bar chart, in which each value is represented by a separate bar, and a stacked bar chart, in which several data points are "stacked" to produce a single bar. Also called bar graph.

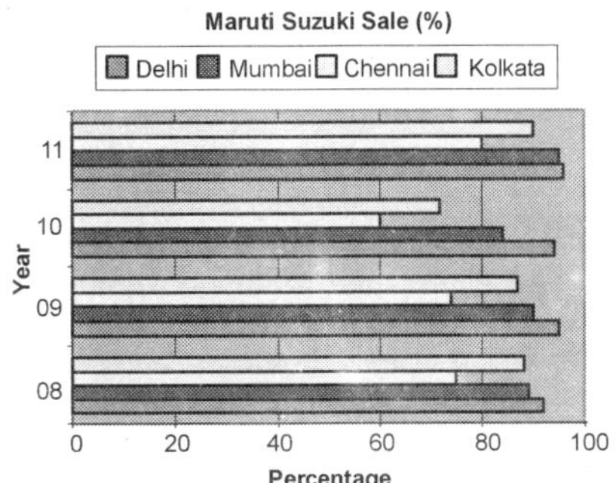

Bar code

The special identification code printed as a set of vertical bars of differing widths on books, grocery products, and other merchandise.

Used for rapid, error-free input in such facilities as libraries, hospitals, and grocery stores, bar codes represent binary information that can be read by an optical scanner. The coding can include numbers, letters, or a combination of the two; some codes include built-in error checking and can be read in either direction.

Bare bones

1. An application that provides only the most basic functions necessary to perform a given task.
2. A computer consisting only of motherboard (equipped with CPU and RAM), cabinet, power supply, floppy disk drive, and keyboard, to which the user must add hard disk, video adapter, monitor, and any other peripherals.

Bare conductor

A conductor not covered with insulating material.

Barretter

A type of bolometer characterized by an increase in resistance as the dissipated power rises.

Barrnet

Bay Area Regional Research Network. Regional network serving the San Francisco Bay Area. The BARRNet backbone is composed of four University of California campuses (Berkeley, Davis, Santa Cruz, and San Francisco), Stanford University, Lawrence Livermore National Laboratory, and NASA Ames Research Center. BARRNET is now part of BBN Planet.

Base

A reference value. A number that is multiplied by itself as many times as indicated by an exponent. Same as radix. The region between the emitter and collector of a transistor that receives minority carriers injected from the emitter. The element in a transistor that controls the flow of current carriers. The element that corresponds to the control grid of an electron tube.

Base address

The lowest address available in an address range.

Base URL

A uniform resource locator (URL) that you can optionally assign to a page to convert relative URLs on that page into absolute URLs. A base URL should end with a document name or a trailing slash.

Baseband

A network medium that uses only one carrier frequency. Examples are Ethernet and PhoneNet.

Base-injection modulator

Similar to a vacuum tube control-grid modulator. The gain of a transistor is varied by changing the bias on its base.

Basic

Beginners All-purpose Symbolic Instruction Code. A commonly used personal-computer language, first developed at Dartmouth during the 1960s.

Bass

Sounds in the lower end of the audio frequency range.

Bass control

A passive circuit used to attenuate frequencies in the higher audio ranges.

Batch file

An ASCII text file containing a sequence of operating-system commands, possibly including parameters and operators supported by the batch command language. When the user types a batch filename at the command prompt, the commands are processed sequentially. Also called batch program.

Batch processing

Originally, a method of organizing work for a computer system, designed to reduce overhead by grouping similar jobs. In one scheme, jobs were collected into batches, each requiring a particular compiler. The compiler was loaded, and the jobs submitted in sequence to the compiler. The term has come to be applied to background processing of jobs not requiring user intervention on multiuser systems.

Batch program

A program that executes without interacting with the user.

Batch query

A query that has been saved so that it can be used more than once and run in the background.

Baud

Unit of signaling speed equal to the number of discrete signal elements transmitted per second. Baud is synonymous with bits per second (bps), if each signal element represents exactly 1 bit.

Baud rate

Generally, the number of bits transferred per second (bps); more accurately, the number of signal changes per second.

BBN

Bolt, Beranek, and Newman, Inc. High-technology company located in Massachusetts that developed and maintained the ARPANET and later, the Internet, core gateway system.

BBN planet

Subsidiary company of BBN that operates a nationwide Internet access network composed in part of the former regional networks BARRNET, NEARNET, and SURAnet.

BC

Committed Burst. Negotiated tariff metric in Frame Relay internetworks. The maximum amount of data (in bits) that a Frame Relay internetwork is committed to accept and transmit at the CIR.

BCC Blind Carbon Copy (sometimes Blind Courtesy Copy)

A recipient of an email that no other recipient knows about. Useful when you have a list of email addresses that you want to keep confidential.

BE

Excess Burst. Negotiated tariff metric in Frame Relay internetworks. The number of bits that a Frame Relay internetwork will attempt to transmit after Bc is accommodated. Be data is, in general, delivered with a lower probability than Bc data because Be data can be marked as DE by the network.

Beacon

Frame from a token ring or FDDI device indicating a serious problem with the ring, such as a broken cable. A beacon frame contains the address of the station assumed to be down.

Bearer channel

One of the 64-Kbps communications channels on an ISDN circuit. A BRI (Basic Rate Interface) ISDN line has 2 bearer channels and 1 data channel.

A PRI (Primary Rate Interface) ISDN line has 23 bearer channels (in North America) or 30 bearer channels (in Europe) and 1 data channel.

Beat-'em-up

A computer game in which you control one or more characters fighting onscreen using karate, kung-fu and so forth. Derives from shoot-'em-up.

BECN

Backward explicit congestion notification. Bit set by a Frame Relay network in frames traveling in the opposite direction of frames encountering a congested path. DTE receiving frames with the BECN bit set can request that higher-level protocols take flow control action as appropriate.

Bellcore

Bell Communications Research. Organization that performs research and development on behalf of the RBOCs.

Benchmark

A test performed t compare a computer process in one set of circumstances to another.

BER

1. Bit error rate. The ratio of received bits that contain errors.
2. Basic encoding rules. Rules for encoding data units described in the ISO ASN.1 standard.

Beta

A beta version of something is not yet ready for prime time but still possibly useful to related developers and other interested parties. Expect beta software to crash more than properly released software does. Traditionally beta versions (of commercial software) are distributed only to selected testers who are often then given a discount on the proper version after its release in exchange for their testing work. Beta versions of non-commercial software are more often freely available to anyone who has an interest.

Beta test

Beta is the second letter of the Greek alphabet. In software, used to signify that this is not the first release for testing, but not the last either.

BGP

Border Gateway Protocol. Interdomain routing protocol that replaces EGP. BGP exchanges reachability information with other BGP systems. It is defined by RFC 1163.

BGP4

BGP Version 4. Version 4 of the predominant interdomain routing protocol used on the Internet. BGP4 supports CIDR and uses route aggregation mechanisms to reduce the size of routing tables.

BIGA

Bus Interface Gate Array. Technology that allows the Catalyst 5000 to receive and transmit frames from its packet-switching memory to its MAC local buffer memory without the intervention of the host processor.

Big-endian

Method of storing or transmitting data in which the most significant bit or byte is presented first.

Big-O notation

A notation for indicating algorithm efficiency by only considering the dominant factor; the big O stands for "on the Order of".

Binary

A file containing one or more strings of data bits which are not printable characters. Some binary files may be computer programs or other forms of data that contain no text characters at all. Binary files cannot be displayed on screen, but can be downloaded for use with appropriate applications on your computer. Binary (base 2) is also the building block of computer information, representing "on" or "off" and "true" or "not true" as 1 or 0.

Binary digit

Either of the two digits in the binary number system, 0 and 1.

Binary file

A file consisting of a sequence of 8-bit data or executable code, as distinguished from files consisting of human-readable ASCII text. Binary files are usually in a form readable only by a program, often compressed or structured in a way that is easy for a particular program to read.

Binary number

A number written using binary notation which only uses zeros and ones. Example: decimal number seven in binary notation is: 111.

Bind

Berkeley Internet Name Domain. The standard TCP/IP naming service that links network names with IP addresses.

Binder

A service that maintains a table of mappings from service names to server ports.

Binding

Specifying a mapping from a name to a particular object.

Biometric

A system that examines biological things like fingerprints or retinas, usually for security purposes.

BIOS

(Basic Input/Output System; pr. "by-oss") A program built into every PC for setting up very basic things, like how many hard and floppy disks you have and what type they are; the first thing that loads when you start your PC. You usually only need to access the BIOS if you are upgrading your hardware, eg adding more RAM or an extra disk drive, or setting a power-on password. BIOS settings are stored in a special type of memory called CMOS.

Biphase coding

Bipolar coding scheme originally developed for use in Ethernet. Clocking information is embedded into and recovered from the synchronous data stream without the need for separate clocking leads. The biphase signal contains no direct current energy.

Bipolar

Electrical characteristic denoting a circuit with both negative and positive polarity. Contrast with unipolar.

BISDN

Broadband ISDN. ITU-T communication standards designed to handle high-bandwidth applications such as video. BISDN currently uses ATM technology over SONET-based transmission circuits to provide data rates from 155 to 622 Mbps and beyond.

Bit

A binary digit, either a 0 or 1. In the U. S., 8 bits make up one byte; in Europe, byte equals one word.

Bit pattern

A sequence of bits that has a specific purpose or meaning.

Bit rate

The total number of bits (ones and zeros) per second that a network connection can support. Note that this bit rate will vary, under software control, with different signal path conditions.

Bitmap

A bitmap is a simplistic representation of an image on a computer, simply indicating whether or not pixels are on or off, and sometimes indicating their color. Often fonts are represented as bitmaps. The term "pixmap" is sometimes used similarly; typically when a distinction is made, pixmap refers to color images and bitmap refers to monochrome images.

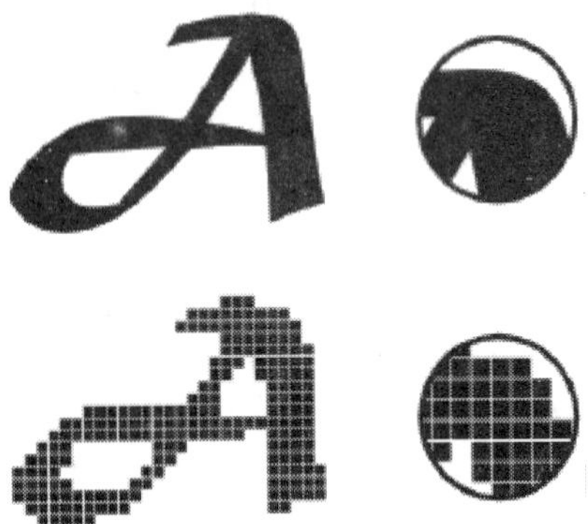

Bitmapped font

A set of characters in a particular size and style in which each character is described as a unique bit map (pattern of dots). Macintosh screen fonts are examples of bitmapped fonts.

Bitmapped graphics

Computer graphics represented as arrays of bits in memory that represent the attributes of the individual pixels in an image (one bit per pixel in a black-and-white display, multiple bits per pixel in a color or gray-scale display). Bitmapped graphics are typical of paint programs, which treat images as collections of dots rather than as shapes.

Bitmapped terminal

A terminal that can turn individual screen dots on or off.

Bitnet

"Because It's Time" Networking Services. Low-cost, low-speed academic network consisting primarily of IBM mainframes and 9600-bps leased lines. BITNET is now a part of CREN.

Bitnet III

Dial-up service providing connectivity for members of CREN.

Bit-oriented Protocol

Class of data link layer communication protocols that can transmit frames regardless of frame content. Compared with byte-oriented protocols, bit-oriented protocols provide full-duplex operation and are more efficient and reliable.

Bits

Binary digits; 0s and 1s.

Bits per second (BPS)

The speed at which bits are transmitted.

Black box

A device that performs a function using mechanisms that are unimportant or impossible to understand.

Black hole

Routing term for an area of the internetwork where packets enter, but do not emerge, due to adverse conditions or poor system configuration within a portion of the network.

Block

A sequence of words or characters written contiguously, such as into a group, by a computer and stored on a disk, diskette, magnetic tape, etc.

Block multiplexer i channel

BM-style channel that implements the FIPS-60 channel, AUS. Channel standard. This channel is also referred to as OEMI channel and 370 block mux channel.

Blocking

In a switching system, a condition in which no paths are available to complete a circuit. The term is also used to describe a situation in which one activity cannot begin until another has been completed.

Blog

(weBLOG) A website documenting someone's life and/or thoughts.

Blogging

Writing on or otherwise using online journals known as web logs or blogs.

Bluetooth

A short range wireless data communication system for smartphones and other computing devices. However Bluetooth devices from different manufacturers wouldn't always communicate with each other reliably, so it hasn't really taken off as the industry had hoped, and it is now under threat from faster wireless technologies.

Blu-Ray Disc

A optical disc storage medium designed to supersede the DVD format.

BMP

BITMAP. A standard type of graphics file. An uncompressed format, so the files tend to be fairly big.

BNC

Bayonet "N" Connector.

1. The locking connector type used in 10Base2 (Thin Ethernet).
2. Any connector similar to the type used by 10Base2 for CATV, and other electronic uses.

BNN

Boundary network node. In SNA terminology, a subarea node that provides boundary function support for adjacent peripheral nodes. This support includes sequencing, pacing, and address translation.

Board

A printed circuit and the substrate on which it lies.

BOC

1. Boxed Order Code is the product code for a boxed Intel® processor
2. Bell operating company.

Body language

Movement of the body and facial expressions to communicate.

Bold

A way of emphasizing a word of text, as in darker type or brighter characters on a video display terminal.

Boldface

A type style that makes the text to which it is applied appear darker and heavier than the surrounding text. Some applications allow the user to apply a "Bold" command to selected text; other programs require that special codes be embedded in the text before and after words that are to be printed in boldface. This sentence appears in boldface.

Bomb

A program planted surreptitiously, with intent to damage or destroy a system in some way—for example, to erase a hard disk or cause it to be unreadable to the operating system.

Bookmarks

Notation that you create to list sites you visit often or would like to quickly return to.

Bookmark file

1. A Netscape Navigator file containing the addresses of preferred Web sites. It is synonymous with the Favorites folder in Internet Explorer and the hotlist in Mosaic. See also Favorites folder, hotlist, Internet Explorer, Mosaic.
2. A rendering of such a file in HTML format, generally posted on a Web page for the benefit of other people.

Boolean

Of, pertaining to, or characteristic of logical (true, false) values. Many languages directly support a Boolean data type, with predefined values for true and false; others use integer data types to implement Boolean values, usually (although not always) with 0 equaling false and "not 0" equaling true.

Boolean network

A Boolean network consists of a discrete set of Boolean variables each of which has a boolean function (possibly different for each variable) assigned to it which takes inputs from a subset of those variables and output that determines the state of the variable it is assigned to. This set of functions in effect determines a topology (connectivity) on the set of variables, which then become nodes in a network. Usually, the dynamics of the system is taken as a discrete time series where the state of the entire network at time t+1 is determined by evaluating each variable's function on the state of the network at time t. This may be done synchronously or asynchronously.

Boot

Starting up an OS is booting it. If the computer is already running, it is more often called rebooting

Boot disk

A floppy disk that contains key system files from a PC-compatible operating system and that can boot, or start, the PC. A boot disk must be inserted in the primary floppy disk drive (usually drive A:) and is used when there is some problem with starting the PC from the hard disk, from which the computer generally boots. Also called bootable disk.

Boot drive

The disk that contains a computers' startup instructions.

Boot PROM

Boot programmable read-only memory. Chip mounted on a printed circuit board used to provide executable boot instruction to a computer device.

Boot sector infector

Virus that infects the boot sector of a floppy or hard disk

Boot, boot up

Usually used to mean "start up the computer". Literally, the process of loading up the operating system and getting the computer ready for use. A "boot password" is a password you have to give to start up the computer.

Booting

In computing, booting (also known as booting up) is the initial set of operations that a computer system performs after electrical power to the CPU is switched on or when the computer is reset. The process begins when a computer is turned on for the first time, is re-energized after being turned off, when it is reset or when the operator invokes a LOAD[NB 1] function from the console, and ends when the computer is ready to perform its normal operations.

Bootp

Bootstrap Protocol. An IP protocol used by diskless workstations to receive boot information from a boot server.

Border gateway

Router that communicates with routers in other autonomous systems.

Bot

(roBOT) An automated program, usually performing a function on the internet such as indexing webpages or sorting email.

Boundary function

Capability of SNA subarea nodes to provide protocol support for attached peripheral nodes. Typically found in IBM 3745 devices.

BPDU

Bridge protocol data unit. Spanning-Tree Protocol hello packet that is sent out at configurable intervals to exchange information among bridges in the network.

BPS

Bits Per Second. A commonly-used measure of the rate of data transmission that specifies the number of bits that are transmitted in one second. May be prefixed with multipliers such as K, M, and G which indicate rates of thousands, millions and billions of bits per second.

BRB

"Be right back", internet/chat slang, also sometimes treated as a synonym of "bathroom break".

Break

An interruption to a transmission; usually a provision to allow a controlled terminal to interrupt the controlling computer.

BRI

Basic Rate Interface. an ISDN service with two bearer channels at 64 KBPS plus a "Data-Link" or control channel at 16 KBPS.

Bridge

A device that connects two networks and passes traffic between them based only on the node address, so that traffic between nodes on one network does not appear on the other network. For example, an Ethernet bridge only looks at the Ethernet.

Bridge forwarding

Process that uses entries in a filtering database to determine whether frames with a given MAC destination address can be forwarded to a given port or ports.

Bridge number

Number that identifies each bridge in an SRB LAN. Parallel bridges must have different bridge numbers.

Bridge static filtering

Process in which a bridge maintains a filtering database consisting of static entries. Each static entry equates a MAC destination address with a port that can receive frames with this MAC destination address and a set of ports on which the frames can be transmitted.

Broadband

A communications medium on which multiple signals are simultaneously transmitted at different frequencies. Also refers to switching capability implemented on this medium that allows communication between devices connected to it. In telecommunications it is defined as any channel with a bandwidth greater than voice grade (4 KHz).

Broadband wi-fi router

Stand-alone Wi-Fi hub that allows any computer that has a Wi-Fi network adapter to communicate with another computer and to connect to the Internet. This device is typically used in a home or small-office environment with a relatively small number of users.

Broadcast

An information transmission that is intended to be interpreted by all entities capable of receiving it.

Broadcast address

Special address reserved for sending a message to all stations. Generally, a broadcast address is a MAC destination address of all ones.

Broadcast communication

Communication in which each packet is transmitted to all of the computers in the network and each computer is responsible for identifying and receiving the packets addressed to it.

Broadcast domain

The set of all devices that will receive broadcast frames originating from any device within the set. Broadcast domains are typically bounded by routers because routers do not forward broadcast frames.

Broadcast search

Propagation of a search request to all network nodes if the location of a resource is unknown to the requester.

Broadcast storm

Undesirable network event in which many broadcasts are sent simultaneously across all network segments. A broadcast storm uses substantial network bandwidth and, typically, causes network time-outs.

Brouter

A device that incorporates the functionality of a bridge and a router in a single unit.

Browser

A program used for viewing World Wide Web pages on the Internet. Usually available free for download. Popular browsers include Internet Explorer (IE), which is built in to Windows, Mozilla Firefox, and Google Chrome. The most popular browser on Apple devices is Safari.

BSC

Binary synchronous communication. Character-oriented data link layer protocol for half-duplex applications.

BSD

Berkeley Software Distribution. UC Berkeley's distribution of the Unix operating system.

BSD UNIX

Acronym for Berkeley Software Distribution UNIX. A UNIX version developed at the University of California at Berkeley, providing additional capabilities such as networking, extra peripheral support, and use of extended filenames. BSD UNIX was instrumental in gaining widespread acceptance of UNIX and in getting academic institutions connected to the Internet. BSD UNIX is now being developed by Berkeley Software Design, Inc.

B-tree

A tree structure for storing database indexes. Each node in the tree contains a sorted list of key values and links that correspond to ranges of key values between the listed values. To find a specific data record given its key value, the program reads the first node, or root, from the disk and compares the desired key with the keys in the node to select a subrange of key values to search. It repeats the process with the node indicated by the corresponding link. At the lowest level, the links indicate the data records. The database system can thus rapidly skip down through the levels of the tree structure to find the simple index entries that contain the location of the desired records or rows.

BT

Bluetooth

BT

Burst tolerance. Parameter defined by the ATM Forum for ATM traffic management. For VBR connections, BT determines the size of the maximum burst of contiguous cells that can be transmitted.

BTW

(By The Way) Internet slang.

BTX

Balanced Technology Extended is a motherboard form factor where the motherboard is typically 12.8x10.5 inches.

Bucket

A region of memory that is addressable as an entity and can be used as a receptacle to hold data.

Buffer

A region of memory reserved for use as an intermediate repository in which data is temporarily held while waiting to be transferred between two locations, as between an application's data area and an input/output device. A device or its adapter may in turn use a buffer to store data awaiting transfer to the computer or processing by the device.

Buffer gate

a logic gate that does not change the logic level of the input, but isolates or amplifies the signal.

Buffered memory

A type of memory module that has a register between the DRAM modules and the system's memory controller. Buffered memory is also called registered memory, it is more stable than unbuffered memory, but also more expensive. Buffered memory is mainly used in servers and workstations.

Bug

Error, especially in a program, that has been missed in testing. The story goes that the original bug was an insect that got itself cremated inside an electrical circuit in an early computer, causing it to fail (and I don't suppose the insect enjoyed it much, either). It took them ages to figure out what was causing the problem, and when they eventually found the bug the story passed into legend.

Bulletin board

A semi-public area which computer users can connect to using a modem, to read and post messages and/or exchange files. Now largely replaced by websites.

Bullets

Can be represented by a range of symbols, usually round dots, which are used to set apart points in paragraph style.

Bundled

Refers to the practice of automatically including an additional application or capability in the sale or delivery of a computing component that is not ordinarily associated with that component.

Bundled software

1. Programs sold with a computer as part of a combined hardware/ software package.
2. Smaller programs sold with larger programs to increase the latter's functionality or attractiveness.

Burn

To write data electronically into a programmable read-only memory (PROM) chip by using a special programming device known variously as a PROM programmer, PROM blower, or PROM blaster. The term is also used in reference to creating read-only memory compact discs (CD-ROMs). Also called blast, blow.

Bus

A collection of wires through which data is Transmitted from one part of a computer to another. You can think of a bus as a highway on which data Travels within a computer. When used reference to Personal computers, the term bus usually refers to Internal bus. This is a bus that connects all the internal computer components to the CPU and main memory. There's also an expansion bus that enables expansion boards to access the CPU and memory. All buses consist of two parts — an address bus and a data bus. The data bus transfers actual data whereas the address bus transfers information about where the data should go. The size of a bus, known as its width, is important because it determines how much data can be transmitted at one time.

Bus and tag channel

IBM channel, developed in the 1960s, incorporating copper multiwire technology. Replaced by the EXCON channel.

BUS topology

Linear LAN architecture in which transmissions from network stations propagate the length of the medium and are received by all other stations.

Business

An organisation that seeks profit by providing goods and services.

Bypass mode

Operating mode on FDDI and Token Ring networks in which an interface has been removed from the ring.

Bypass relay

Allows a particular Token Ring interface to be shut down and thus effectively removed from the ring.

Byte

A group of adjacent binary digits, usually 8, on which a computer operates as a unit; often used to represent a single character.

Byte reversal

Process of storing numeric data with the least-significant byte first. Used for integers and addresses on devices with Intel microprocessors.

Bytecode

Platform-independent instructions created by the Java compiler for the JVM.

Byte-oriented protocol

Class of data-link communications protocols that use a specific character from the user character set to delimit frames. These protocols have largely been replaced by bit-oriented protocols.

C

C

C is one of the most popular computer languages in the world, and quite possibly the most popular. It is a compiled langauge widely supported on many platforms. It tends to be more portable than FORTRAN but less portable than Java; it has been standardized by ANSI as "ANSI C" — older versions are called either "K&R C" or "Kernighan and Ritchie C" (in honor of C's creators), or sometimes just "classic C". Fast and simple, it can be applied to all manner of general purpose tasks. C compilers are made by several companies, but the free GNU version (gcc) is still considered one of the best. Newer C-like object-oriented languages include both Java and C++.

C++

C++ is a compiled object-oriented language. Based heavily on C, C++ is nearly as fast and can often be thought of as being just C with added features. It is currently probably the second most popular object-oriented language, but it has the drawback of being fairly complex — the much simpler but somewhat slower Java is probably the most popular object-oriented language. Note that C++ was developed independently of the somewhat similar Objective-C; it is however related to Objective-C++.

Cable

An assembly of one or more insulated conductors, or optical fibers, or a combination of both, within an enveloping jacket. Either a stranded conductor (single-conductor cable) or a combination of conductors insulated from one another (multiple conductor cable). Small sizes are commonly referred to as stranded wire or as cords. A conductor with insulation, or a stranded conductor with or without insulation and other coverings (single-conductor cable), or a combination of conductors insulated from one another (multiple-conductor cable).

Cable armour

A covering of steel, wire, tape or some other material used to protect the internal conductors.

Cable assembly

A cable that is ready for installation in specific applications and usually terminated with connectors. .

Cable carrier

A device that holds a cable. Also refer to a detailed definition of Cable Carrier. In some case it may be called a cable retracter.

Cable clamp

A mechanical clamp attached to the wire entrance of a connector to support the cable or wire bundle, provide stress relief, and absorb vibration and shock. Also called a cable adapter bracket.

Cable harness

A group of wires or ribbons of wiring used to interconnect electronic systems and subsystems. Also refer to more detail on Specifying a Cable Harness, part of the equipment chassis design section.

Cable leakage

Shielded cables with gaps in their shielding, which allows the center conductor to radiate. Cable signal leaks can be caused by loose connectors, or cracked or unterminated cables.

Cable modem

A PC modem which interfaces between a personal computer and a cabled internet connection, normally coax. .

Cable range

Range of network numbers that is valid for use by nodes on an extended AppleTalk network. The cable range value can be a single network number or a contiguous sequence of several network numbers. Node addresses are assigned based on the cable range value.

Cable sheath

A non-conductive protective covering applied to cables. .

Cable splitter

It refers to a 3-port component, or Y-Cable as it refers to a cable with 3 ends or terminations.

Cable tray

A lattice work or mesh of intersecting metal used to support some number of cables running between different points. A cable tray is normally metal but may also be plastic or fiber-glass. Cable Trays may also be a solid section of metal instead of a wire frame work.

Cable, coaxial

A cable in which an insulated conductor is centered inside another. The outer conductor is usually a metal braid or metal sheath. Braided cables usually have an outer insulating jacket over the braid. Coaxial cables are used primarily for transmission of RF signals.

Cache

A temporary storage area for frequently or recently used data, either in memory, on your hard disk or the internet. For example, if you go back to a webpage you have recently visited, your PC will usually be able to display it from the internet cache on your hard disk, so it won't need to download it from the internet again.

CAD

(Computer Aided Design) Software used to produce complex technical drawings by designers and engineers.

Cage code

Commercial and Government Entity Code. A five-position alphanumeric code with a numeric in the first and last positions (e.g. 27340, 2A345, or 2AAA5), assigned to United States and Canadian organizations which manufacture and/or control the design of items supplied to a Government Military or Civil Agency or assigned to United States and foreign organizations, primarily for identifying contractors in the mechanical interchange of data.

Calculated field

A field that displays the result of a calculation in a query.

Call admission control

Traffic management mechanism used in ATM networks thatdetermines whether the network can offer a path with sufficient bandwidth for a requested VCC.

Call priority

Priority assigned to each origination port in circuit-switched systems. This priority defines the order in which calls are reconnected. Call priority also defines which calls can or cannot be placed during a bandwidth reservation.

Call setup time

The time required to establish a switched call between DTE devices.

Call stream

A communication facility that combines synchronous and asynchronous RPCs so that the different forms of communication are invisible to servers.

Call waiting

Where a caller is put on hold and can be listening to music, the radio or messages.

CAM

Content-addressable memory.

Can bus

A differential 2-wire interface running over either a Shielded Twisted Pair (STP), Un-shielded Twisted Pair (UTP), or Ribbon cable. A number of different Protocols are used with CAN bus. The CanBus is primarily used as an Automotive Bus, but is also one of the major Field Buses.

Cancel character

[CAN] A control character used by some conventions to indicate that the data with which it is associated are in error or are to be disregarded.

Candidate key

A minimal set of attributes that uniquely identifies an object or link.

Capacitance

The property of an electrical circuit that opposes changes in voltage. Also refer to the dictionary of Capacitor Terms. That property of a system of conductors and dielectrics that permits the storage of electricity when potential difference exists between the conductors. Its value is expressed as the ratio of quantity of electricity to a potential difference. A capacitance value is always positive.

Capacitive coupling

The transfer of energy from one circuit to another by means of the mutual capacitance between the circuits.

Capacitive load

A load where the current leads the voltage.

Capacitive reactance

The opposition, expressed in ohms, offered to the flow of an alternating current by capacitance. The symbol for capacitive reactance is XC.

Capacitor

A circuit component that provides a known amount of capacitance (ability to store an electric charge). A capacitor typically consists of two conductive plates separated by an insulating (dielectric) material. If other factors remain constant, capacitance increases as the plates are made larger or brought closer together. A capacitor blocks direct current but passes alternating current to an extent that depends on its capacitance and on the frequency of the current.

Capacitor microphone

A microphone that uses one plate of a capacitor as the diaphram.

Capacitor-start motor

A type of single-phase, ac induction motor in which a starting winding and a capacitor are placed in series to start the motor. The values of XC and R are such that the main-winding and starting-winding currents are nearly 90 degrees apart and the starting torque is produced as in a two-phase motor.

Capture ratio

A measure of an FM tuner's ability to reject an interfering signal of the same frequency as the desired signal.

Carbon microphone

A microphone in which sound waves vary the resistance of a pile of carbon granules. May be single-button or double-button.

Carbon resistor

A resistor that uses either a slug of carbon or a film impregnated with carbon as the resistive element.

Card

A circuit board that plugs into a computer's bus to extend the computer's capability.

Card cage

That portion of an equipment chassis that holds the circuit cards. An open or closed frame which has card guides or slots and allows attachment of a backplane to allow the interconnection of the cards within the cage.

Card extractor

A device specifically designed to remove a circuit card assembly.

Card stiffener

A rigid item mounted to a printed wiring board.

Cardbus

One of the different types of PCMCIA interfaces. CardBus implements the 32-bit PCI bus standard into the PCMCIA form factor.

Carriage return

The or key on your keyboard. On-line commands often must be followed by.

Carrier

Electromagnetic wave or alternating current of a single frequency, suitable for modulation by another, data-bearing signal.

Carrier card

A host card designed to hold two or more mezzanine cards, and having the primary function of supporting the cards by providing a site for the mezzanine card. The VME card to the right acts as a carrier card for one or two PMC mezzanine cards which would plug into the pair of black connectors just to the right of the white VME connector.

Carrier frequency
The base frequency of a transmitted electromagnetic pulse or wave on which information can be imposed by varying the signal strength, varying the base frequency, varying the wave phase, or other means. The frequency of an unmodulated transmitter output.

Carrier wave
The Carrier Frequency component of a modulated wave, or the signal wave that is intended to be modulated.

Carry flag (CY)
the first bit in the PSW register; a dual-purpose flag that signifies whether there is a carry-over during arithmetic, and is also used as a Boolean accumulator.

Cartridge fuse
An instrument fuse. A fuse with a cylindrical body usually made of plastic or ceramic and terminated with metal end caps. Also called a ribbon fuse when the body of the fuse is glass. A ferrule fuse.

Cascade amplifier
Two or more amplifiers connected together, with each output connected to the input of the following stage. Several amplifiers connected in series, forming a chain.

Cascading
Connecting two or more circuits together so that one circuit feeds the other.

Case insensitive
Referring to a system in which upper case letters are not differentiated from their lower case form.

Case sensitive
Referring to a system in which upper case letters are differentiatedfrom their lower case form.

Case sensitive search
A search in a database in which capitalization of key words must exactly match the capitalization of words in the database. A case-sensitive search for “north and south” would fail to find a database entry for “North and South.”

Case temperature
The temperature measured at a specified point on the case of a semiconductor device.

Caster
A wheel mounted in a swivel frame.

Category 1 cabling
One of five grades of UTP cabling described in the EIA/TIA-586 standard. Category 1 cabling is used for telephone communications and is not suitable for transmitting data.

Category 2 cabling
One of five grades of UTP cabling described in the EIA/TIA-586 standard. Category 2 cabling is capable of transmitting data at speeds up to 4 Mbps.

Category 3 cabling
One of five grades of UTP cabling described in the EIA/TIA-586 standard. Category 3 cabling is used in 10Base T networks and can transmit data at speeds up to 10 Mbps.

Category 4 cabling
One of five grades of UTP cabling described in the EIA/TIA-586 standard. Category 4 cabling is used in Token Ring networks and can transmit data at speeds up to 16 Mbps.

Category 5 cabling
One of five grades of UTP cabling described in the EIA/TIA-586 standard. Category 5 cabling is used

for running CDDI and can transmit data at speeds up to 100 Mbps.

Catenet

Network in which hosts are connected to diverse networks, which themselves are connected with routers. The Internet is a prominent example of a catenet.

Catv

Cable television. Communication system where multiple channels of programming material are transmitted to homes using broadband coaxial cable. Formerly called Community Antenna Television.

CBDS

Connectionless Broadband Data Service. European high-speed, packet-switched, datagram-based WAN networking technology.

CBR

Constant bit rate. QOS class defined by the ATM Forum for ATM networks. CBR is used for connections that depend on precise clocking to ensure undistorted delivery.

CC

Carbon Copy

CCD

(Charge Coupled Device) The component of a scanner or digital camera which actually takes the pictures. The quality of image it is capable of is usually measured in Megapixels the higher the number, the more detailed the image.

CCITT

Consultative Committee for International Telegraph and Television and Telephone. International organization responsible for the development of communications standards. Now called the ITU-T.

CCS

Common Channel Signaling. Signaling system used in telephone networks that separates signaling information from user data. A specified channel is exclusively designated to carry signaling information for all other channels in the system.

CD

Carrier Detect. Signal that indicates whether an interface is active. Also, a signal generated by a modem indicating that a call has been connected.

CD burner

A CD drive that can create ("burn") CDs.

CDDI

Copper Distributed Data Interface. Implementation of FDDI protocols over STP and UTP cabling. CDDI transmits over relatively short distance (about 100 meters), providing data rates of 100Mbps using a dual-ring architecture to provide redundancy. Based on the ANSI Twisted-Pair Physical Medium Dependent (TPPMD) standard.

CDE

The common desktop environment is a popular commercial window manager (and much more — as its name touts, it is more of a desktop environment) that runs under X-Windows. Free work-alike versions are also available.

CDEV

The designation of a Control Panel Device in Macintosh System 6 and earlier.

CDFS

A designation used with UNIX computers to indicate that a file system resides on a read-only removable medium (that is a CD-ROM). This usually implies that the compact disc is compliant with the ISO 9660 standard. CDFS is also used as a part of commands that mount media (hard drives, tape drives, remote networked drives, and CD-ROMs) for use on a computer.

CDPD

Cellular Digital Packet Data. Open standard for two-way wireless data communication over high-frequency cellular telephone channels. Allows data transmissions between a remote cellular link and a NAP. Operates at 19.2 Kbps.

CD-PLUS

A compact disc encoding format that allows mixing of audio recordings and computer data on the same CD, without the possibility of audio equipment becoming damaged by attempting to play the data sections.

CD-ROM

(Compact Disk - Read Only Memory). Optical (CD) disks that are mastered and then can only be read; i.e., the data cannot be manipulated, removed, etc.

CD-ROM

(compact Disk Read Only Memory). An optical 120mm diameter disk with 650 megabytes capacity. It is used to store text, graphics, sound and video. The digital data is recorded in a spiral from the centre to the outermost edge

CD-ROM, CD-R

(Compact Disk-Read Only Memory) A misnomer, as strictly speaking it is not memory but storage. Identical to standard music CDs. A popular medium for releasing programs. Now being replaced by DVD, which has a much higher capacity.

CD-RW

(Compact Disk-ReWriter) A CD drive which can create CDs, either audio or data, using special rewriteable CDs which are also often called CD-RWs. A CD-RW drive can also create ordinary CDs, though not rewrite them.

CDVT

(Cell Delay Variation Tolerance). Parameter defined by the ATM Forum for ATM traffic management. In CBR transmissions, determines the level of jitter that is tolerable for the data samples taken by the PCR.

CEDI

Cayman Encapsulated DDP in IP. An Apple Talk tunneling protocol developed by Cayman.

Cell

The basic unit for ATM Switching and multiplexing. Cells contain identifiers that specify the data stream to which they belong. Each cell consists of a 5-byte header and 48 bytes of payload.

Cell relay

Network technology based on the use of small, fixed-size packets, or cells. Because cells are fixed-length, they can be processed and switched in hardware at high speeds. Cell relay is the basis for many high-speed network protocols including ATM, IEEE802.6, and SMDS.

Cells
The rectangles created at the intersection of columns and rows.

Cellular radio
Technology that uses radio transmissions to access telephone-company networks. Service is provided in a particular area by a low-power transmitter.

Centrex
AT&T PBX that provides direct inward dialing and automatic numbering identification of the calling PBX.

CEPT
Conférence Européenne des Postes et des Télécommunications. Association of the 26 European PTTs that recommends communication specifications to the ITU-T.

CERT
Acronym for Computer Emergency Response Team. An organization that provides a round-the-clock security consultation service for Internet users and provides advisories whenever new virus programs and other computer security threats are discovered.

Certificate
Used for client authentication. A certificate is registered on the authentication server (for example, RADIUS server) and used by the authenticator.

Certnet
California Education and Research Federation Network. TCP/IP network, based in Southern California, that connects hundreds of higher-education centers internationally while also providing Internet access to subscribers. CERFnet was founded in 1988 by the San Diego Supercomputer Center and General Automics and is funded by the NSF.

CGI
Common Gateway Interface — conventions for data communication between a Web server and an auxiliary program; Computer Generated Image — a physical object modeled and represented as a realistic three-dimensional graphic.

Chaining
SNA concept in which RUs are grouped together for the propose of error recovery.

Channel
Any medium by which information can be transmitted. For example, the air is a channel for our voices just as much as a fiber optic line can be data for a video signal.

Channel I/O
In computer science, channel I/O is a generic term that refers to a high-performance input/output (I/O) architecture that is implemented in various forms on a number of computer architectures, especially on mainframe computers.

Channel-attached
Pertaining to attachment of devices directly by data channels (input/output channels) to a computer.

Channelized E1
Access link operating at 2.048 Mbps that is subdivided into 30 B-channels and 1 D-channel, Supports DDR, Frame Relay, and X.25.

Channelized T1
Access link operating at 1.544 Mbps that is subdivided into 24 channels (23 B-channels and 1D-channel) of 64 Kbps each. The individual channels

or groups of channels connect to different destinations. Supports DDR, Frame Relay, and X.25. Also referred to as fractional T1.

CHAP

Challenge Handshake Authentication Protocol. Security feature supported on lines using PPP encapsulation that prevents unauthorized access. CHAP does not itself prevent unauthorized access, it merely identifies the remote end. The router or access server than determines whether that user is allowed access.

Character

1. A symbol such as a letter, number or punctuation mark that canbe arranged to represent higher units of meaning, such as wordsand sentences.
2. The group of bits that represent such a symbol.

Character map

In text-based computer graphics, a block of memory addresses that correspond to character spaces on a display screen. The memory allocated to each character space is used to hold the description of the character to be displayed in that space.

Character set

A set of characters handled by a specified machine; sets include alphabetic characters, numbers, symbols, graphics characters, a space character and control characters. Graphics characters denote a printed mark; control characters produce some particular effect. Two of the most widely used sets are ASCII and EBCDIC.

Chart

A graphic or diagram that displays data or the relationships between sets of data in pictorial rather than numeric form.

Chassis

The framework on a computer that supports its components including the motherboard, hard drives, and memory

Chat

Chatting is like e-mail, only it is done instantaneously and can directly involve multiple people at once. While e-mail now relies on one more or less standard protocol, chatting still has a couple competing ones. Of particular note are IRC and Instant Messenger. One step beyond chatting is called MUDding

Chat script

String of text that defines the login “conversation” that occurs between two systems. Consist of expect-send pairs that define the string that the local system expects to receive from the remote system and what the local system should send as a reply.

Chatroom

A website where you can meet and chat live (via the keyboard) with other internet users. Most such websites have multiple “rooms”, each dedicated to a particular topic or theme.

Cheapernet

Industry term used to refer to the IEEE 802.3 10Base2 standard or the cable specified in that standard.

Checked exception

An exception checked by the compiler which requires a programmer to write explicit exception handlers.

Checkpointing

The process of writing data items to a recovery file along with status entries and intentions lists.

Checksum

The result of a mathematical operation that uses the binary representation of a group of data as its basis, usually to check the integrity of the data.

Chip

A tiny piece of semi-conductive material, usually based on silicon, used in the manufacture of electronic components.

Chip (integrated circuit)

A miniaturized electronic circuit (consisting mainly of semiconductor devices, as well as passive components) that has been manufactured in the surface of a thin substrate of semiconductor material.

Chipset

A chipset, PC chipset, or chip set refers to a group of integrated circuits, or chips, that are designed to work together. They are usually marketed as a single product.

Choke packet

Packet sent to a transmitter to tell it that congestion exists and that it should reduce its sending rate.

Chrome

A popular internet browser, free from the Google Corporation.

Cicnet

Regional network that connects academic, reserach, nonprofit, and commercial organizations in the Midwestern United States. Founded in 1988, CICNet was a part of the NSF NET and was funded by the NSF until the NSFNET dissolved in 1995.

CICS

(Customer Information Control System). IBM application subsystem allowing transactions entered at remote terminals to be processed concurrently by user applications.

CIDR

(Classless interdomain routing). Technique supported by BGP4 and based on route aggregation. CIDR allows routers to group routes together in order to cut down on the quantity of routing information carried by the core routers. With CIDR, several IP networks appear to networks outside the group as a single, larger entity.

CIR

(Committed information rate). The rate at which a Frame Relay network agrees to transfer information under normal conditions, averaged over a minimum increment of time. CIR, measured in bits per second, is one of the key negotiated tariff metrics.

Circuit

1. Any electrical pathway.
2. An arrangement of electrical andelectronic devices and the conductive paths between them.

Circuit group

Grouping of associated serial lines that link two bridges. If one of the serial links in a circuit group is in the spanning tree for a network, any of the serial links in the circuit group can be used for load balancing. This load-balancing strategy avoids data ordering problems by assigning each destination address to a particular serial link.

Circuit switching

Switching system in which a dedicated physical circuit path must exist between sender and receiver for the duration of the "call." Used heavily in the telephone company network. Circuit switching can be contrasted with contention and token passing as a channel-access method, and with message switching and packet switching as a switching technique.

CISC

Acronym for complex instruction set computing. The implementation of complex instructions in a microprocessor design so that they can be invoked at the assembly language level. The instructions can be very powerful, allowing for complicated and flexible ways of calculating such elements as memory addresses. All this complexity, however, usually requires many clock cycles to execute each instruction.

Class

The definition of an object's attributes and operations; A "blueprint" for a group of objects with common attributes, operations, and semantics.

Class attribute

an attribute whose value is common to a class of objects rather than a value peculiar to each instance.

Classic ip over atm

Specification for running IP over ATM in a manner that takes full advantage of the features of ATM.

Classification

a grouping of objects with the same data structure and behavior.

CLAW

(Common Link Access for Workstations). Data link layer protocol used by channel-attached RISC System/6000 series systems and by IBM 3172 devices running TCP/IP off-load. CLAW improves efficiency of channel use and allows the CIP to provide the functionality of a 3172 in TCP/IP environments and support direct channel attachment. The output from TCP/IP mainframe processing is a series of IP datagrams that the router can switch without modifications.

Clean boot

Booting or starting a computer using the minimum system files in the operating system. The clean boot is used as a troubleshooting method for isolating problems associated with software that may be calling on the same system resources at the same time, causing conflicts that lower the performance of the system, make some programs inoperable, or crash the computer.

Clean install

Reinstallation of software in a manner that ensures that no application or system files from a previous installation will remain. The procedure prevents "smart" installer programs from skipping file installations where a file already exists, which could potentially keep a problem from being removed.

Click

To press a mouse button. When done twice in rapid succession, it is referred to as a double-click

Client

A computer program that uses the services of another computer program. Software that extracts information from a server; your auto-dial phone is a client, and the phone company is its server.

Client module

A module that extends the operations of the flat file service and the directory service under a single API.

Client-server

A type of relationship between two computers where the two havedifferent roles in the relationship. Typically, the client computerdrives the relationship and uses a resource of the servercomputer.

Client-server computing

The model or scheme underlying practically all programs running on the Internet (as well asother network and database software). In this design, the work of an application (such as FTP orGopher) is divided up between two programs-the client (or "front end") and the server (or "back end"). The client program handles the work of connecting to the server and requesting files or information, and the server handles the work of finding and "serving up" the information (or of providing some other service, such as directing print jobs to a printer). See also Archie, client, File Transfer Protocol, Gopher server Domain Name System, Wide Area Information Servers.

Client-server interface

An architecture that provides for the splitting of user requests (usually called clients) and a related server function, most commonly across a network. The combined effect is to provide the clients with access to some service such as databases, printing, etc.

Client-server model

A program design approach in which one program, the server, provides a service to another program, the client, which is requesting that service.

Clipboard

A temporary storage area in Windows. When you cut (Ctrl-X) or copy (Ctrl-C) highlighted text, documents or whatever in Windows they are sent to the clipboard; when you paste (Ctrl-V) they are copied from the clipboard to the cursor position. Sending something to the clipboard automatically overwrites its previous contents.

Clipper chip

An integrated circuit that implements the SkipJack algorithm, an encryption algorithm created by the National Security Agency that encrypts 64-bit blocks of data with an 80-bit key. The Clipper is manufactured by the U.S. government to encrypt telephone data. It has the added feature that it can be decrypted by the U.S. government, which has tried unsuccessfully to make the chip compulsory in the United States.

CLNP

(Connectionless Network Protocol). OSI network layer protocol that does not require a circuit to be established before data is transmitted.

CLNS

CLNS routes messages to their destinations independently of any other messages.

Clock

1. A component in a computer that provides a timing pulse forother components.
2. The timing pulse of a network transmission.

Clock rate

The rate at which the clock in an electronic device, such as a computer, oscillates. The clock rate is normally given in hertz (Hz, one cycle per second), kilohertz (kHz, one thousand cycles per second), or megahertz

(MHz, one million cycles per second). Clock rates in personal computers increased from about 5 MHz to about 50 MHz between 1981 and 1995. Also called clock speed, hertz time.

Clock speed

The clock speed is the frequency which determines how fast devices that are connected to the system bus operate. The speed is measured in millions of cycles per second (MHz or megahertz) and is generated by a quartz crystal on the motherboard which acts as a kind of metronome. Devices that are synchronized with the clock may run faster or slower but their speed is determined by multiplying or dividing a factor by the clock speed.

Clone

A copy; in microcomputer terminology, a look-alike, act-alike computer that contains the same microprocessor and runs the same programs as a better-known, more prestigious, and often more expensive machine.

Closely synchronized group

A group of servers in which the members execute all requests immediately after receiving them.

Cloud, the

Remote storage via the internet, or sometimes just the internet in general. Called "the cloud" because you don't know where your data is physically located, it's just out there somewhere.

CLP

(Cell Loss Priority). Field in the ATM cell header that determines the probability of a cell being dropped if the network becomes congested. Cell with CLP = 0 are insured traffic, which is unlikely to be dropped. Cells with CLP = 1 are best-effort traffic, which might be dropped in congested conditions in order to free up resources to handle insured traffic.

Cluster

1. An aggregation, such as a group of data points on a graph.
2. A communications computer and its associated terminals.
3. In data storage, a disk-storage unit consisting of a fixed number of sectors (storage segments on the disk) that the operating system uses to read or write information; typically, a cluster consists of two to eight sectors, each of which holds a certain number of bytes (characters).

Cluster controller

1. Generally, an intelligent device that provides the connections for a cluster of terminals to be data link. 2. In SNA, a programmable device that controls the input/ output operations of attached devices. Typically, an IBM 3174 or 3274 device.

CMI

(Coded Mark Inversion). ITU-T line coding technique specified for STS-3c transmissions. Also used in DS-1 systems.

CMIP

Common Management Information Protocol.

CMIS

Common Management Information Services. OSI network management service interface created and standardized by ISO for the monitoring and control of heterogeneous networks.

CMNS

(Connection-Mode Network Service). Extends local X.25 switching to a variety of media (Ethernet, FDDI, Token Ring).

CMOS

(Complementary Metal Oxide Semiconductor; pr. "see-moss") A special type of memory which retains its data when the PC is switched off, used to store settings for things like what type of hard disk you have, and how much memory. The settings are accessed via the BIOS.

CMT

Connection management. FDDI process that handles the transition of the ring through its various states (off, active, connect, and so on), as defined by the ANSI X3T9.5 specification.

CMY

Acronym for cyan-magenta-yellow. A model for describing colors that are produced by absorbing light, as by ink on paper, rather than by emitting light, as on a video monitor. The three kinds of cone cells in the eye respond to red, green, and blue light, which are absorbed (removed from white light) by cyan, magenta, and yellow pigments, respectively. Percentages of pigments in these subtractive primary colors can therefore be mixed to get the appearance of any desired color. Absence of any pigment leaves white unchanged; adding 100 percent of all three pigments turns white to black.

CMYK

(Cyan, Magenta, Yellow, Keystone black) The standard four colours used by most printers - almost any colour can be created out of these.

Coaxial cable

An electrical cable in which the conductors share a common axis.

COBOL

Stands for Common Business Oriented Language. A computer programming language invented during the second generation of computers and designed to meet the needs of business. Although less often used today, it was well-suited for writing programs that process large files and generate report

Code

A language for expressing operations to be performed by a computer. To write in such a language.

Code of practice

Guidelines that should be implemented to maintain safe work practices.

CODEC

(COmpressor/DECompressor) A small piece of computer code that tells the computer how to decode particular types of information, usually video files. If your video player won't play a particular format, you can usually download and install a codec which will tell it how from the internet.

Coding

Electrical techniques used to convey binary signals.

Collapsed backbone

Nondistributed backbone in which all network segments are interconnected by way of an internetworking device. A collapsed backbone might be a virtual network segment existing in a device such as a hub, a router, or a switch.

Collection
an object that encapsulates a data structure for storing other objects.

Collision
The result of two nodes transmitting at the same time on a multiple access network such as Ethernet. Both packets may be lost or partial packets may result.

Collision avoidance
A Media Access Control (MAC) method in which any node maytake control of the network after taking certain steps to insure thatthe cable is not in use or about to be used by another node.

Collision detection
A MAC method in which any node may take control of the networkwhen it is not in use by another node. While transmitting, stationscontinue to listen for incoming signals (collisions) and emit a jamming signal to notify all other stations of the collision.

Collision domain
In Ethernet, the network area within which frames that have collided are propagated. Repeaters and hubs propagate collisions; LAN switches, bridges and routers do not.

Color bits
A predetermined number of bits assigned to each displayable pixel that determine its color when it is displayed on a monitor. For example, two color bits are required for four colors; eight color bits are required for 256 colors.

Color box
In the Microsoft NT and Windows 95 Paint accessory, a graphic screen element in the form of a paint box that is used to select foreground and background colors.

Color management
In printing, the process of producing accurate, consistent color using any of a variety of output devices. Color management includes accurate conversion of RGB input from a scanner, camera, or monitor to CMYK output for a printer; application of a device profile for the printer or other output device on which the image will be reproduced; and allowance for environmental variations such as humidity and barometric pressure.

Color saturation
The amount of a hue contained in a color; the more saturation, the more intense the color.

Column
A vertical arrangement of characters or other expressions.

COM port
Short for communications port, the logical address assigned by MS-DOS (versions 3.3 and higher) and Microsoft Windows (including Windows 95 and Windows NT) to each of the four serial ports on an IBM Personal Computer or a PC compatible. COM ports also have come to be known as the actual serial ports on a PC's CPU where peripherals, such as printers, scanners, and external modems, are plugged in.

Command
A request, typed from a terminal or embedded in a file, to perform an operation or to execute a particular program.

Command key
On the original Macintosh keyboard, a key labeled with the special symbol, sometimes called the propeller or

puppy foot. This key is found on one or both sides of the Spacebar, depending on the version of the Apple keyboard. The key serves some of the same functions as the Control key on IBM keyboards.

Command line

A string of text written in the command language and passed to the command interpreter for execution.

Common carrier

Licensed, private utility company that supplies communication services to the public at regulated prices.

Common gateway interface (CGI)

An Interface that allows a program, or application called a CGIscript usually written in a computer language such as "PERL" or "C++" to perform some useful task based on a users input. Typical CGI scripts do things like :read an Image Map, count the number hits to your page, or accept and filter data from a forms page.

Communicate

Successfully convey an idea from one person to another using some form of medium – verbal, non-verbal.

Communication

Transmission of information.

Communication breakdown

Failure to communicate or be understood for some reason.

Communication controller

In SNA, a subarea node (such as an IBM 3745 device) thatcontains an NCP.

Communication identifier

the main part of a resolved name that generally identifies the sender or receiver of some communication.

Communication server

Communications processor that connects asynchronous devicesto a LAN or WAN through network and terminal emulation software. Performs only asynchronous routing of IP and IPX.

Communications line

The physical link (such as wire or a telephone circuit) that connects one or more devices to one or more other devices.

Communications program

A program that makes a computer act as a terminal to another computer. Communications programs usually provide for file transfer between microcomputers and mainframes.

Community

In SNMP, a logical group of managed devices and NMSs in the same administrative domain.

Community string

Text string that acts as a password and is used to authenticate messages sent between a management station and a router containing a SNMP agent. The community string is sent in every packet between the manager and the agent.

Companding

Contraction derived from the opposite processes of compression and expansion. Part of the PCM process whereby analog signal values are logically rounded to discrete scale-step values on a nonlinear scale. The decimal step number is then coded in its binary equivalent prior to transmission. The process is reversed at the receiving terminal using the same nonlinear scale.

Compatible

Compatible pieces of equipment can work together; incompatible ones can't.

Compile

To translate all the source code of a program from a high-level language into object code prior to execution of the program. Object code is executable machine code or a variation of machine code. More generally, compiling is sometimes used to describe translating any high-level symbolic description into a lower-level symbolic or machine-readable format. A program that performs this task is known as a compiler.

Compiler

A program that translates human-readable programs into a form the computer understands. The input (source code) to the compiler is a description of an algorithm in a problem- oriented language; its output (object code) is an equivalent description of the algorithm in a machine-oriented language.

Complete class

A class which contains no abstract parts.

Component

An indivisible unit of functionality, usually embodied in hardware.

Compose

To produce or put together an idea, usually written.

Compressed file

A file whose contents have been compressed by a special utility program so that it occupies less space on a disk or other storage device than in its uncompressed (normal) state.

Compression

A way of making files smaller, either to fit into restricted storage space or to speed up transmission over the Internet. Popular compression standards include JPEG and GIF for pictures, MP3 for music files,MPEG, MP4, AVI and MOV for movie footage, and zip for just about everything else.

Computer

A device or system that is capable of carrying out a sequence of operations in a distinctly and explicitly defined manner. The operations are frequently numeric computations or data manipulations, but also include data input and output. The ability to branch within sequences is its key feature.

Computer case

A computer case (also known as a computer chassis, cabinet, box, tower, enclosure, housing, system unit or simply case) is the enclosure that contains most of the components of a computer (usually excluding the display, keyboard and mouse).

Computer form factor

In computing, the form factor is the name used to denote the dimensions, power supply type, location of mounting holes, number of ports on the back panel, etc.

Computer graphics interface

Acronym CGI. A software standard applied to computer graphics devices, such as printers and plotters. Computer Graphics Interface is an offshoot of a widely recognized graphics standard called GKS (Graphical Kernel System), which provides applications programmers with standard methods of creating, manipulating, and displaying or printing computer graphics.

Computer graphics metafile

A software standard related to the widely recognized GKS (Graphical Kernel System) that provides applications programmers with a standard means of describing a graphic as a set of instructions for re-creating it. A graphics metafile can be stored on disk or sent to an output device; Computer Graphics Metafile provides a common language for describing such files in relation to the GKS standard. See also Graphical Kernel System.

Computer literacy

Knowledge and an understanding of computers combined with the ability to use them effectively. On the least specialized level, computer literacy involves knowing how to turn on a computer, start and stop simple application programs, and save and print information. At higher levels, computer literacy becomes more detailed, involving the ability of power users to manipulate complex applications and, possibly, to program in languages such as Basic or C. At the highest levels, computer literacy leads to specialized technical knowledge of electronics and assembly language.

Computer science

The study of algorithms, including their formal and mathematical properties, hardware realizations, linguistic realizations, and applications; the science of algorithmic problem solving.

Computing agent

the thing carrying out the steps of an algorithm.

Concentrator

A device that brings together at a common center connections to a particular kind of network (such as Ethernet), and implements that network internally.

Concrete class

A class that can have direct instances.

Concurrency

A situation in which multiple processes exist in a single system.

Concurrency transparency

a type of transparency that enables several processes to operate concurrently using shared information objects without interference between them.

Concurrent

Two or more tasks, activities, or events whose execution may overlap in time.

Condition

A Boolean function of object values valid over an interval of time.

Conductor

The current-carrying component of a transmission cable, typicallya copper wire.

Conference

An electronic meeting place dedicated to a particular subject where users come to participate in discussions or group projects. Conferences can be used to post a variety of information such as news services, newsletters, and statistics; also called "newsgroups," "bulletin boards," or "echoes." An electronic conference provides a many-to-many communication medium, as opposed to the person-to-person nature of e-mail. All conferences have a particular subject or purpose, and the topics and responses they contain might provide items of news, ideas, questions, or other information in almost any form. Some special-purpose conferences may have restricted access, allowing some users to write messages, some only to read, and some neither. The person responsible for the technical maintenance and/or community communication is called the "conference facilitator."

Conference call

This is where several people are calling by telephone from different locations and everyone can be heard simultaneously.

Configsys

A special text file that controls certain aspects of operating-system behavior in MS-DOS and OS/2. Commands in the CONFIG.SYS file enable or disable system features, set limits on resources (for example, the maximum number of open files), and extend the operating system by loading device drivers that control hardware specific to an individual computer system.

Configuration

The particular hardware elements and their interaction in a computer system for a particular period of operation.

Configuration management

One of five categories of network management of OSI networks. Configuration management subsysems are responsible for detecting and determining the state of a network.

Congestion

Traffic in excess of network capacity.

Connect time

Time that elapses while the user of a terminal is connected to a time-sharing system; it is measured by the duration between logon and logoff.

Connectionless

The opposite of connectionless, a type of relationship betweentwo devices where each information packet must contain theaddress of the partner device.

Connection-oriented

In data networks, a type of computer relationship in which the network equipment constructs a circuit between the two devices for the duration of their relationship. Once the circuit is established, the devices pass information back and forth through the circuit without regard to their physical addresses. The circuit may be physical or virtual.

Connectivity

1. The nature of the connection between a user's computer and another computer, such as a server or a host computer on the Internet or a network. This may describe the quality of the circuit or telephone line, the degree of freedom from noise, or the bandwidth of the communications devices.
2. The ability of hardware devices or software packages to transmit data between other devices or packages.
3. The ability of hardware devices, software packages, or a computer itself to work with network devices or with other hardware devices, software packages, or a computer over a network connection.

Connector

A device that establishes a physical connection between oneconductor or circuit and another.

CONP
Connection-Oriented Network Protocol, OSI protocol providing connection-oriented operation to upper-layer protocols.

Console
In SNMP (Simple Network Management Protocol), a software program that has the capability of interacting with an agent, including examining or changing the values of the data objects in the agent's Management Information Base (MIB).

Constraint
a functional relationship between objects, classes, attributes, links, and associations; a statement about some condition or relationship that must be maintained as true.

Constructor
A special member function that performs initialization and is called automatically when an object is instantiated.

Consumables
Items that need to be replaced such as toners, ink cartridges, paper, blank disks etc.

Container class
a class of container objects, such as sets, arrays, dictionaries, and associations.

Contention
A network access method where all the devices on the network have equal changes of gaining control of the network at any time. Includes avoidance (CSMA/CA) access methods.

Context switch
The transition between contexts that takes place when switching between threads.

Control
The aspect of a system that describes the sequences of operations that occur in response to stimuli.

Control character
One of 32 characters of the ASCII character set that defines a control function for a character entry and display device such as a terminal. Examples are carriage return, tab, form feed and bell.

Control flow
A Boolean value that affects whether a process is executed.

Control key
A key that, when pressed in combination with another key, gives the other key an alternative meaning. In many application programs, Control (labeled CTRL or Ctrl on a PC keyboard) plus another key is used as a command for special functions.

Control panel
In the Macintosh, a software application that has the ability to control an aspect of system configuration, such as the pixel depth of the monitor (Monitors), the choice of network type (Network), etc.

Control store
The memory that stores the microcode of a CPU; originally read-only memory was employed.

Control unit
A device or circuit that performs an arbitrating or regulating function. For example, a memory controller chip controls access to a computer's memory and is the control unit for that memory.

Conventional PCI

Conventional PCI (PCI is an initialism formed from Peripheral Component Interconnect, part of the PCI Local Bus standard and often shortened to PCI) is a computer bus for attaching hardware devices in a computer.

Convergence

The speed and ability of a group of internetworking devices running a specific routing protocol to agree on the topology of an internetwork after a change in that topology.

Convergence sublayer

One of the two sublayers of the AAL CPCS, responsible for padding and error checking. PDUs passed from the SSCS and appended with a 8-byte trailer (for error checking and other control information) and padded, if necessary, so that the length of the resulting PDU is divisible by 48. These PDUs are then passed to the SAR sublayer of the CPCS for further processing.

Conversation

In SNA, an LU 6.2 session between two transaction programs.

Cookie

A small data file stored on your computer by a website, in theory to allow it to "remember" your preferences, but in practise mostly used to track which adverts you have seen. You can set most browsers to reject all cookies, or to ask your permission before storing them, but this can generate multiple error messages on some websites and is generally more hassle than it's worth they are pretty harmless.

Cookies

Text files that visit Web sites store information on your computer's hard disk.

Copy

A function that reads data from a source, leaving the source data unchanged and writes it elsewhere. One example would be to copy a deck of punched cards onto magnetic tape.

Core gateway

The primary routers in the Internet.

Core memory

in modern usage, a synonym for main memory, dating back from the time when the dominant main memory technology was magnetic core memory.

Core router

In a packet-switched star topology, a router that is part of the backbone and that serves as the single pipe through which all traffic from peripheral networks must pass on its way to other peripheral networks.

COS

1. **Class of service.** Indication of how an upper-layer protocol requires that a lower-layer protocol treat its messages. In SNA subarea routing, COS definitions are used by subarea nodes to determine the optimal route to establish to given session. A COS definition comprises a virtual route number and a transmission priority field. Also called TOS (type of service).
2. **Corporation for Open Systems.** Organization that promulgates the use of OSI protocols through conformance testing, certification, and related activities.

COSINE

Cooperation for Open Systems Interconnection Networking in Europe. European project financed by the European Community (EC) to build a communication network between scientific and industrial entities in Europe. The project ended in 1994.

Cost

Arbitrary value, typically based on hop count, media bandwidth, or other measures, that is assigned by a network administrator and used to compare various paths through an internetwork environment. Cost values are used by routing protocols to determine the most favorable path to a particular destination: the lower the cost, the better the path. Sometimes called path cost.

Count to Infinity

Problem that can occur in routing algorithms that are slow to converge, in which routers continuously increment the hop count to particular networks. Typically, some arbitrary hop-count limit is imposed to prevent this problem.

CPCS

Common part convergence sublayer. One of the two sublayers of any AAL. The CPCS is service-independent and is further divided into the CS and the SAR sublayers. The CPCS is responsible for preparing data for transport across the ATM network, including the creation of the 48-byte payload cells that are passed to the ATM layer.

CPE

Customer premises equipment. Terminating equipment, such as terminals, telephones, and modems, supplied by the telephone company, installed at customer sites, and connected to the telephone company network.

CPI-C

Common Programming Interface for Communications. Platform-independent API developed by IBM and used to provide portability in APPC applications.

CPM (cost per thousand)

The practice of calculating a cost per 1000 ad displays. It is used by programs that pay on an impression basis — with the CPM rate being the amount you earn for every 1000 times an advertisement is displayed. For example, a $5 CPM means you earn $5 every time 1000 ads are displayed on your site. CPM can also be calculated for pay-per-sale, pay-per-lead and pay-per-click programs by using this formula

CPS

(Characters Per Second) A measure of how quickly information, particularly text, is being transferred over a modem link or network.

CPS

Cells per second.

CPU

(Central Processing Unit) The nerve centre of the computer: everything flows through it. Often just called "the processor".

The best known PC processors are Intel's Pentium and AMD's Athlon.

CPU bound

A computing activity or network interaction whose speed is limitedby the speed at which the CPU can perform the necessary computing tasks.

CPU ID

An earlier revision of utilities such as the Intel® Frequency ID Utility and the Intel® Processor ID Utility

Crack, cracked

A crack is a small program intended to defeat software's copy protection, thus allowing unlicensed copies to be made - stealing it, in effect. Software that is distributed with its copy protection disabled or bypassed has been "cracked".

Crash

When a computer program or operating system stops working completely or almost completely it (or the computer) is said to have "crashed". When a computer crashes it usually needs to be rebootedbefore it can be used again.

Crawler

A program that indexes pages on the World Wide Web for search engines.

CRC

Cyclic Redundancy Check. A method of insuring data integritywhere a calculation is performed using the binary representationof the data itself as the basis of the calculation. The CRC is thenumerical result of this calculation and is held separately from thedata. The integrity of the data is checked by calculating a newCRC. If the two CRC's match, then there is a high degree of confidence that the data has not changed.

CREN

Corporation for Research and Educational Networking. The result of a merger of BITNET and CSNET. CREN is devoted to providing Internet connectivity to its members, which include the alumni, students, faculty, and other affiliates of participating educational and research institutions, via BITNET III.

Criteria

A specific set of conditions that you want records to meet in order to be displayed in a query, form or report.

Crosstalk

In electronic signaling, an error condition caused when the signal from one circuit causes a disturbance to the signal of thenearby circuit.

CRT

The basis of the television screen and the standard microcomputer display screen. A CRT display is built around a vacuum tube containing one or more electron guns whose electron beams rapidly sweep horizontally across the inside of the front surface of the tube, which is coated with a material that glows when irradiated. Each electron beam moves from left to right, top to bottom, one horizontal scan line at a time. To keep the screen image from flickering, the electron beam refreshes the screen 30 times or more per second. The clarity of the image is determined by the number of pixels on the screen.

CSLIP

Compressed Serial Link Internet Protocol. Extension of SLIP that, when appropriate, allows just header information to be sent across a SLIP connection, reducing overhead and increasing packet throughput on SLIP lines.

CSMA/CD

Carrier sense multiple access collision detect. Media-access mechanism wherein devices ready to transmit data first check the channel for a carrier. If no carrier is sensed for a specific period of time, a device can transmit. If two devices transmit at once, a collision occurs and is detected by all colliding devices. This collision subsequently delays retransmissions from those devices for some random length of time. CSMA/CD access is used by Ethernet and IEEE 802.3.

CSNET

Computer Science Network. Large internetwork consisting primarily of universities, research institutions, and commercial concerns. CSNET merged with BITNET to form CREN.

CSNP

Complete sequence number PDU. PDU sent by the designated router in an OSPF network to maintain database synchronization.

CSS

Cascading Style Sheets; while HTML dictates the content of page, CSS regulates the format, including headers, footers, navigation bars, etc. While all of these elements can be created in HTML, such a method would have to be repeated on every web page. CSS on the other hand, is applied to all pages of a website.

CSU

Channel Service Unit. Digital interface device that connects end-user equipment to the local digital telephone loop. Often referred to together with DSU, as CSU/DSU.

Cryptography

The use of codes to convert data so that only a specific recipient will be able to read it, using a key. The persistent problem of cryptography is that the key must be transmitted to the intended recipient and may be intercepted. Public key cryptography is a recent significant advance.

CTS

1. Clear To Send. Circuit in the EIA/TIA-232 specification that is activated when DCE is ready to accept data from DTE.
2. Common transport semantic. Cornerstone of the IBM strategy to reduce the number of protocols on networks. CTS provides a single API for developers of network software and enables applications to run over APPN, OSI, or TCP/IP.

CUI

Common User Interface is a term for the user interface used to manage Intel® Graphics Driver

Cursor

A symbol on a display screen that indicates the position at which the next character entered will be displayed. The symbol often blinks so that it can be easily noticed.

Cursor control

The keyboard keys used to position the cursor on a display screen. They are usually keys labeled with arrows indicating the direction of movement.

CUT

Control Unit Terminal.

Cut and paste

A procedure in which the computer acts as an electronic combination of scissors and glue for reorganizing a document or for compiling a document from different sources. In cut and paste, the portion of a document to be moved is selected, removed to storage in memory or on disk, and then reinserted into the same or a different document.

Cut-through packet switching

Packet switching approach that streams data through a switch so that the leading edge of a packet exits the switch at the output port before the packet finishes entering the input port. A device using cut-through packet switching reads, processes, and forwards packets as soon as the destination address is looked up, and the outgoing port determined. Also known as on-the-fly packet switching.

Cyberbully

A bully who harasses his or her victims online through various means such as spamming, defaming or negative impersonation of the victim.

Cyberdog

Apple's Internet suite for HTML browsing and e-mail, based on OpenDoc for easy integration with other applications.

Cybernaut

One who spends copious time online, exploring the Internet.

Cybersex

Communication via electronic means, such as e-mail, chat, or newsgroups, for the purpose of sexual stimulation or gratification.

Cyberspace

The nebulous "place" where humans interact over computer networks (the Internet is considered Cyberspace). Coined by William Gibson in Neuromancer.

Cybersquatter

Someone who buys up internet domain names in order to sell them on at a profit.

D

D channel

1. Data channel. Full-duplex, 16-kbps (BRI) or 64-kbps (PRI) ISDN channel.
2. In SNA, a device that connects a processor and main storage with peripherals.

D flip flop

A style of flip flop who's output follows the input when the device is clocked. The Truth Table for a D-Type flip flop is shown to the right. The output changes on the edge of the clock. The most common IC is the 7474; Dual Positive-Edge-Triggered D-Type Flip-Flops with Set and Reset.

DAC

(Dual-Attached Concentrator). FDDI or CDDI concentrator capable of attaching to both rings of an FDDI or CDDI network. It can also be dual-homed from the master ports of other FDDI or CDDi concentrators.

Daemon

In the UNIX operating system, a computing process that, oncestarted, is not under user control, but continues to run in the background. Daemons usually perform a particular purpose on demand, such as supplying information to another processor. An example in AppleTalk networking is the atalkad daemon, which supplies AppleTalk tunneling information to routers on request.

Daisy chain

In LocalTalk, a daisy chain is made by linking LocalTalkconnectors together with patch cord. In telephony, a daisy chainrefers to the method of linking a series of wall outlets togetherwith twisted pair cabling rather than the normal practice of connecting the wall outlets to a central location (home run). In telephony, "daisy chaining" is equivalent to the "backbone" method of LocalTalk construction.

DAL

Data Access Language. A data base metalanguage designed byApple. A superset of SQL.

Damped natural frequency

The frequency of an oscillator or other circuit that occurs following a transient input, which might be a step function.

Damped oscillation

An Oscillation that gradually decreases over time.

Damped wave

A sinusoidal wave in which the amplitude steadily decreases with time. Often associated with energy loss.

Damping

The process of smoothing out oscillations. The progressive decay with time in the amplitude of the free oscillations in a circuit. The progressive diminution with time of certain quantities characteristic of a phenomenon. In a meter, this process is used to keep the pointer of the meter from over-shooting the correct reading. A mechanical or electrical technique used in synchro receivers to prevent the rotor from oscillating or spinning. Damping is also used in servosystems to minimize overshoot of the load.

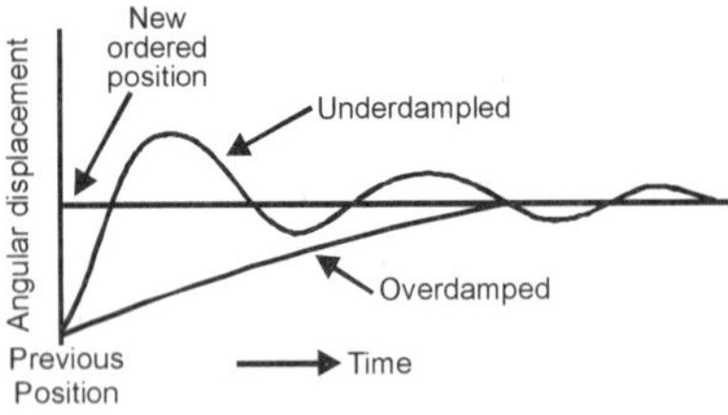

Damping coefficient

The ratio of damping to critical damping.

Darlington

[Darlington Pair] A transistor pair configured as a dual Emitter amplifier. A transistor configuration that produces a gain equal to the product of both transistors. A transistor pair in which the emitter current of the first transistor equals the Base current of the second transistor.

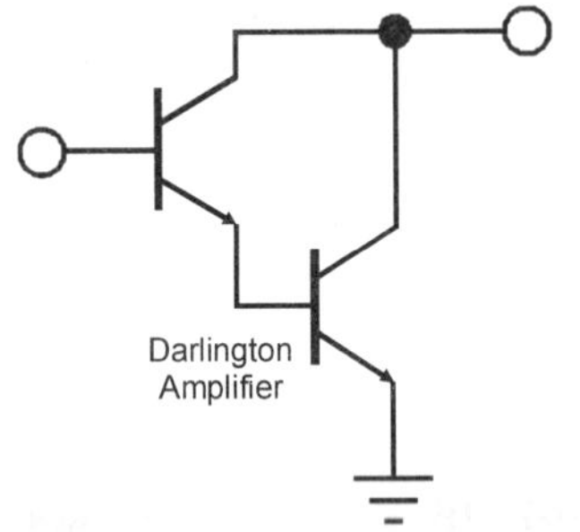

DARPA

Defense Advanced Research Projects Agency. US. government agency that funded research for and experimentation with the Internet. Evolved from ARPA, and then, from 1994, back to ARPA.

Darpa internet

Obsolete term referring to the Internet.

D'arsonval meter movement

The permanent-magnet moving-coil movement used in most analog meters. Note that most meters use digital displays. A common Analog meter movement is shown to the right.

DAS

Dual attachment station. Device attached to both the primary and the secondary FDDI rings. Dual attachment provides redundancy for the FDDI ring; if the primary ring fails, the station can wrap the primary ring to the secondary ring, isolating the failure and retaining ring integrity. Also known as a Class A station.

DASD (direct access storage device)

Mainframe terminology introduced by IBM denoting secondary storage with random access, typically (arrays of) hard disk drives.

DAT

Digital Audio Tape. A type of storage media used for the backupof computing data.

Data

Information suitable for communication, interpretation or processing by a computer.

Data acquisition

The process of obtaining data from another source, usually one outside a specific system.

Data bandwidth

The difference between the highest and lowest frequency of the data to be transmitted, usually defined by the -

3dB points.

Data base

A collection of data that can be selectively retrieved by a type ofapplication knows as a Data Base Management System.

Data block

A block transfer that moves a unit of data as a complete unit, normally without much of the associated overhead required with a single data transfer. Any required interaction to gain control of an interface bus is only done with the first data transfer, while all other transfers within the block do not require this over-head.

Data bit

In asynchronous communications, one of a group of from 5 to 8 bits that represents a single character of data for transmission. Data bits are preceded by a start bit and followed by an optional parity bit and one or more stop bits. See also asynchronous transmission, bit, communications parameter.

Data bus

A group of parallel conductors (circuit traces) found on the motherboard that is used by the CPU to send and receive data from all the devices in the computer. Also called the external data bus.

Data collection

The gathering and recording of facts, changes and forecasts for reporting and future planning.

Data communication

The collection and redistribution of data through communications channels, often including operations such as coding, decoding and validation.

Data compaction

The reduction of the number of data elements, bandwidth, cost, and time for the generation, transmission, and storage of data without loss of information by eliminating unnecessary redundancy, removing irrelevancy, or using special coding.

Data compression

Increasing the amount of data that can be stored in a given domain, such as space, time, or frequency, or contained in a given message length. Reducing the amount of storage space required to store a given amount of data, or reducing the length of message required to transfer a given amount of information.

Data conversion

The process of changing data from one form of representation to another.

Data dictionary

A textual description of each class, its associations, attributes, and operations.

Data encryption standard

A cryptographic algorithm for the protection of unclassified computer data and published by the National Institute of Standards and Technology in Federal Information Processing Standard Publication 46-1.

Data entry

The entry of data into a computer or onto a computer-readable medium by an operator from a single data device, such as a card reader or keyboard.

Data flow

The connection between the output of one object or process and the input to another.

Data flow control layer

Layer 5 of the SNA architectural model. This layer determines and manages interactions between session partners, particularly data flow. Corresponds to the session layer of the OSI model.

Data flow diagram

a graphical representation of the functional model, showing dependencies between values and the computation of output values from input values without regard for when or if the functions are executed.

Data frame

A packet of transmitted information that contains at a minimum, the destination address and information being transmitted. Additional information also being transmitted may include the source address, a check word or CRC, and frame length.

Data integrity

The condition in which data are identically maintained during any operation, such as transfer, storage, and retrieval.

Data link

A connection between any two devices capable of sending and receiving information, such as a computer and a printer or a main computer and a terminal. Sometimes the term is extended to include equipment, such as a modem, that enables transmission and receiving. Such devices follow protocols that govern data transmission.

Data link layer

Layer 2 of the OSI reference model. This layer provides reliable transit of data across a physical link. The data link layer is concerned with physical addressing, network topology, line discipline, error notification, ordered delivery of frames, and flow control. The IEEE has divided this layer into two sublayers: The MAC sublayer and the LLC sublayer. Sometimes simply called link layer. Roughly corresponds to the data link control layer of the SNA model.

Data link protocol

The protocol that controls the network signaling and receivinghardware, performing data integrity checks and formatting information according to the rules of the data link.

Data multiplexing

The process of combining two or more signals into a single composite signal.

Data processing

The systematic performance of operations upon data, for example, handling, merging, sorting and computing.

Data signaling rate

The aggregate rate at which data pass a point in the transmission path of a data transmission system.

Data sink

Network equipment that accepts data transmissions.

Data store

A passive object that stores data for later access.

Data stream

All data transmitted through a communications line in a single read or write operation.

Data transfer rate

The average number of bits, characters, or blocks per unit time passing between corresponding equipment in a data transmission system.

Data transmission

The transfer of information from one place to another or from one part of a system to another. The sending of data from one place to another by means of signals over a channel.

Data type

The attribute for a field that determines what type of data it can contain.

Database

A collection of interrelated data values that may be integrated permanently into a single connected structure or integrated temporarily for each interrogation, known as a query. In its most technical sense, database implies that any of the data may be used as a key for specific queries. In more common usage it means any accessible collection of information and that only a limited set of data values may be used to specify queries.

Database management system

A systematic approach to storing, updating, securing and retrieving information stored as data items, usually in the form of records in one or more files.

Datagram

Logical grouping of information sent as a network layer unit over a transmission medium without prior establishment of a virtual circuit. IP datagrams are the primary information units in the Internet. The terms frame, message, packet, and segment are also used to describe logical information grouping at various layers of the OSI reference model and in various technology circles.

Dataset

A file or group of files associated with one part of a study.

Datum

A datum is the origin from which the location or geometric characteristics of features of a part are established.

Daughter card

A printed circuit board that plugs into another circuit board (usually the motherboard). A daughter card is similar to an expansion board, but it accesses the motherboard components (memory and CPU) directly instead of sending data through the slower expansion bus.

DB connector

Database bus connector. Type of connector used to connect serial and parallel cables to a data bus. DB connector names are of the format DB-x, where x represents the number of (wires) within the connector. Each line is connected to a pin on the connector, but in many cases, not all pins are assigned a function. DB connectors are defined by various EIA/TIA standards.

DBMS

Database Management System

DCA

Defence Communications Agency. US. government organization responsible for DDN networks such as MILNET. Now called DISA.

DCC

Data Country Code. One of two ATM Address formats developed by the ATM Forum for use by private networks. Adapted from the subnetwork model of addressing in which the ATM layer is responsible for mapping network layer addresses to ATM Addresses.

DCITA

Department of Communication Technology and Arts

DDM

Distributed Data Management. Software in an IBM SNA environment that provides peer-to-peer communication and file sharing. One of three SNA transaction services.

DDN

Defense Data Network. US. military network composed of an unclassified network (MILNET) and various secret and top-secret networks. DDN is operated and maintained by DISA.

DDP

Datagram Delivery Protocol. Apple Computer network layer protocol that is responsible for the socket-to-socket delivery of datagrams over an AppleTalk internetwork.

DDR

Double data rate is a type of memory where data is transferred on both the rising and falling edges of the clock signal.

DDR

Dial-on-demand routing. Technique whereby a Cisco router can automatically initiate and close a circuit-switched session as transmitting stations demand. The router spoofs keepalives so that end stations treat the session as active. DDR permits routing over ISDN or telephone lines using an external ISDN terminal adapter or modem.

DDR2

Double data rate type 2 memory, double pumps the data bus. DDR2 allows higher bus speed and requires lower power by running the internal clock at half the speed of the data bus.

DDR3

Double Data Rate Type 3 memory is a type of memory with a high bandwidth interface, and has been in use since 2007.

De facto standard

Standard that exists by nature of its widespread use.

De jure standard

Standard that exist because of its approval by an official standards body.

Deadlock

1. Unresolved contention for the use of a resource.
2. In APPN, when two elements of a process each wait for action by or a response from the other before they resume the process.

Debug

To detect, trace and eliminate errors in computer programs.

Debugger

A program designed to aid in debugging another program by allowing the programmer to step through the program, examine the data, and monitor conditions such as the values of variables.

Decay

A loss in the clarity or readability of an electronic signal caused bythe interaction of the signal with its carrier and electrical environment.

Decibel

Abbreviated dB. One tenth of a bel (named after Alexander Graham Bell), a unit used in electronics and other fields to measure the strength of a sound or signal. Decibel measurements fall on a logarithmic scale and compare the measured quantity against a known reference.

Decimal

A base 10 number system; a number system with ten digits: 0 1 2 3 4 5 6 7 8 9.

Decimal fraction

A fraction whose denominator is a power of 10.

Decision

The removal of uncertainty with respect to a course of action for an organization that consumes resources.

Decision documentation

The recording of the terms and results of a decision and the assumptions and reasoning behind the decision.

Decision event

State in the progress of a project when a decision is required before the start of any succeeding activity.

Decision tree

Similar to a decision table, an analysis instrument where possible outcomes of some condition are represented as branches, which may in turn generate other branches.

Decnet

Group of communications products (including a protocol suite) developed and supported by Digital Equipment Corporation. DECnet/OSI (also called DECnet Phase V) is the most recent iteration and supports both OSI protocols and proprietary Digital protocols. Phase IV Prime supports inherent MAC addresses that allow DECnet nodes to coexist with systems running other that have MAC address restrictions.

Decnet Routing

Proprietary routing scheme introduced by Digital Equipment Corporation in DECnet Phase III. In DECnet Phase V, DECnet completed its transition to OSI routing protocols (ES-IS and IS-IS).

Decoder

A circuit or device that restores a coded signal to its original form based on knowledge of the process used to code the signal.

Decompiler

A program that attempts to generate high-level source code from assembly language code or machine code. This can be a difficult task, as some assembly language code has no corresponding high-level source code.

Decomposing

The process of reducing a project scope into its various elements resulting in a work breakdown structure.

Decryption

The reverse application of an encryption algorithm to encrypted data, thereby restoring that data to its original, unencrypted state.

Dedicated LAN

Network segment allocated to a single device. Used in LAN switched network topologies.

Dedicated line

Communications line that is indefinitely reserved for transmissions, rather than switched as transmission is required.

Default

A default setting is one you haven't changed - what a program will do (or use) if you don't tell it any different.

"Accept the defaults" means leave any settings as they are.

Default button

The control that is automatically selected when a window is introduced by an application or operating system, typically activated by pressing the Enter key.

Default drive

The disk drive that an operating system reads to and writes from when no alternative is specified.

Default home page

On a Web server, the file that is returned when a directory is referenced without a specific filename. This is specified by the Web server software and is typically the file called index.html or index.htm.

Default printer

The printer to which a computer sends documents for printing unless an alternative is specified.

Default route

Routing table entry that is used to direct frames for which a next hop is not explicitly listed in the routing table.

Default values

Values that software programs insert into fields automatically when no information is provided by the user.

Delay

The time between the initiation of a transaction by a sender and the first response received by the sender. Also, the time required to move a packet from source to destination over a given path.

Delegation

An implementation mechanism in which an object, responding to an operation on itself, forwards the operation to another object; a mechanism in which methods may be attached directly to instances and where the method resolution is performed by searching a chain of instance pointers, rather than by searching a class heirarchy.

Delete key

Personal computers normally allow deletion of typing mistakes by either the backspace key or the Del key. Users must either specify which of these keys they wish to use, or set their communication software to match whichever key the network expects.

Delimiter

A special character that sets off, or separates, individual items in a program or set of data. In the following example, commas separate the fields in a database record (each non-numeric field is enclosed by double quotation marks).

Demand priority

Media access method used in 100VG-AnyLAN that uses a hub that can handle multiple transmission requests and can process traffic according to priority, making it useful for servicing time-sensitive traffic such as multimedia and video. Demand priority eliminates the overhead of packet collisions, collision recovery, and broadcast traffic typical in Ethernet networks.

Demarc

Demarcation point between carrier equipment and CPE.

Demodulation

Process of returning a modulated signal to its original form. Modems perform demodulation by taking an analog signal and returning it to its original (digital) form.

Demultiplexing

The separating of multiple input streams that have been multiplexed into a common physical signal back into multiple output streams.

Density

A measure of the quantity of information bits that can be stored on a storage medium. Higher density allows greater volumes of data to be stored in the same physical space.

Derived association

An association that is defined in terms of other associations.

Derived attribute

An attribute that is computed from other attributes.

DES

Data Encryption Standard. Standard cryptographic algorithm developed by the US.

Descendent class

A class that is a direct or indirect subclass of a given class.

Designated bridge

The bridge that incurs the lowest path cost when forwarding a frame from a segment to the route bridge.

Designated router

OSPF router that generates LSAs for a multiaccess network and has other special responsibilities in running OSPF. Each multiaccess OSPF network that has at least two attached routers has a designated router that is elected by the OSPF Hello protocol. The designated router enables a reduction in the number of adjacencies required on a multiaccess network, which in turn reduces the amount or routing protocol traffic and the size of the topological database.

Desktop

A desktop system is a computer designed to sit in one position on a desk somewhere and not move around. Most general purpose computers are desktop systems. Calling a system a desktop implies nothing about its platform. The fastest desktop system at any given time is typically either an Alpha or PowerPC based system, but the SPARC and PA-RISC based systems are also often in the running. Industrial strength desktops are typically called workstations.

Desktop computer

A computer that fits conveniently on the surface of a business desk. Most personal computers as well as some workstations can be considered desktop computers.

Desktop conferencing

The use of computers for simultaneous communication among geographically separated participants in a meeting. This communication may include input to and display from application programs as well as audio and video communication.

Desktop publisher

A program for creating newspapers, magazines, books, etc. Some common desktop publishing programs include FrameMaker, PageMaker, InDesign, and GeoPublish.

Despatcher

A procedure (on the server) that uses the procedure identifier of a client request message to select one of the server procedures and pass the client's arguments to it.

Destination address

Address of a network device that is receiving data.

Detail section

The section of form and report design that contains the records of the table (in Micros).

Deterministic load distribution

Technique for distributing traffic between two bridges across a circuit group. Guarantees packet ordering between source-destination pairs and always forwards traffic for a source-destination pair on the same segment in a circuit group for a given circuit-group configuration.

Device driver

Software that acts as an intermediary between a CPU and aperipheral device. The CPU sends a command to the devicedriver, which translates that command into a command meaningful to the peripheral device.

DFP

Digital Flat Panel is a type of video connector for flat panel displays

DFT

Distributed Function Terminal.

DHCP

Dynamic Host Configuration Protocol. Supports booting workstations and other devices that need information from outside before they can complete the booting process, such as an IP number or name of program file to download.

DIA

Document Interchange Architecture. Defines the protocols and data formats needed for the transparent interchange of documents in an SNA network. One of three SNA transaction services.

Diagnostic

A test or the data from a test which indicates the condition of thestate of a computer or network's health.

Dialogue box

Dialog boxes prompt the user to enter information.

Dial-up

A method of connection to the internet using existing copper phone lines using a modem on the client's end to send information at a slow speed, normally reaching maximum speed at about 56 kbit/s. This technology uses the voice spectrum of the telephone lines to transmit data using a system of sounds that only the receiving modem or ISP understand.

Dial-up Line

Communications circuit that is established by a switched-circuit connection using the telephone company network.

Dictionary file

A special form of machine-readable codebook that contains information about the structure of a datafile and the locations and, often, the names of variables variables in the datafile. Typically, you use a dictionary file and a datafile together with statistical software; the statistical software uses the dictionary so that you may specify variables by name, rather than having to specify their locations in the file.

Differential backup

Any files that have changed since the last full backup, are duplicated

Differential encoding

Digital encoding technique whereby a binary value is denoted by a signal change rather than a particular signal level.

Differential manchester encoding

Digital coding scheme where a mid-bit-time transition is used for clocking, and a transition at the beginning of each bit time denotes a zero. The coding scheme used by IEEE802.5 and Token Ring networks.

Digital

Literally "to do with numbers". Often used to describe a device using computer technology to replace older, traditional technologies.

Digital audio tape

A magnetic tape storage medium for recording digitally encoded audio information.

Digital audio/video connector

An interface on some high-end video cards or TV tuner cards that allows the simultaneous transmission of digital audio and video signals. Also called DAV connector.

Digital camera

A type of camera that stores photographed images electronically instead of on traditional film. A digital camera uses a CCD (charge-coupled device) element to capture the image through the lens when the operator releases the shutter in the camera; circuitry within the camera then stores the image captured by the CCD in a storage medium such as solid-state memory or a hard disk. After the image has been captured, it is downloaded by cable to the computer using software supplied with the camera. Once stored in the computer, the image can be manipulated and processed much like the image from a scanner or related input device.

Digital display

A video display capable of rendering only a fixed number of colors or gray shades. Examples of digital displays are IBM's Monochrome Display, Color/Graphics Display, and Enhanced Color Display.

Digital photography

Photography by means of a digital camera. Digital photography differs from conventional photography in that a digital camera does not use a silver halide-based film to capture an image. Instead, a digital camera captures and stores each image electronically.

DIMM

DIMM which means (dual in-line memory module) comprises a series of dynamic random-access memory integrated circuits. These modules are mounted on a printed circuit board and designed for use in personal computers, workstations and servers. DIMM replaced SIMM which is the single in-line memory module.

DIN

Deutsche Industrie Norm. German national standards organization.

DIN connector

Deutsche Industrie Norm connector. Multipin connector used in some Macintosh and IBM PC-compatible computers, and on some network processor panels.

Dingbat

A small graphical element used for decorative purposes in a document. Some fonts, such as Zapf Dingbats, are designed to present sets of dingbats.

DIR

Department of Industrial Relations

Direct access

The ability to read or write data directly from or to any location on a storage device without having to refer to data that was previously written. Files written with direct access do not have to be read sequentially starting at the beginning.

Directed search

Search request sent to a specific node known to contain a resource. A directed search is used to determine the continued existence of the resource and to obtain routing information specific to the node.

Directory

Also called "folder", a directory is a collection of files typically created for organizational purposes. Note that a directory is itself a file, so a directory can generally contain other directories. It differs in this way from a partition

Directory service

A service that provides a mapping between file names and their UFIDs.

Directory tree

A graphic display listing the directories and subdirectories on a hard disk in tree form, with subdirectories shown as branches of the main directory.

Directx*

A set of Microsoft* APIs for handling tasks related to items such as games and video

Disa

Defence Information Systems Agency. US. military organization responsible for implementing and operating military information systems, including the DDN.

Disaster recovery plan

Detailed, written plan describing how an organisation will restore computer operations, in the event of a disaster.

Discovery architecture

APPN software that enables a machine configured as an APPN EN to automatically fine primary and backup NNs when the machine is brought onto an APPN network.

Discovery mode

Method by which an AppleTalk interface acquires information about an attached network from an operational node and then uses this information to configure itself. Also called dynamic configuration.

Discrete graphics

The graphics controller is not built into the chipset but is a separate component

Discriminator

An attribute of enumeration type that indicates which property of a class is being abstracted by a particular generalization.

Disk

A round, flat piece of flexible plastic (floppy disk) or inflexible metal (hard disk) coated with a magnetic material that can be electrically influenced to hold information recorded in digital (binary) form. In most computers a disk is the primary means of storing data on a permanent or semi-permanent basis. Floppy disks are encased in a protective plastic jacket to protect them from damage and contamination. A hard disk is enclosed in a rigid case and can be exposed only in a dust-free environment. Types of disks used with microcomputers include floppy disks, microfloppy disks, hard disks, and removable cartridges that can be used with some hard disk drives and units, such as the Bernoulli box.

Disk drive

The device that operates (reads and writes) to the floppy disk, HDD, DVD and CD-ROM.

Disk or diskette

A small, flat, either rigid or floppy magnetic disk for storing data permanently. Magnetic medium for data storage. Either "floppy" diskettes (720K to 1.4 megabytes), or "hard" disks (usually 20 megabytes or more).

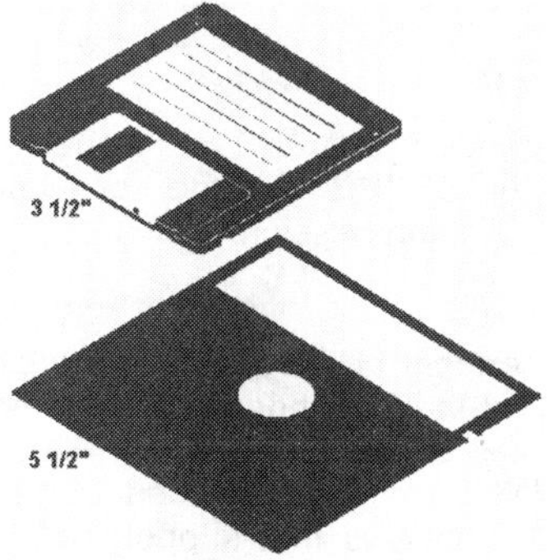

Display

A device that enables information, either textual or pictorial, to be seen but not permanently recorded. The most widely used kind is the cathode-ray tube.

Displayport

DisplayPort is a digital display interface developed by the Video Electronics Standards Association (VESA). The interface is primarily used to connect a video source to a display device such as a computer monitor, though it can also be used to transmit audio, USB, and other forms of data.

Distance vector routing algorithm

Class of routing algorithms that iterate on the number of hops in a route to find a shortest-path spanning tree. Distance vector routing algorithms call for each router to send its entire routing table in each update, but only to its neighbors. Distance vector routing algorithms can be prone to routing loops, but are computationally simpler than link state routing algorithms. Also called Bellman-Ford routing algorithm.

Distortion

A change in a electronic signal that occurs when different frequen-cy components of the signal decay at different rates. In a signalmade up of many frequency components (such as a squarewave), the higher frequency components of a signal typicallydecay faster than the lower frequency components.

Distortion delay

Problem with a communication signal resulting from nonuniform transmission speeds of the components of a signal through a transmission medium. Also called group delay.

Distributed

Processing resides in more than one computer in a network.

Distributed application

Application designed so that components run on different - but cooperating - systems on a network.

Distributed database

The data resides in more than one physical database in a network. Access to the data involves more than one database server. Clients may have to connect to more than one server directly and integrate the data they receive according to the applications needs.

Distributed file system

Allows files on remote nodes of a network to appear locally connected.

Distributed mutual exclusion

A mechanism for controlling resource access that involves allowing access to only one process at a time.

Distributed system

A collection of autonomous computers linked by a computer network and equipped with distributed system software that enables the computers to coordinate their activities and to share hardware, software and data.

Dithering

A graphics term where colors are intentionally mixed of adjacent pixels. Dithering is usually needed for 8-bit color and sometimes for 16-bit. It allows a limited color set to approximate a broader range, by mixing groups of varying-color pixels in a semi-random pattern. Without dithering, color gradients like sky or sunset tend to show "banding" artifacts.

DIY

Do It Yourself is someone who does a task themselves rather than relying on a professional

DLCI

Data-link connection identifier. Value that specifies a PVC or SVC in a Frame Relay network. In the basic Frame Relay specification, DLCIs are locally significant (connected devices might use different values to specify the same connection). In the LMI extended specification, DLCIs are globally significant (DLCIs specify individual end devices).

DLL

Dynamically Linked Libraries. A component of Microsoft's OLE.

DLSW

Data-link switching. Interoperability standard, described in RFC 1434, that provides a method for forwarding SNA and NetBIOS traffic over TCP/IP networks using data link layer switching and encapsulation. DLSw uses SSP (Switch-to-Switch Protocol) instead of SRB, eliminating the major limitations of SRB, including hop-count limits, broadcast and unnecessary traffic, timeouts, lack of flow control, and lack of prioritization schemes.

DLU

Dependent LU. An LU that depends on the SSCP to provide services for establishing session with other LUs.

DLUR

Dependent LU Requester. The client half of the Dependent LU Requester/ Server enhancement to APPN. The DLUR component resides in APPN ENs and NNs that support adjacent DLUs by securing services from the DLUS.

DLUR node
In APPN networks, an EN or NN that implements the DLUR component.

DLUS
Dependent LU Server. The server half of the Dependent LU Requester/ Server enhancement to APPN. The DLUS component provides SSCP services to DLUR nodes over an APPN network.

DLUS node
In APPN networks, an NN that implements the DLUS component.

DMA (Direct Memory Access)
Hardware devices attached to PCs (ranging from keyboards to sound cards) can be designed to send their instructions to and from main memory in one of two ways. The default is to ask the CPU to do the work. The more efficient way is to allocate one of the PC's DMA channels to send instructions directly to memory. This leaves the CPU free to do more important things. Like IRQs, DMA channels are limited in number, and you can't allocate one channel to more than one device (unless you want to grind your system to a halt). Most users come in contact with DMA when they install a sound card that—if they're lucky—picks the right channel during setup.

DMAC
Destination MAC. The MAC address specified in the Destination Address field of a packet.

DNA
Digital Network Architecture. Network architecture developed by Digital Equipment Corporation. The products that embody DNA (including communications protocols) are collectively referred to as DECnet.

DNIC
Data Network Identification Code. Part of an X.121 address. DNICs are divided into two parts: the first specifying the country in which the addressed PSN is located and the second specifying the PSN itself.

DNS
(Domain Name Service/System) An internet service that converts a human web address such as www.jonstorm.com into the numeric address that computers use, called the IP address. "Can't resolve DNS" usually means that this conversion has failed and therefore the website can't be found.

DNSIX
Department of Defense Intelligence Information System Network Security for Information Exchange. Collection of security requirements for networking defined by the US. Defense Intelligence Agency.

Document
A medium and the data recorded on it for human use; for example, a report sheet or book. By extension, any record that has permanence and that can be read by human or machine.

Documentation
A collection of organized documents or the information recorded in documents. Also instructional material specifying the inputs, operations and outputs of a computer program or system.

DOD

Department of Defence. US. government organization that is responsible for national defense. The DoD has frequently funded communication protocol development.

Domain

1. In the Internet, a portion of the spanning hierarchy tree that refers to general groupings of networks based on organization type or geography.
2. In SNA, an SSCP and the resources it controls.
3. In IS-IS, a logical set of networks.

Domain transition

A switch between execution environments.

Dongle

A small hardware device used for copy protection with some software. The dongle must be plugged in to a port on the computer, often the printer port, or the software won't function. They are unpopular with users because if the dongle gets lost or broken, the software won't function.

DOS

(Disk Operating System; pr. "doss") Usually refers to MS-DOS, which was the standard operating system for PCs until Windows 95came out, now pretty much obsolete. Controlled by typing in text commands and has several serious limitations, but requires a much less powerful computer than Windows 95.

DOS

(Denial of Service) A form of attack on (usually) an internet service, which aims to prevent the service from operating properly, often by bombarding it with more information than it can process.

DOT

1. In the UNIX, MS-DOS, OS/2, and other operating systems, the character that separates a filename from an extension as in TEXT.DOC (pronounced "text-dot-doc").
2. In computer graphics and printing, a small spot combined with others in a matrix of rows and columns to form a character or a graphic element in a drawing or desig The dots forming an image on the screen are called pixels. The resolution of a display or printing device is often expressed in dots per inch (dpi).
3. In an Internet address, the character that separates the different parts of the domain name, such as the entity name from the domain.

DOT address

Refers to the common notation for IP addresses in the form <n.n.n.n> where each number n represents, in decimal, 1 byte of the 4-byte IP address. Also called dotted notation or four-part dotted notation.

Dot-matrix printer

Any printer that produces characters made up of dots using a wire-pin print head. The quality of output from a dot-matrix printer depends largely on the number of dots in the matrix, which might be low enough to show individual dots or might be high enough to approach the look of fully formed characters. Dot-matrix printers are often categorized by the number of pins in the print head—typically 9, 18, or 24.

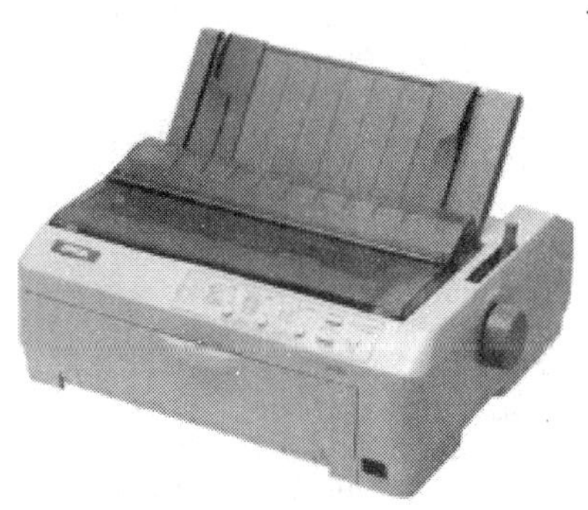

Double-sided

A memory module where DRAM chips are on both sides of the module.

Down

A computer is down when it is not running. It may be shut down for maintenance, hardware failure, or failure of the operating system or user program.

Download

The transfer of information from a remote computer system to the users system. Opposite of upload.

Downsizing

The transfer of computing tasks previously performed by main frame or minicomputers to personal computers.

Downtime

1. A temporary interruption in the usability of a computer system.
2. A work stoppage caused by the temporary lack of usability of acomputer system.

DPI

(Dots Per Inch) A measure of picture quality, often used to measure printer capabilities. The higher the number, the better the quality.

DQDB

Distributed Queue Dual Bus. Data link layer communication protocol, specified in the IEEE802.6 standard, designed for use in MANs. DQDB, which permits multiple systems to interconnect using two unidirectional logical buses, is an open standard that is designed for compatibility with carrier transmission standards and is aligned with emerging standards for BISDN. SIP (SMDS Interface Protocol) is based on DQDB.

Drag and drop

A protocol supported by OPEN LOOK and Macintosh System 7 that allows a user to specify the input file to an application by dragging the icon representing the file onto the applications icon and dropping it there. OPEN LOOK also recognizes dragging the icon into the applications input panel. For example, dragging a files icon into the printool application causes it to be printed.

DRAM

Dynamic Random-Access Memory. RAM that stores information in capacitors that must be periodically refreshed. Delays can occur because DRAMs are inaccessible to the processor when refreshing their contents. However, DRAMs are less complex and have greater capacity than SRAMs.

Dreamweaver

A superb graphical editor for websites, widely used by professional web designers.

Drive

A device for storing and/or retrieving data. Some drives (such as disk drives, zip drives, and tape drives) are typically capable of having new data written to them, but some others (like CD-ROMs or DVD-ROMs) are not. Some drives have random access(like disk drives, zip drives, CD-ROMs, and DVD-ROMs), while others only have sequential access (like tape drives)

Driver

Operating systems and applications use a general system call to operate hardware devices. The driver is a software routine that translates it into the specific instructions needed to control the hardware device.

DRM

(Digital Rights Management) Software intended to prevent the unauthorised duplication of copyrighted audio, video or software. Unpopular with users because if there is ever a problem with it, such as the rights management company folding, your legally-purchased content becomes unplayable. Following a lot of problems of this kind it has largely been abandoned by the music industry.

Drop

Point on a multipoint channel where a connection to a networked device is made.

Drop cable

Generally, a cable that connects a network device (such as a computer) to a physical medium. A type of AUI.

DS-0

Digital signal level 0. Framing specification used in transmitting digital signals over a single channel at 64-kbps on a T1 facility.

DS-1

Digital signal level 1. Framing specification used in transmitting digital signals at 1.544-Mbps on a T1 facility (in the United States) or at 2.108-Mbps on an E1 facility (in Europe).

DS-1/dti

DS-1 domestic trunk interface. Interface circuit used for DS-1 applications with 24 trunks.

DS-3

Digital signal level 3. Framing specification used for transmitting digital signals at 44.736-Mbps on a T3 facility.

DSAP

Destination service access point. The SAP of the network node designated in the Destination field of a packet.

DSP

Domain specific part. The part of a CLNS address that contains an area identifier, a station identifier, and a selector byte.

DSPU

Downstream physical unit. In SNA, a PU that is located downstream from the host.

DSR

Data set ready. EIA/TIA-232 interface circuit that is activated when DCE is powered up and ready for use.

DSU

Data service unit. Device used in digital transmission that adapts the physical interface on a DTE device to a transmission facility such as T1 or E1. The DSU is also responsible for functions such as signal timing. Often referred to together with CSU, as CSU/DSU.

DSX-1

Cross-connection point for DS-1 signals.

DTE

Data Terminal Equipment. The X.25 term for an end node. Device at the user end of a user-network interface that serves as a data source, destination, or both. DTE connects to a data network through a DCE device (for example, a modem) and typically uses clocking signals generated by the DCE. CTE includes devices such as computers, protocol translators, and multiplexers.

DTMF

Dual tone multifrequency. Use of two simultaneous voice-band tones for dialing (such as touch tone).

DTP

Desk Top Publisher(ing) - A PC Term that describes a program that enables you to design, create and print a variety of projects such as letterheads, birthday cards, calendars, business cards, invitations etc. that would have previously only been possible by using the services of an outside printers business.

DTR

Data terminal ready. EIA/TIA 232 circuit that is activated to let the DCE know when the DTE is ready to send and receive data.

DTS

Distributed Time Service.

Dual

Diffusing Update Algorithm. Convergence algorithm used in Enhanced IGRP that provides loop-free operation at every instant throughout a route computation. Allows routers involved in a topology change to synchronize at the same time, while not involving routers that are unaffected by the change.

Dual core, dual-core

PC processors which have two complete processors on the same chip, allowing computers to handle multiple tasks faster.

Dual counter-rotation ring

Network topology in which two signal paths, whose directions are opposite one another, exist in a token-passing network. FDDI and CDDI are based on this concept.

Dual homing

Network topology in which a device is connected to the network by way of two independent access points (points of attachment). One access point is the primary connection, and the other is a standby connection that is activated in the event of a failure of the primary connection.

Dual layer

A technology allowing two layers of data to be written to a DVD instead of the usual one, thus increasing its capacity.

Dual-channel mode

This mode is enabled when the installed memory capacities of both DIMM channels are equal. Also known as interleaved mode.

Dual-homed Station

Device attached to multiple FDDI rings to provide redundancy.

Dump

A printed representation of the contents of a computer storage device, usually main memory, backed-up when a system crash or other failure has occurred. As a verb, refers to a large amount of data.

Duplex

Capable of carrying information in both directions over a communications channel. A system is full-duplex if it can carry information in both directions at once; it is half-duplex if it can carry information in only one direction at a time.

Duplex printer

A printer capable of printing on both sides of the page.

DVD

(Digital Versatile Disk) A more advanced version of the standard CD which can hold far more information, now standard on most PCs. Widely used for high-quality digital movies and software. DVD drives can also read ordinary CDs.

Dvd RW, DVD Writer

(Digital Versatile Disk ReWriter) A DVD drive that can create ("write") rewriteable DVDs. There are several competing formats at the moment, but most recent drives support more than one format. It is likely that one of these formats will become standard in time, but at the moment it is not clear which. To add to the confusion, they tend to have very similar names : for example DVD+RW and DVD-RW are completely different formats, and incompatible with each other.

DVI

Digital Visual Interface (DVI) is a video display interface developed by the Digital Display Working Group (DDWG). The digital interface is used to connect a video source to a display device, such as a computer monitor.

DVMRP

Distance Vector Multicast Routing Protocol. Internetwork gateway protocol, largely based on RIP, that implements a typical dense mode IP multicast scheme. DVMRP uses IGMP to exchange routing datagrams with its neighbours.

DVMT

Dynamic Video Memory Technology is a system memory that is dynamically allocated as video memory.

DXI

Data Exchange Interface. ATM Forum specification, described in RFC 1483, that defines how a network device such as a bridge, router, or hub can effectively act as an FEP to an ATM network by interfacing with a special DSU that performs packet segmentation and reassembly.

Dynamic address resolution

Use of an address resolution protocol to determine and store address information on demand.

Dynamic addressing

A system of addressing in which the computer selects it s own address without the user's intervention.

Dynamic memory allocation

The allocation of memory to a process or program at run time. Dynamic memory is allocated from the system heap by the operating system upon request from the program.

Dynamic method binding

Choosing the correct method to call at runtime based on an object's actual type, and not the type of reference referring to it.

Dynamic model

A description of aspects of a system concerned with control, including time, sequencing of operations, and interaction of objects.

Dynamic programming language

A programming language where programs can dynamically change in structure as they are run.

Dynamic routing

Routing that adjusts automatically to network topology or traffic changes. Also called adaptive routing.

E

E channel

Echo channel. 64-Kbps ISDN circuit-switching control channel. The E channel was defined in the 1984 ITU-T ISDN specification, but was dropped in the 1988 specification.

E.164

ITU-T recommendation for international telecommunication numbering, especially in ISDN, BISDN, and SMDS. An evolution of station telephone numbers.

E1

Wide-area digital transmission scheme used predominantly in Europe that carries data at a rate of 2.048 Mbps. E1 lines can be leased for private use from common carriers.

E3

Wide-area digital transmission scheme, used predominantly in Europe, that carries data at a rate of 34.368 Mbps. E3 lines can be leased for private use from common carrier.

Eap

Extensible Authentication Protocol is an authentication framework that is often used in wireless networks and defines message formats. Short for Extensible Authentication Protocol, EAP sits inside of Point-to-Point Protocol's (PPP) authentication protocol and provides a generalized framework for several different authentication methods. EAP is supposed to head off proprietary authentication systems and let everything from passwords to challenge-response tokens and public-key infrastructure certificates all work smoothly.

Early token release

Technique used in Token Ring networks that allows a station to release a new token onto the ring immediately after transmitting, instead of waiting for the first frame to return. This feature can increase the total bandwidth on the ring.

Earphone

A transducer placed near the ear or over the ear. A small speaker placed over one or both ears. A smaller version of Headphones.

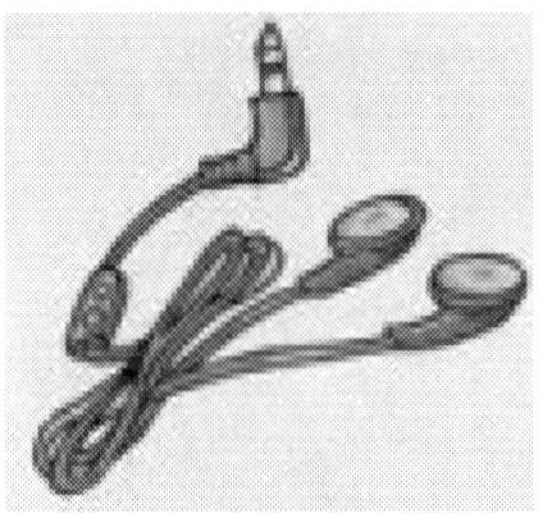

Earth ground

The connection to earth. Ground. The most common connection to earth is via a water pipe. The graphic shows how to connect a Printed Circuit Board ground to chassis ground. In many cases chassis ground will also connect to earth ground.

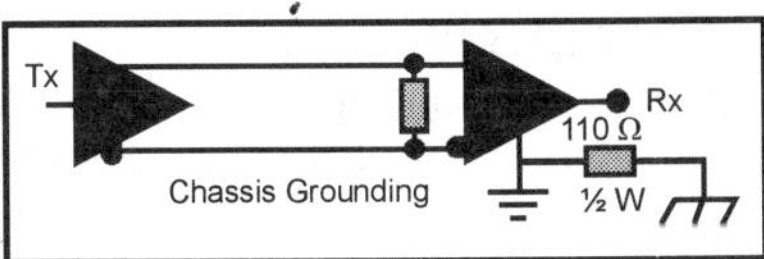

EBCDIC

Extended binary code decimal interchange code. Any of a number of coded character sets developed by IBM consisting of 8-bit coded characters. This character code is used by older IBM systems and telex machines.

E-book

The concept behind an e-book is that it should provide all the functionality of an ordinary book but in a manner that is (overall) less expensive and more environmentally friendly. The actual term e-book is somewhat confusingly used to refer to a variety of things: custom software to play e-book titles, dedicated hardware to play e-book titles, and the e-book titles themselves. Individual e-book titles can be free or commercial (but will always be less expensive than their printed counterparts) and have to be loaded into a player to be read. Players vary wildly in capability level. Basic ones allow simple reading and bookmarking; better ones include various features like hypertext, illustrations, audio, and even limited video. Other optional features allow the user to mark-up sections of text, leave notes, circle or diagram things, highlight passages, program or customize settings, and even use interactive fiction. There are many types of e-book; a couple popular ones include the Newton book and Palm DOC.

ECC

Error-correcting code allows data to be checked for errors and corrected when required.

Echo

1. In electronic signaling, the reflection of a signal caused by asudden change in the impedance of the carrier.
2. A networkcontinuity test where packets are sent to a distant node that isobligated to immediately send the packets back.

Echo box

A resonant cavity device that is used to check the overall performance of a radar system. It receives a portion of the transmitted pulse and retransmits it back to the receiver as a slowly decaying transient.

Echo protocol

In the AppleTalk protocol family, a protocol that allows a computer to return test packets. The purpose of Echo Protocol is t testthe delivery conditions to a remote node, including reachability,reliability and round trip time.

Echo test

A diagnostic test in which packets are sent by one node to another node, which immediately returns them to the original node. Thedata recorded by the echo test includes the success rate of thereturn as well as the time needed to complete the round trip.

Echoplex

Mode in which keyboard characters are echoed on a terminal screen upon return of a signal from the other end of the line indicating that the characters were received correctly.

ECL

A type of digital logic using transistors that do not go into saturation, allowing the devices to operate faster [as it takes longer for the transistor to come out of saturation]. An ECL OR gate symbol is shown to the right. Note that most gates use differential inputs and outputs, although the I/O can be made into single ended lines too. The normal supply voltage level [Vee] is -5.2 volts as opposed to TTL logic which is 5 volts. However ECL also uses a Vcc of between 0 volts to 7 volts. Although ECL 'logic' gates function the same as TTL gates, the greater speed, differential un-saturated logic [analog] signals and impedance matching requirements impose a completely different design approach.

Eclipse

A condition in which the satellite is not in view or in direct line of sight with the sun. This happens when the earth is between them.

ECMA

European Computer Manufacturers Association. Group of European computer vendors who have done substantial OSI standardization work.

E-commerce

Conducting business over the internet, and particularly the World Wide Web.

E-core

E-Cores expose the winding so heat does not get trapped inside and also makes it easier to bring out connections from several windings.

EDBIC

The EDBIC character set is similar to (but less popular than) the ASCII character set in concept, but is significantly different in layout. It tends to be found only on old machines..

Eddy current

Induced circulating currents in a conducting material that are caused by a varying magnetic field. The current induced in a conductor subjected to a varying magnetic field.

Eddy current loss

Losses caused by random current flowing in the core of a transformer. Power is lost in the form of heat.

Edge connector

A male connector formed by running conductive copper traces to the edge of a printed wiring board to act as a plug for another connector. The standard connector system used for expansion cards in personal computers.

Edge skew

The difference in the arrival between two edges from the same device. For a flip flop, the difference in time between when Q output goes high and the Q-bar output goes low. The difference in time between the outputs of a digital counter changing, with reference to each other [A, B, C, D].

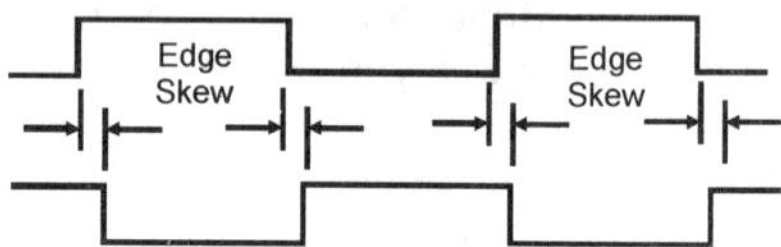

Edge triggered flip flop

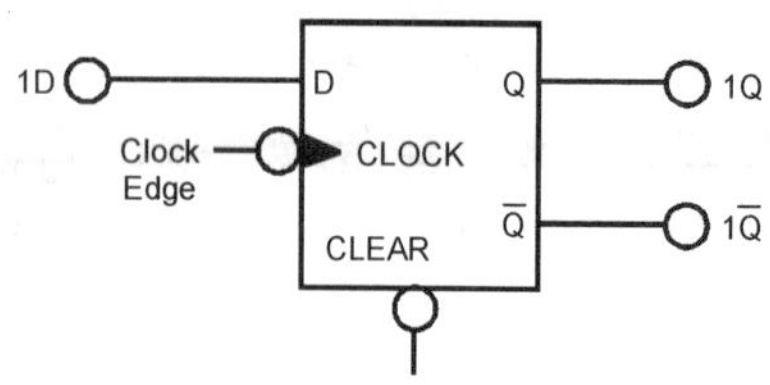

A type of Flip Flop [FF] that requires either a rising edge or falling edge of a clock edge to force the output to change to the level of the input signal.

Edge triggering

A method of activating a circuit by means of a pulse transition from either high to low or low to high. Normally components such as flip flops are edge triggered while components like latches are level triggered.

EDI

Electronic Document (or Data) Interchange. The term EDI usuallyconnotes a system where authentication and security methodsguarantee the integrity and origin of the information.

EDID

Extended Display Identification Data is data given from a display device to a graphics driver that defines its capabilities

EDIFACT

Electronic Data Interchange for Administration, Commerce, and Transport. Data exchange standard administered by the United Nations to be a multi-industry EDI standard.

Edison cap

Also called an Edison Base A type of screw cap used with light bulbs.

Edison cell

Another name for a nickel-iron cell or battery [NiFe].

Edison effect

Also called Richardson Effect. The phenomenon wherein electrons emitted from a heated element within a vacuum tube will flow to a second element that is connected to a positive potential.

Edit

1. To make a change to an existing file or document. Changes to the existing document are saved in memory or in a temporary file but are not added to the document until the program is instructed to save them. Editing programs typically provide safeguards against inadvertent changes, such as by requesting confirmation before saving under an existing filename, by allowing the user to assign a password to a file, or by giving the option of setting the file to read-only status.
2. To run software that makes extensive, predictable changes to a file automatically, such as a linker or a filter for graphics.

Edit key

In a software application, a predefined key or combination of keys that, when pressed, causes the application to enter edit mode.

Edit mode

The mode of a program in which a user can make changes to a document, as by inserting or deleting data or text.

Editor

A program that creates files or makes changes to existing files. An editor is usually less powerful than a word processor, lacking the latter's capability for text formatting, such as use of italics. Text or full-screen editors allow the user to move through the document using direction arrows. In contrast, line editors require the user to indicate the line number on which text is to be edited.

EDP

Embedded DisplayPort is an interface that is primarily used to connect a video source to a display device such as a computer monitor or television set.

EDRAM

Embedded DRAM [Memory]. eDRAM is used as embedded memory blocks within ASIC ICs. eDRAM does not exist as a individual integrated circuit, IC or component.

EDO RAM

Acronym for extended data out random access memory. A type of dynamic RAM that keeps data available for the CPU while the next memory access is being initialized, resulting in increased speed. Pentium-class computers using Intel's Triton chip set are designed to take advantage of EDO RAM.

Eeprom

EEPROM (also written E2PROM and pronounced "e-e-prom," "double-e prom," "e-squared," or simply "e-prom") stands for Electrically Erasable Programmable Read-Only Memory and is a type of non-volatile memory used in computers and other electronic devices to store small amounts of data that must be saved when power is removed.

Efficiency

Careful use of resources, such as time and space.

EFI BIOS

Extensible Firmware Interface BIOS is a newer BIOS specification

Egosurfer

Someone who searches the Internet for references of himself/herself.

EGP

Exterior Gateway Protocol. Internet protocol for exchanging routing information between autonomous systems. Documented in RFC 904. Not to be confused with the general term exterior gateway protocol. EGP is an obsolete protocol that has been replaced by BGP.

EHCI

Enhanced Host Controller Interface is a high speed controller standard

EIA

Electronic Industries Association. Group that specifies electrical transmission standards. The EIA and TIA have developed numerous well-known communications standards, including EIA/TIA-232 and EIA/TIA-449.

Eia/tia-232

Common physical layer interface standard developed by EIA and TIA, that supports unbalanced circuits at signal speeds of up to 64 kbps. Closely resembles the V.24 specification. Formerly known as RS-232.

Eia/tia-449

Popular physical layer interface developed by EIA and TIA. Essentially, a faster (up to 2Mbps) version of EIA/TIA-232 capable of longer cable runs. Formerly called RS-449.

Eia/tia-586

Standard that describes the characteristics and applications for various grades of UTP cabling.

Eia-530

Refers to two electrical implementations of EIA/TIA-449: RS-422 (for balanced transmission) and RS-423 (for unbalanced transmission).

EIDE

(Enhanced Integrated Development Environment), also called EIDE, is a

term that Western Digital coined in 1994 to represent a particular set of extensions it devised to the original AT Attachment standard. At that time, the official ATA standard was rather limiting, and work was progressing towards the new ATA-2 standard. Western Digital decided that it did not want to wait for the new standard, and also that it could better position itself as a market leader by creating a new feature set for future drives. The name "Enhanced IDE" was presumably selected to build upon the common name for ATA then in popular use: IDE.

EISA

(Extended Industry Standard Architecture; pr. "ee-icer") An upgraded version of ISA, now obsolete; usually used with reference to expansion cards.

ELAN

Emulated LAN. ATM network in which an Ethernet or Token Ring LAN is emulated using a client-server model. ELANs are composed of an LEC, an LES, a BUS, and an LECS. Multiple ELANs can exist simultaneously on a single ATM network. ELANs are defined by the LANE specification.

Elapsed duration

The amount of time needed to complete a task.

Elapsed time

The total number of calendar days (excluding non-work days such as weekends or holidays) that is needed to complete an activity. It gives a "real world view" of how long an activity is scheduled to take for completion.

Election algorithm

An algorithm that chooses a unique process to play a particular role.

Electromagnetic

Interference in the integrity of a signal caused by radiation.

EMA

Enterprise Management Architecture. Digital Equipment Corporation network management architecture, based on the OSI network management model.

E-mail

E-mail is short for electronic mail. It allows for the transfer of information from one computer to another, provided that they are hooked up via some sort of network (often the Internet. E-mail works similarly to FAXing, but its contents typically get printed out on the other end only on demand, not immediately and automatically as with FAX. A machine receiving e-mail will also not reject other incoming mail messages as a busy FAX machine will; rather they will instead be queued up to be received after the current batch has been completed. E-mail is only seven-bit clean, meaning that you should not expect anything other than ASCIIdata to go through uncorrupted without prior conversion via something like uucode or bcode. Some mailers will do some conversion automatically, but unless you know your mailer is one of them, you may want to do the encoding manually.

E-mail filter

A feature in e-mail-reading software that automatically sorts incoming mail into different folders or mailboxes based on information contained in the message. For example, all incoming mail from a user's Uncle Joe might be placed in a folder labeled "Uncle Joe." Filters may also be used either to block or accept e-mail from designated sources.

E-mail address
The way you specify where an E-Mail message should be delivered.

E-mail server
A computer system that provides MTA, mailbox storage and directory services and optionally UA services.

E-mail service
UA, MTA, mailbox storage, and directory service.

EMI
Electromagnetic interference. Interference by electromagnetic signals that can cause reduced data integrity and increased error rates on transmission channels.

EMIF
ESCON Multiple Image Facility. Mainframe I/O software function that allows one ESCON channel to be shared among multiple logical partitions on the same mainframe.

Emoticon
(EMOTion ICON) A group of symbols used to indicate emotions inemail or newsgroups. The most popular is the smiley :-) or :) (look at it sideways), but there are lots of variations including the sad face :-(, the wink ;-) , and the astonished face :-0 .

EMP
Electromagnetic pulse. Caused by lightning and other high-energy phenomena. Capable of coupling enough energy into unshielded conductors to destroy electronic devices.

Empathy
The ability to see things from the other person's point of view.

Emulation
A network activity in which a computer acts as if it is another kindof computer or terminal. An example is when a Macintosh useropens a remote terminal session to a VAX, it may run a programthat emulates a DEC VT240 terminal.

Emulation mode
Function of an NCP that enables it to perform activities equivalent to those performed by a transmission control unit.

EN
End node. APPN end system that implements the PU 2.1, provides end-user services, and supports sessions between local and remote CPs. ENs are not capable of routing traffic and rely on an adjacent NN for APPN services.

Encapsulation
Combining or defining a data structure of attributes and a group of associated functions and behaviours as a single object.
The process of placing one protocol inside of another. Usually implies that the encapsulated protocol was not originally intended by its designers to be carried by the encapsulating protocol.

Encapsulation bridging
Carries Ethernet frames from one router to another across disparate media, such as serial and FDDI lines. Contrast with translational bridging.

Encoder
Device that modifies information into the required transmission format.

Encrypt, encryption
Coding data so that it can't be read by hackers etc when transmitted over the internet. For example, any reputable website selling goods by credit card will encrypt your credit card number and personal details.

Energy star*

Energy Star* is a program run by the U.S. Environmental Protection Agency and the U.S. Department of Energy that promotes energy efficient products

End-user license agreement

A legal agreement between a software manufacturer and the software's purchaser with regard to terms of distribution, resale, and restricted use.

Engineering process

The set of activities relating to a construction output.

Enhanced IGRP

Enhanced Interior Gateway Routing Protocol. Advanced version of IGRP developed by Cisco. Provides superior convergence properties and operating efficiency, and combines the advantages of link state protocols with those of distance vector protocols.

Enhancement

An extension of functional or performance requirements.

ENIAC

An 1800-square-foot, 30-ton computer containing 17,468 vacuum tubes and 6,000 manual switches. Developed between 1942 and 1946 for the U.S. Army by J. Presper Eckert and John Mauchly at the University of Pennsylvania, ENIAC is considered to have been the first truly electronic computer. It remained in operation until 1955.

Enter key

A special function key on a keyboard used to transmit a line or screen of data from a display screen to a computer. Often used interchangeably with return key.

Enterprise network

A networking system that allows communication and resourcesharing among all of a company's business functions andworkers. In some circles, this would even include the company'sbusiness including its suppliers and distributors.

Enterprise resource planning systems ("ERPS")

Enterprisewide applications/ processes/systems that support ERP by handling a wide variety of planning, transaction processing and accounting functions in an integrated manner across many functional areas.

Entity

A hardware (or firmware) device or software process capable ofinitiating or responding to communication. Entities typicallypossess a unique address.

Entity-relationship diagram

It's a diagram that represents entities and how they are related to each other.

Entropy

1. A measure of the disorder of a system.
2. The thermodynamictendency of a system to reduce its overall energy state by increasing its disorder. Theoretically, an equilibrium is reached where the energy reduction that can be gained by a further increase in entropy is offset by the energy necessary to contain that increase.

Enumeration

A group of related, named constants.

Environment

The setting in which computing takes place that is the aggregate of the hardware, software, policies and procedures relating to their use. The computing environment may be influenced by software, such as the operating system (for example, a UNIX environment) or the vendor (for example, an IBM environment).

EOT

End of Transmission. Generally, a character that signifies the end of a logical group of characters or bits.

EPROM

Erasable programmable read-only memory. Nonvolatile memory chips that are programmed after they are manufactured and, if necessary, can be erased by some means and reprogrammed.

Equalization

Technique used to compensate for communications channel distortions.

Erase

To remove data from a data medium, leaving the medium available for recording new data.

Ergonomics

The study of the work environment in relation to the user.

Error checking

Uploading or downloading transfer check employed to identify errors in data transmission.

Error control

Technique for detecting and correcting errors in data transmissions.

Error message

A message that reports the detection of an error.

Error-correcting Code

Code having sufficient intelligence and incorporating sufficient signaling information to enable the detection and correction of many errors at the receiver.

Error-detecting Code

Code that can detect transmission errors through analysis of received data based on the adherence of the data to appropriate structural guidelines.

ES

1. End system. Generally, an end-user device on a network.
2. End system. Nonrouting host or node in an OSI network.

E-SATA

External Serial ATA* is an external interface for SATA devices

Escon

Enterprise System Connection. IBM channel architecture that specifies a pair of fiber-optic cables, with either LEDs or lasers as transmitters and a signaling rate of 200 Mbps.

Escon channel

IBM channel for attaching mainframes to peripherals such as storage devices, backup units, and network interfaces. This channel incorporates fiber channel technology. The ESCON channel replaces the bus and tag channel.

ESD

Electrostatic discharge. Discharge of stored static electricity that can damage electronic equipment and impair electrical circuitry, resulting in complete or intermittent failures.

ESF

Extended Superframe Format. Framing type used on T1 circuits that consists of 24 frames of 192 bits each, with the 193rd bit providing timing and other functions. ESF is an enhanced version of SF.

ES-IS

End System-to Intermediate System. OSI protocol that defines how end systems (hosts) announce themselves to intermediate systems (routers).

ESNET

Energy Sciences Network. Data communications network managed and funded by the U.S. Department of Energy Office of Energy Research (DOE/OER). Interconnects the DOE to educational institutions and other research facilities.

Ethernet

A local area network originally developed by Xerox for linking personal computers. Later adapted by DEC and Intel as well and subsequently adopted as an international standard called 802.3. It transmits data at 10 megabits per second. All computers on a network were originally connected to a coaxial cable up to one kilometer. Each computer monitors all transmissions, looking for packets containing its identifier as the destination. Only one signal may be present on the channel at a time and no single computer controls transmissions. Several upper layer protocols, such as DECnet and TCP/IP use Ethernet as an underlying transport mechanism. Ethernet is to be contrasted with other data link protocols such as token ring, DDCMP or SDLC. Uses CSMA/CD.

Ethertalk

1. EtherTalk Link Access Protocol (ELAP), the protocol that placesAppleTalk's DDP formatted packets in Ethernet frames.
2. Theimplementation of AppleTalk using Ethernet as a delivery system.In AppleTalk Phase 1, Ethernet V.2 is used; in Phase 2, 802.3 isused.

ETSI

European Telecommunication Standards Institute. Organization created by the European PTTs and the European Community (EC) to propose telecommunications standards for Europe.

EUNET

European Internet. European commercial Internet service provider. EUnet is designed to provide electronic mail, news and other Internet services to European markets.

Event

Network message indicating operational irregularities in physical elements of a network or a response to the occurrence of a significant task, typically the completion of a request for information.

Event listener

It is an interface of JAVA responsible for handling events.

Excel

The most popular spreadsheet program for PCs, part of the Microsoft Office suite.

Excess rate

Traffic in excess of the insured rate for a given connection. Specifically, the excess rate equals the maximum rate minus the insured rate. Excess traffic is delivered only if network resources are available and can be discarded during periods of congestion.

Exe (or .exe)

(EXEcutable; pr. "exie", "dot exie") A file which is usually the main part of a

program. A program may consist of just an exe file and nothing else, or there may be dozens of files, including more exes.

Exec

The interactive command process of the Cisco IOS software.

Execute

To interpret a computer instruction and carry out the operations specified in the instruction.

Execution environment

a collection of kernel-managed resources to which threads have access; consists of an address space and resources for synchronization and communication.

Expansion

The process of running a compressed data set through an algorithm that restores the data set to its original size.

Expansion card (or board)

A circuitboard which can be plugged in to an expansion slot on the PC's motherboard, to give the PC extra capabilities. A lot of the features originally provided by expansion cards, like sound, graphics and network connections, are now built in.

Expansion card (expansion board, adapter card or accessory card)

A printed circuit board that can be inserted into an expansion slot of a computer motherboard to add functionality to a computer system.

Expedited delivery

Option set by a specific protocol layer telling other protocol layers, or the same protocol layer in another device, to handle specific data more rapidly.

Explicit route

In SNA, a route from a source subarea to a destination subarea, as specified by a list of subarea nodes and transmission groups that connect the two.

Explorer frame

Frame sent out by a networked device in a SRB environment to determine the optimal route to another networked device.

Explorer packet

Generated by an end station trying to find its way through a SRB network. Gathers a hop-by-hop description of a path through the network by being marked (updated) by each bridge that it traverses, thereby creating a complete topological map.

Export

The process of taking (exporting) data from an application, i.e. a database, and placing it into another application, i.e. a spreadsheet.

Express chipset

Part of the product name for Intel chipsets such as the Intel® G33 Express Chipset.

Express chipset family

Part of the product name for a group of Intel chipsets that are all in the same family of chipsets (for example, the Intel® 3 Series Chipset family includes chipsets such as the Intel® G33 Express Chipset, the Intel® G35 Express Chipset, and the Intel® P31 Express Chipset).

Expressxcard

ExpressCard is an interface to allow peripheral devices to be connected to a computer, usually a laptop computer.

Peripherals include Firewire 800,USB 2.0/3.0,soundcards, TV Tuner cards, PCIe graphics cards and CAC cards.

Extension

Filename extensions originate back in the days of CP/M and basically allow a very rough grouping of different file types by putting a tag at the end of the name. To further complicate matters, the tag is sometimes separated by the name proper by a period "." and sometimes by a tab. While extensions are semi-enforced on CP/M, MS-DOS, and MS-Windows, they have no real meaning aside from convention on other platforms and are only optional.

Exterior gateway protocol

Any internetwork protocol used to exchange routing information between autonomous systems. Not to be confused with Exterior Gateway Protocol EGP), which is a particular instance of an exterior gateway protocol.

Exterior router

Router connected to an AURP tunnel, responsible for the encapsulation and deencapsulation of AppleTalk packets in a foreign protocol header.

External gateway protocol

A protocol for distributing information regarding availability to the routers and gateways that interconnect networks.

External style sheet

A cascading style sheet is a file with a .css file extensio The .css file is comprised solely of style rules in valid .css syntax, without any surrounding HTML tags. By defining styles in one or more external style sheets and linking them to pages in your web, you ensure consistency of appearance throughout those pages. If you change a style in the external style sheet, the change will be reflected in all of the pages linked to that style sheet.

External lines

Telephone access from outside the organisation or company.

External pager

A server that stores page data for virtual memory implementation.

Extranet

An extranet is a private network that uses the Internet protocols and the public tele-communication system to share a business's information , data or operations with external suppliers, vendors or customers. An extranet can be viewed as the external part of a company's Intranet.

F-connector

A coaxial connector, used primarily in video applications, that requires a screw-on attachment.

F2f

Short for face-to-face. In person, rather than over the Internet. The term is used in e-mail.

Facsimile (FAX) machine

Operated via telephone lines, producing a hard copy for the receiver.

Factor

Any of the elements, quantities, or symbols that, when multiplied together, form a product.

Fading

In a received signal, the variation (with time) of the amplitude or relative phase, or both, of one or more of the frequency components of the signal.

Fail

The opposite of "win", "fail" expresses an ability to incorrectly perform acts ranging from idiotically simple to impossibly difficult, often consisting of an amusing element.

Failsafe

Built-in safety characteristics of a unit or system so that unit or system failure or a loss of control power will not result in an unsafe condition. The design feature of a part, unit or equipment which allows the item to fail only into a non-hazardous mode. Of a device, the capability to fail without detriment to other devices or danger to personnel. If a component were to fail, it will fail in a safe condition.

Fail-stop server

a server that, when it is about to fail, changes to a state that allows other servers to detect the failure, then it stops.

Failure

The inability of a component or system to perform its required function.

Failure domain

Area in which a failure has occurred in a Token Ring, defined by the information contained in a beacon. When a station detects a serious problem with the network (such as a cable break), it sends a beacon frame that includes the station reporting the failure, its NAUN, and everything in between. Beaconing in turn intitiates a process called autoreconfiguration.

Failure mode

a way of failing in which conditions in the system determine the method or severity at which the system fails.

Failure rate

The amount of units failing per unit time, or over the units life. Failure rate over time is divided into three general time periods; early failures [infant mortality], normal usage over time having a constant failure rate, and an end-of-life wear-out failure period. Failure rates are higher during both the early life and wear-out periods and much lower and consistent during the devices useful life. One method of reducing early failures is by a Burn In test.

Failure semantics

A description of the ways in which a server may fail.

Failure transparency

a type of transparency that enables the concealment of faults, allowing users and programs to complete tasks despite the failure.

Fair and reasonable cost

Costs that do not exceed what an ordinary, prudent person in the conduct of competitive business would incur.

Fair market price

A price based on reasonable costs under normal competitive conditions and not on lowest possible cost.

Fall time

The time required for the amplitude of a pulse to decrease (fall) from a specified value (usually 90 percent of the peak value exclusive of overshoot or under-shoot) to another specified value (usually 10 percent of the peak value exclusive of overshoot or undershoot).

False clock

A condition where a phase-locked loop controlling a clock locks on a frequency other than the correct frequency.

False lock

A condition where a phase-locked loop locks to a frequency other than the correct one, or to an improper phase.

Families of programs

Sets of programs that are related by sharing significant portions of requirements, design, and code, e.g., a program family might include one version of a program developed for an English-speaking audience, a second version of a program developed for a German-speaking audience, and a third version for a Japanese-speaking audience.

Family

A series of hardware or software products that have some properties in common, such as a series of personal computers from the same company, a series of CPU chips from the same manufacturer that all use the same instruction set, or a set of fonts that are intended to be used together, such as Times New Roman.

Fan

The cooling mechanism built into computer cabinets, laser printers, and other such devices to prevent malfunction due to heat buildup. Fans are the main source of the continuous humming associated with computers and other hardware; to flip through a stack of printer paper to ensure that the pages are loose and will not stick together or jam the printer.

Fan-heatsink

This solution incorporates active (fan) and passive (heatsink) cooling components. The heatsink provides absorption for the heat and the fan provides the airflow necessary to remove the heat from the processor.

Fanout

The number of IC gates an Integrated circuit can drive is determined by the current it can source and sink.

Fan-out Unit

Device that allows multiple devices on a network to communicate using a single network attachment.

FAQ

Frequently Asked Questions. A collection of information on the basics of any given subject. Often put together and archived on a server so that people don't waste bandwidth asking simple questions.

Farad

The basic unit of capacitance. A capacitor has a capacitance of 1 farad when a voltage potential of 1 volt across it produces a charge of 1 coulomb.

Faraday cage

A enclosure composed of a conducting material that shields the contents of the cage from electric fields and electromagnetic radiation. Although the amount of electromagnetic interference that is blocked depends not only on the frequency of the EMI but the spacing of the mesh used as the cage. A solid metal cage blocks all EMI regardless of the frequency.

Faraday constant

The magnitude of electric charge per mole of electrons; 96,485.3365 C mol^{-1}.

Faraday rotation

The rotation of the plane of polarization of electromagnetic energy when it passes a substance influenced by a magnetic field that has a component in the direction of propagation.

Faraday shield

A common conductor connection at one end to provide electrostatic shielding without effecting electro-magnetic waves. The common point connection is normally grounded, while the other side of the conductor is left un-connected.

Far-end Crosstalk

Crosstalk that is propagated in a disturbed channel in the same direction as the propagation of a signal in the disturbing channel.

Fast bus

IEEE Std 960-1993, FastBus defined the Mechanical, Electrical, and Protocol for a board-to-backplane interface. This interface is obsolete.

Fast ethernet

A 100 MB network using 4 twisted pairs.

Fast recovery diode

A diode that can switch between forward and reverse bias is a relativly small amount of time, compared to other diode types. The 1N5615 represents a fast recovery diode.

Fast SCSI

A form of the SCSI-2 interface that can transfer data 8 bits at a time at up to 10 megabytes per second. The Fast SCSI connector has 50 pins. Also called Fast SCSI.

Fast switching

Cisco feature whereby a route cache is used to expedite packet switching through a router.

Fast time-constant circuit

Differentiator circuit in the first video amplifier that allows only the leading edges of target returns, no matter how small or large, to be used.

Fast track

The starting or implementation of a project by overlapping activities, commonly entailing the overlapping of design and construction (or manufacturing) activities.

FAT

(File Allocation Table; pr. "fat") A sort of index of where data is stored on a hard disk, used by the operating system.

Fault

An accidental condition that causes a functional unit to fail to perform its required function. A defect that causes a reproducible or catastrophic malfunction.

Fault current

Any current that is not in its intended path. A current that flows as a result of a fault.

Fault indicator

A component or device that indicates a failure or defect in the equipment being monitored either by audio or visual indication.

Fault management

One of five categories of network management defined by ISO for management of OSI networks. Fault management attempts to ensure that network faults are detected and controlled.

Fault tolerance

The extent to which a functional unit focused at infinity, the far-field region is sometimes will continue to operate at a defined performance level even though one or more of its components are malfunctioning.

Fault-tolerant system

A system which can detect a fault and either fail gracefully or hide the fault from the user.

Favorite

In Microsoft Internet Explorer, a user-defined shortcut to a page on the World Wide Web, analogous to a bookmark in Netscape Navigator.

Favorites folder

In Microsoft Internet Explorer, a collection of shortcuts to Web sites that a user has selected for future reference. Other Web browsers refer to this collection by other names, such as bookmarks or hotlists.

Fax modem

A modem that sends (and possibly receives) data encoded in a fax format (typically CCITT fax format), which a fax machine or another modem decodes and converts to an image. The image must already have been encoded on the host computer. Text and graphic documents can be converted into fax format by special software usually provided with the modem; paper documents must first be scanned i Fax modems may be internal or external and may combine fax and conventional modem capabilities.

FB-DIMM

Fully buffered dual in-Line memory module is a type of computer memory that includes an advanced memory buffer between the memory controller and the memory module; usually used in server environments.

FCC

Federal Communications Commission. The United States government agency that regulates electronic communications and the domestic manufacture and importation of communication equipment.

FDD

(Fixed Disk Drive, Floppy Disk Drive). The slot on the PC which accepts floppy disks, almost always referred to as "Drive A:" by the computer.

FDDI

Fiber Distributed Data Interface is a Local Area Network [LAN] using Fiber-Optic cable in a Dual Token Ring topology. FDDI is defined in ISO 9314-1/2/3.

FDDI II

ANSI standard that enhances FDDI. FDDI II provides isochronous transmission for connectionless data circuits and connection-oriented voice and video circuits.

FDM

Frequency-division multiplexing. Technique whereby information from multiple channels can be allocated bandwidth on a single wire based on frequency.

FDHP

Acronym for Full Duplex Handshaking Protocol. A protocol used by duplex modems to determine the source type of the transmission and match it.

Feature

Either an attribute or an operation of a class.

FECN

Forward explicit congestion notification. Bit set by a Frame Relay network to inform DTE receiving the frame that congestion was experienced in the path from source to destination. DTE-receiving frames with the FENC bit set can request that higher-level protocols take flow-control action as appropriate.

Feedback

The return of a portion of the output, or processed portion of the output, of a (usually active) device to the input. The feedback may be in phase with the input signal [positive feedback], or out of phase with the input signal [negative feedback].

Feed-forward

A signal that is passed from the origin of a circuit to another portion of the circuit.

Feed-through capacitor

A bulk-head mount filter used to pass signals into an enclosure. The most common filter element is a shunt capacitor. .

Feed-thru terminal

A terminal that feeds through a front panel, metal plate or some other barrier so that there is a terminal accessible on either side of a panel. A terminal designed to be mounted on a chassis or other partition, and having through connected wire mounting facilities. It may or may not be insulated. It is fabricated into a single item whose parts are not separable.

Female connector

Also called "jack". A connector which joins with a male connector by providing recesses into which the male connector inserts its contact points or pins.

Female contact

A contact that accepts a mating contact by having it inserted within the contact.

FEP

Fluorinated Ethylene Propylene, A synthetic type of insulation.

FEP
Front-end processor. Device or board that provides network interface capabilities for a networked device. In SNA, typically an IBM 3745 device.

Ferrite
A powdered and compressed ferric oxide material that has both magnetic properties and light resistance to current flow.

Ferrite bead
A surface mount choke used as a low pass filter used to suppress noise..

Ferrite switch
A ferrite device that blocks the flow of energy through a waveguide by rotating the electric field 90 degrees. The rotated energy is then reflected or absorbed.

Ferromagnetic material
A highly magnetic material, such as iron, cobalt, nickel, or their alloys.

Ferrule
A short metal tube used to make crimp connections to shielded or coaxial cables. The cylindrical metallic ends of a cartridge fuse or wire.

FET
A semiconductor device.

FFS
*(For F***'s Sake)* Internet slang, not suitable for polite company.

Fiber channel
An interface using fiber as the net.

Fiber optic
A technology for the transmission of light beams along optical fibers. A light beam, such as that produced in a laser, can be modulated to carry information. Because light has a higher frequency on the electromagnetic spectrum than other types of radiation, such as radio waves, a single fiber-optic channel can carry significantly more information than most other means of information transmission. Optical fibers are thin strands of glass or other transparent material, with dozens or hundreds of strands housed in a single cable. Optical fibers are essentially immune to electromagnetic interference.

Fiber optic cable
A fiber, multiple fiber or fiber bundle in a cable structure fabricated to meet optical mechanical and environmental specifications.

Fiber optic connector
A fiber optic component normally assembled onto a cable and attached to a piece of apparatus for the purpose of providing interconnecting/ disconnecting of fiber optic cables.

Fiber optic link
A communications link that transmits signals by means of modulated light propagated in an optical fiber.

Fibrous braid
An outer covering used to protect a conductors insulating material. Commonly made from cotton, linen, silk, rayon, or fiberglass. Cable braid is also made off metal and used as a conductor shield or signal conductor.

FID1
Format indicator 1. One of several formats that an SNA TH can use. An FID1 TH encapsulated messages between two subarea nodes that do not support virtual and explicit routes.

FID2

Format indicator 2. One of several formats that an SNA TH can use. An FID2 TH is used for transferring messages between a subarea node and a PU 2 , using local addresses.

FID3

Format indicator 3. One of several formats that an SNA TH can use. An FID3 TH is used for transferring messages between a subarea node and a PU 1, using local addresses.

FID4

Format indicator 4. One of several formats that an SNA TH can use. An FID4 TH encapsulates messages between two subarea nodes that are capable of supporting virtual and explicit routes.

Field

Usually the smallest data element in a record; a specified area used for a particular category of data; for example, columns used to represent a particular item of data, such as an employees wage (fixed field). The particular field is always used to record the same kind of information. In free field records, each field has an identifier that is present in the record and linked to the contents of the field.

Field name

Label used to identify the data stored in a field.

Field property

An attribute of a field that affects its appearance or behaviour.

File

A collection of any form of data that is stored beyond the time of execution of a single job. A file may contain program instructions or data, which may be numerical, textual or graphical information.

File allocation table

A table or list maintained by some operating systems to manage disk space used for file storage. Files on a disk are stored, as space allows, in fixed-size groups of bytes (characters) rather than from beginning to end as contiguous strings of text or numbers. A single file can thus be scattered in pieces over many separate storage areas. A file allocation table maps available disk storage space so that it can mark flawed segments that should not be used and can find and link the pieces of a file. In MS-DOS, the file allocation table is commonly known as the FAT.

File attribute

A restrictive label attached to a file that describes and regulates its use—for example, hidden, system, read-only, archive, and so forth. In MS-DOS, this information is stored as part of the file's directory entry.

File compression

Refers to files that have been reduced in size using file compression software.

File conversion

The process of transforming the data in a file from one format to another without altering its contents—for example, converting a file from a word processor's format to its ASCII equivalent.

File format

The type of file, such as picture or text; represented as a suffix at the end of the filename (text = TXT or .txt, etc.).

File handle

In MS-DOS, OS/2, and Windows, a token (number) that the system uses to identify or refer to an open file or, sometimes, to a device.

File infector
Virus that attack and modify program files, usually .exe and .com files. When the program is run the virus is executed.

File maintenance
Broadly, the process of changing information in a file, altering a file's control information or structure, or copying and archiving files. A person using a terminal to enter data, the program accepting the data from the terminal and writing it to a data file, and a database administrator using a utility to alter the format of a database file are all forms of file maintenance.

File manager
A module of an operating system or environment that controls the physical placement of and access to a group of program files.

File retrieval
The act of transferring a data file from a storage location to the machine where it is to be used.

File server
A computer designated to store software, courseware, administrative tools, and other data on a local- or wide-area network. It "serves" this information to other computers via the network when users enter their personal access codes.

File service
A distributed system component that is analogous to a file system.

File sharing
The use of computer files on networks, wherein files are stored on a central computer or a server and are requested, reviewed, and modified by more than one individual. When a file is used with different programs or different computers, file sharing can require conversion to a mutually acceptable format. When a single file is shared by many people, access can be regulated through such means as password protection, security clearances, by file locking to prohibit changes to a file by more than one person at a time.

File system
In an operating system, the overall structure in which files are named, stored, and organized. A file system consists of files, directories, and the information needed to locate and access these items. The term can also refer to the portion of an operating system that translates requests for file operations from an application program into low-level, sector-oriented tasks that can be understood by the drivers controlling the disk drives.

File transfer
Popular network application that allows files to be moved from one network device to another.

Filter
1) A device which allows you to use an ordinary phone over a telephone line set up for an ADSL internet connection. Also called a micro-filter.
2) A program or set of programs that automatically removes spam from your email.

Filter keys
A Windows 95 accessibility control panel feature that enables users with physical disabilities to use the keyboard. With FilterKeys, the system ignores brief and repeated keystrokes

that result from slow or inaccurate finger movements.

Finder

A software application included with Macintosh system software that allows users to perform basic file access and management functions using icons and pull-down menus.

Finger

A collection of software routines used by computers running theIP protocol stack, which allows a user to read public informationabout a user on the same, or a remote machine, often including:full name, telephone number and extension, snail-mail address,time and place of last login, whether user has any pending un-read mail, and witticisms selected by the user.

Firefox

A popular browser, available free from Mozilla, which you can use instead of Internet Explorer or Google Chrome.

Firewall

Originally a dedicated computer between you and the internet, preventing hackers, spammers and similar undesirables from taking over your PC. Now often just a program running on your PC, performing the same task. Recent versions of Windows have one built-in.

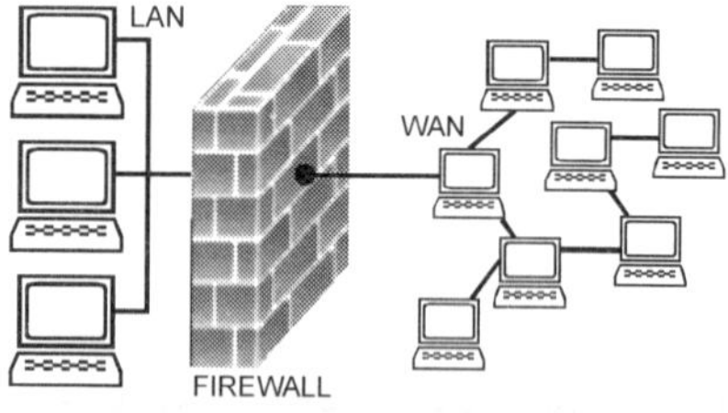

Firewire

A fast (up to 50megabyes per second) serial bus with support for 63 hot swap, plug and play devices. Has the potential to replace serial, parallel, IDE and SCSI hard disk type interfaces.

Firmware

Sort of in-between hardware and software, firmware consists of modifiable programs embedded in hardware. Firmware updates should be treated with care since they can literally destroy the underlying hardare if done improperly. There are also cases where neglecting to apply a firmware update can destroy the underlying hardware, so user beware

Flag

In a packet, a bit (or sometimes a group of bits) that indicates acondition. For example, the ZIP GetNetInfo Reply includes a 1-bitflag that indicates whether the zone name specified either is or isnot a valid home zone name for the node that requested the information.

Flag byte

In LocalTalk signaling, the bit pattern "01111110", which signalsthe beginning and ending of a LLAP frame. The Flag Bytes preceding the packets establish the synchronization of the framesimilar to the function of an Ethernet preamble.

Flame

Internet slang for an email or newsgroup post insulting or telling someone off.

Flamer

A flamer is someone who makes degrading or insulting remarks on a forum or other Internet message board, the verb of which is "flame".

Flamewar

A public trading of insults in a newsgroup or forum. Sometimes flamewars get so out of hand that there are hundreds of flames in the newsgroup and almost nothing else.

Flapping

Routing problem where an advertised route between two nodes alternates (flaps) back and forth between two paths due to a network problem that causes intermittent interface failures.

Flash

A technology for displaying animations (mostly) on webpages, created by the Macromedia Corporation. The Flash Player is a plugin which enables internet browsers to display the animations.

Flash drive

A removable data storage device, usually thumb sized and plugged into a PC's USB port.

Flash memory

A type of nonvolatile memory. Flash memory is similar to EEPROM memory in function but it must be erased in blocks, whereas EEPROM can be erased one byte at a time. Because of its block-oriented nature, flash memory is commonly used as a supplement to or replacement for hard disks in portable computers. In this context, flash memory either is built into the unit or, more commonly, is available as a PC Card that can be plugged into a PCMCIA slot. A disadvantage of the block-oriented nature of flash memory is that it cannot be practically used as main memory (RAM) because a computer needs to be able to write to memory in single-byte increments.

Flash update

Routing update sent synchronously in response to a change in the network topology.

Flat file service

A file service that is responsible for implementing operations on the the contents of files

Float

A primitive data type that models floating-point numbers.

Floating-point

Numbers of fixed precision that are associated with measurements and are used typically in scientific and engineering applications.

Flooding

Traffic-passing technique used by switches and bridges in which traffic received on an interface is sent out all of the interfaces of that device except the interface on which the information was originally received.

FLOP

Floating-Point Operations per Second. A measure of a computer's performance.

Floppy

An extremely common type of removable disk. Floppies do not hold too much data, but most computers are capable of reading them. Note though that there are different competing format used for floppies, so that a floppy written by one type of computer might not directly work on another. Also sometimes called "diskette"

Floppy disk

A round piece of flexible plastic film coated with ferric oxide particles that can hold a magnetic field. When placed inside a disk drive, the floppy disk rotates to bring different areas, or sectors, of the disk surface under the drive's read/write head, which can detect and alter the orientation of the particles' magnetic fields to represent binary 1s and 0s. A floppy disk 5.25 inches in diameter is encased in a flexible plastic jacket and has a large hole in the center, which fits around a spindle in the disk drive; such a disk can hold from a few hundred thousand to over one million bytes of data. A 3.5-inch disk encased in rigid plastic is also called a floppy disk or a microfloppy disk. In addition, 8-inch floppy disks were common in DEC and other minicomputer systems.

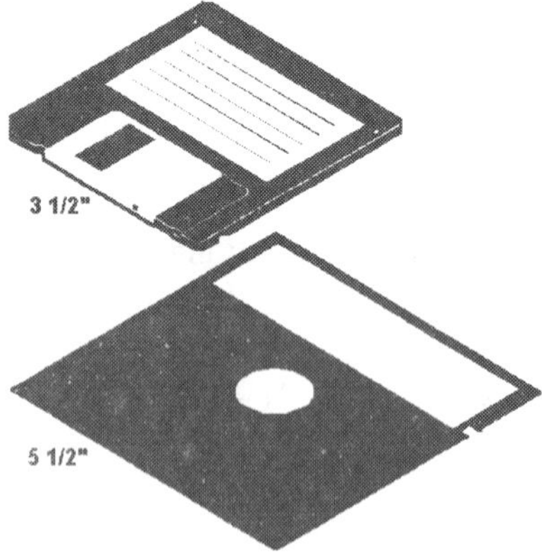

Flow
Stream of data traveling between two endpoints across a network (for example, from one LAN station to another). Multiple flows can be transmitted on a single circuit.

Flow control
Technique for ensuring that a transmitting entity, such as a modem, does not overwhelm a receiving entity with data. When the buffers on the receiving device are full, a message is sent to the sending device to suspend the transmission until the data in the buffers has been processed. In IBM networks, this technique is called pacing.

FM
Frequency Modulation. In data transmission, a system of signaling in which the data is encoded by varying the frequency of the signal.

Foad
(<bleep> Off And Die) Internet slang. Pretty self-explanatory really.

Focus
In television and raster-scan displays, to make an electron beam converge at a single point on the inner surface of the screen.

Fogging
A graphics term where to add the effect of density to the atmosphere. Objects farther away from the viewer appears more "cloudy" or "foggy."

FOIRL
Fiber Optic Inter Repeater Link. An asynchronous fiber optic connection that links two Ethernet repeaters (hubs) with a maximum transmission distance of 2 kilometers when used at 10MBits/sec.

Folder
A place where a user's e-mail messages may be stored. Every user has a folder for new messages, and on most systems may create other folders for specific purposes.

Font
In a simplistic sense, a font can be thought of as the physical description of a character set. While the character set will define what sets of bits map to what letters, numbers, and other symbols, the font will define what each letter, number, and other symbol looks like. Fonts can be either fixed width or variable width and independently, either bitmapped or

vectored. The size of the large characters in a font is typically measured in points.

Font cartridge

A plug-in unit available for some printers that contains fonts in several different styles and sizes. Font cartridges, like downloadable fonts, enable a printer to produce characters in sizes and styles other than those created by the fonts built into it.

Font editor

A utility program that enables the user to modify existing fonts or to create and save new ones. Such an application commonly works with a screen representation of the font, with a representation that can be downloaded to a PostScript or other printer, or with both.

Footer

Information that appears at the bottom of a page.

Foreground

High-priority processing, usually for realtime activities, automatically given precedence, by means of interrupts, over lower-priority processing.

Form

A database object used primarily for data entry and making changes to existing records.

Form factor

Form factor is a standard size and shape for a computer motherboard.

Form feed

The feature that automatically advances a roll of paper to the top of the next page or the next form when the printer has finished printing a document or form of one or more pages.

Format

The manner in which data is stored; its organization. For example, VHS, SVHS, and Beta are three different formats of video tape. They are not 100% compatible with each other, but information can be transferred from one to the other with the proper equipment (but not always without loss; SVHS contains more information than either of the other two). Computer information can be stored in literally hundreds of different formats, and can represent text, sounds, graphics, animations, etc. Computer information can be exchanged via different computer types provided both computers can interpret the format used.

Format bar

A toolbar within an application used for modifying the format of the document being displayed, such as changing font size or type.

Formula

An equation that performs operations on worksheet data.

FORTRAN

FORmula TRANslator. Developed in 1954 by IBM, it is a high-level programming language, most widely used for scientific and engineering applications because it has excellent mathematical functions. Many programmers consider it to sacrifice "elegance" for speed of numerical manipulations.

Forum

A public or semi-public area on a website or bulletin board where you can read and post messages on a particular topic, allowing public debate.

Forward channel

Communications path carrying information from the call initiator to the called party.

Forward delay interval

Amount of time an interface spends listening for topology change information after that interface has been activated for bridging and before forwarding actually begins.

Forwarding

Process of sending a frame toward its ultimate destination by way of an internetworking device.

Fourier transform

Technique used to evaluate the importance of various frequency cycles in a time series pattern.

FPS

1. *(Frames Per Second)* A measure of the smoothness and quality of animations, particularly in computer games. The more frames per second, the better the quality.
2. *(First Person Shooter)* A computer game where you shoot things, played from a first person perspective, ie with you standing behind the gun(s). Also known as a shoot-'em-up.

FQDN

Fully Qualified Domain Name. Includes host name, as well as allenclosing domains, and is often distinguished by the use of aterminating dot: (host.subdomain.domain.).

Frad

Frame Relay access device. Any network device that provides a connection between a LAN and a Frame Relay WAN.

Frag

Shoot someone in a computer game.

Fragment

Piece of a larger packet that has been broken down to smaller units.

Fragmentation

Process of breaking a packet into smaller units when transmitting over a network medium that cannot support a packet of the original size.

Frame

In data networks, the information packet and all of the precedingand succeeding signals necessary (flag bytes, preambles, framechecks, abort sequences, etc.) to convey it along the data link.

Frame relay

Industry-standard, switched data link layer protocol that handles multiple virtual circuits using HDLC encapsulation between connected devices. Frame relay is more efficient than X.25, the protocol for which it is generally considered a replacement.

Frame relay bridging

Bridging technique, described in RFC 1490, that uses the same spanning-tree algorithm as other bridging functions, but allows packets to be encapsulated for transmission across a Frame Relay network.

Free-trade Zone

Part of an AppleTalk internetwork that is accessible by two other parts of the internetwork that are unable to directly access one another.

Free format

A physical file structure that specifies the order of variables in a file and that they are delimited from each other by a special character or characters (usually a blank or other white pace). Free format files may have variable physical record lengths; when they do, they are typically delimited by a newline character at the end of each line. Contrast with Fixed Format.

Free space

Space on a floppy disk or a hard drive not currently occupied by data.

Freenet

A community-based computer BBS and Internet service provider, usually operated by volunteers and providing free access to subscribers in the community or access for a very small fee. Many freenets are operated by public libraries or universities.

Freeware

Software that is distributed for free, with no license fee.

Frequency

The measure of how often a periodic event occurs, such as a signal going through a complete cycle. Frequency is usually measured in hertz (Hz), with 1 Hz equaling 1 occurrence (cycle) per second. In the United States, household electricity is alternating current with a frequency of 60 Hz. Frequency is also measured in kilohertz (kHz, or 1,000 Hz), megahertz (MHz, or 1,000 kHz), gigahertz (GHz, or 1,000 MHz), or terahertz (THz, or 1,000 GHz).

Friending

the act of making and adding friends online through social networking sites such as Facebook and MySpace.

Front end

It is an interface through which a program can be accessed by common users.

FSB

Front Side Bus is the physical component that carries information between the computer's processor and other components such as system memory.

FST

Fast Sequenced Transport. Connectionless, sequenced transport protocol that runs on top of the IP protocol. SRB traffic is encapsulated inside of IP datagrams and is passed over an FST connection between two network devices (such as routers). Speeds up data delivery, reduces overhead, and improves the response time of SRB traffic.

FTAM

The OSI standard for File Transfer, Access and Management.

FTP

File Transfer Protocol. Lowest-common-denominator protocolfor the point-to-point transfer of text and binary files between IP connected hosts.

FUD

Fear, Uncertainty and Doubt. "FUD factor"

Full backup

All files in the system, including program files and data files, are duplicated

Full mesh

Term describing a network in which devices are organized in a mesh topology, with each network node having either a physical circuit or a virtual circuit connecting it to every other network node. A full mesh provides a great deal of redundancy, but because it can be prohibitively expensive to implement, it is usually reserved for network backbones.

Full-duplex

A term applied to data transmission in which data can be sent and received simultaneously.

Function

A predefined formula that performs calculations by using specific values, called arguments

Function key

A keyboard key that gives an instruction to a computer, as opposed to keys that produce letters, numbers, marks of punctuation, etc.

Functional model

Description of aspects of a system that transform values using functions, mappings, constraints, and functional dependencies.

Fundamental principle of fractions

The basic rule used in obtaining equivalent fractions, which states that multiplying or dividing the numerator and denominator by the same non-zero number results in a fraction that is equivalent to the original fraction.

Fuzzball

Digital Equipment Corporation LSI-11 computer system running IP gateway software. The NSFnet used these systems as backbone packet switches.

G

G.703/g.704

ITU-T electrical and mechanical specifications for connections between telephone company equipment and DTE using BNC connectors and operating at E1 data rates.

G.804

ITU-T framing standard that defines the mapping of ATM cells into the physical medium.

Gain block

A component that provides amplification, which normally contains additional circuitry in addition to a simple amplifier.

Gain-bandwidth product

The number that results when the gain of a circuit is multiplied by the bandwidth of that circuit. For an operational amplifier, the gain-bandwidth product for one configuration will always equal the gain-bandwidth product for any other configuration of the same amplifier.

Galvanic isolation

The separation in movement of charge-carrying particles from one section to another. A current moving in one section of a circuit does not flow in another section of the circuit. Isolation between the ground reference of two power systems such that the potential difference between the two ground references, up to some maximum voltage, would not cause damage or interference to normal operations.

Galvanometer

A meter used to measure small values of current by electromagnetic or electrodynamic means.

Gamma

The transistor emitter-to-base current ratio in a common-collector configuration. Gamma Ray; Emissions of a specific frequency produced from sub-atomic particle interaction.

Ganged tuning

The process used to tune two or more circuits with a single control.

Gantt bar

A graphic element on a Gantt Chart representing the duration of a task.

Gantt chart

A chart using time lines and other symbols that illustrates multiple, time-based activities or projects on a horizontal time scale. A Gantt chart is a time-phased graphic display of activity durations. It is also referred to as a bar chart. Activities are listed with other tabular information on the left side with time intervals over the bars. Activity durations are shown in the form of horizontal bars. A graphic display of schedule related information. In the typical Gantt Chart, activities are listed down the left side of the chart, dates are shown across the top, and planned activity durations are shown as date-placed horizontal bars. Also called a "bar chart."

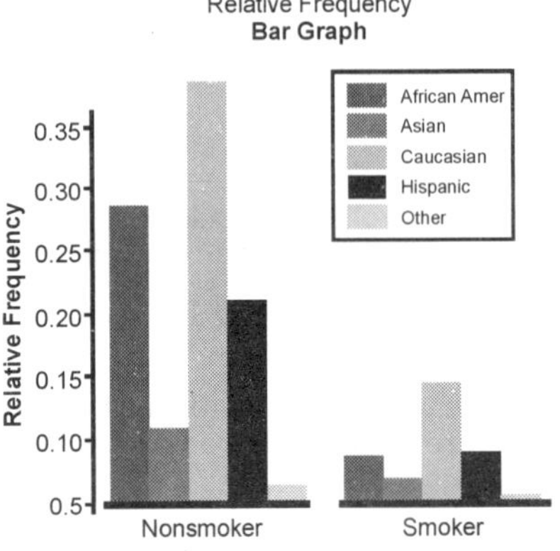

A view that includes a list of tasks and a graphical representation of those tasks using Gantt bars. A graphic display of activity durations. Activities are listed with other tabular information on the left side with time intervals over the bars. Activity durations are shown in the form of horizontal bars.

Gapped clock

A periodic clock stream which is missing clock pulses at arbitrary intervals for arbitrary lengths of time. A clock signal which has had one or more clock pulses removed from the series.

Garbage

Unwanted or meaningless information in memory, on disk or on a tape.

Garble

An error in transmission or reception, that results in incorrect or un-decryptable information.

Gas-discharge display

A type of flat-panel display, used on some portable computers, containing neon between a horizontal and a vertical set of electrodes. When one electrode in each set is charged, the neon glows (as in a neon lamp) where the two electrodes intersect, representing a pixel. Also called gas-plasma display.

Gas-discharge tube

A gas filled tube that illuminates by ionizing the gas within the tube with an applied voltage.

Gas filled tube

Gas Tube. A two-electrode vacuum tube with a cathode and plate. The evacuated tube contains a small amount of gas, such as neon, which is sealed inside the tube. When sufficient voltage is applied to the tube, ionization of the gas molecules occurs and is responsible for the current passing through the tube during operation.

Gasket

A preformed shapeable component that is placed between two adjoining parts to prevent electromagnetic radiation into or escaping from an enclosure or system.

Gate

As applied to logic circuitry, one of several different types of electronic devices that will provide a particular output when specified input conditions are satisfied. Gate; as in AND Gate, OR Gate, NOR Gate, NAND Gate or Inverter. Also, a circuit in which a signal switches another signal on or off. The electrode associated with the region in which the electric field due to the control voltage is effective.

Gate pulse
A signal pulse use to gate or allow another signal through a circuit.

Gate terminal
The gate lead of a Field Effect Transistor.

Gate turn-off thyristor
A Thyristor that may be turned on or off by a signal applied to the gate, as opposed to only being turned on with a normal thyristor. .

Gated AGC
Circuit that permits automatic gain control to function only during short time intervals.

Gated-beam detector
An FM demodulator that uses a special gated-beam tube to limit, detect, and amplify the received FM signal. Also known as a quadrature detector.

Gateway
An electronic door between one computer network and another. A device or set of devices that connects two or more networks, enabling data transfer between them. When the networks are similar, a gateway routes packets or messages. When the networks differ, a gateway also performs extensive protocol conversion.

Gateway host
In SNA, a host node that contains a gateway SSCP.

Gateway NCP
NCP that connects two or more SNA networks and performs address translation to allow cross-network session traffic.

Gating
The process of selecting those portions of a wave that exist during one or more selected time intervals or that have magnitudes between selected limits. Also, the application of a specific waveform to perform electronic switching.

Gauge
The thickness of a wire, as in the American Wire Gauge.

Gaussian noise
Noise whose amplitude is characterized by the normal distribution.

GB
A unit of memory storage that is equal to 1,024 megabytes (or 1,073,741,824 bytes).

GB
Gigabyte.

GB
Gigabit.

GBPS
Gigabytes per second.

GBPS
Gigabits per second.

GDP
Gateway Discovery Protocol. Cisco protocol that allows hosts to dynamically detect the arrival of new routers as well as determine when a router goes down. Based on UDP.

Gender changer
A component that changes the Gender of a connector or cable assembly. An SMA male to female gender changer is shown to the right.

General public license
The agreement under which software, such as the GNU (GNU's Not UNIX) utilities, is distributed by the Free

Software Foundation. Anyone who has a copy of such a program may redistribute it to another party and may charge for distribution and support services, but may not restrict the other party from doing the same. A user may modify the program, but if the modified version is distributed, it must be clearly identified as such and is also covered under the General Public Licence. A distributor must also either provide source code or indicate where source code can be obtained. Also called copyleft.

Generalization

The relationship between a class and one or more refined or specialized versions of it.

Generator

A machine that converts mechanical energy to electrical energy by applying the principle of magnetic induction. A machine that produces ac or dc voltage, depending on the original design.

Germanium

Symbol Ge in the periodic table. A grayish-white metal having semiconductor properties, similar to tin. Many transistors once used Germanium as the semiconductor material [example Germanium diodes; 1N270, 1N276, 1N277, 1N3287 and Germanium transistors 2N384, 2N539, 2N1120].

Germanium photodiode

A germanium-based PN- or PIN-junction photodiode.

GET

In SNMP, a command given by the Console to retrieve a single data structure from a MIB.

GGP

Gateway-to-Gateway Protocol. MILNET protocol specifying how core routers (gateways) should exchange reachability and routing information. GGP uses a distributed shortest-path algorithm.

GHz

Gigahertz - billions of cycles per second. Often used as a measurement of a PC processor chip's speed and power, with bigger numbers meaning a bit more speed, and a higher price. 1000 MHz = 1.0 GigaHertz.

GIF

(Graphics Interchange Format) A popular type of compressed graphics (picture) file, widely used on the WWW. Best for artwork with 256 colours or less.

Giga

A prefix denoting a billion.

Gigabyte (or Gig)

Unit of measurement for pieces of information : approximately 1 billion bytes, 1 million kilobytes, or 1000 megabytes. Hard disk sizes are usually measured in gigabytes. Often shortened to "GB", "Gig" or just G.

GIGO

(Garbage In Garbage Out; pr. "guy-go") A fundamental principle of computing, that if you feed a computer bad data, you will get bad results, even if the program is working perfectly.

GM

Part of the product name for specific mobile Intel chipsets with integrated graphics.

GMA

Intel® Graphics Media Accelerator (Intel® GMA) is part of the product name for specific Intel graphics controllers such as the Intel GMA 900

GMCH

Graphics and Memory Controller Hub is the chipset component that handles communication between the CPU and all other devices

GNS

Get Nearest Server. Request packet sent by a client on an IPX network to locate the nearest active server of a particular type. An IPX network client issues a GNS request to solicit either a direct response from a connected server or a response from a router that tells it where on the internetwork the service can be located. GNS is part of the IPX SAP.

Google

Started out as search engine and rapidly became so much better at it than everyone else that "to google" was (and is) widely used to mean "to look up via the internet". Now a huge, rich and influential corporation with fingers in many pies, owners of the Android operating system. Its headquarters are in California and it has offices and data centers all over the world.

Googling

searching through the Google search engine.

Gopher

A simple, menu-based system (named after the mascot of the University of Minnesota, where it was created) for searching and retrieving information from resources across the Internet. Gopher uses a simple protocol that allows a single Gopher client to access information from any accessible Gopher server, providing the user with a single menu of informatio Menu topics may lead to hierarchically organized subtopics. Depending on the context, the term "Gopherspace" refers either to the whole collection of documents available from Gopher servers or to what's available based on the menu selections you've already made. Public domain versions of the client and server are available. The system can be accessed by typing a Gopher URL in the Open URL dialog box.

GOSIP

Government OSI Profile. US Government procurement standard that specified interoperability standards for computing equipmentand software purchased.

GQM (goal, question, metric) paradigm

A technique for defining meaningful metrics for any part of the software process.

Gossip architecture

a replication architecture in which the replica managers periodically exchange messages to notify each other of updates.

GPF

(General Protection Fault) A common error message in early versions of Windows, seen when a program tried to do something Windows thought it shouldn't, often locking up the PC.

Grade

Also Level or Category. In the specification of wiring for data networks, a standard designation used to describe the electricalquality of the wiring with regard to its suitability to carry high-speed signals.

Grade of service

Measure of telephone service quality based on the probability that a call will encounter a busy signal during the busier hours of the day.

Graph

In Quality Management, a visual comparison of variables that yield data in numerical facts. Examples include trend graphs, histograms, control charts, frequency distributions arid, scatter diagrams. In Time Management, the display or drawing that shows the relationship between activities. Pictorial representation of relative variables.

Graphic

A computer-generated picture produced on a computer screen or paper, ranging from simple line or bar graphs to colorful and detailed images.

Graphical user interface (GUI)

A GUI is a software "front end" which lets the user use pictures and "point-and-click" technology to access the software application. It allows a computer user to interact with the computer by manipulating graphic representations (icons) with a mouse or other pointing device instead of typing text commands. Many modern Internet clients are based on GUI principles and technology. NetCruiser is a GUI.

Graphics controller

A term used to describe the graphics hardware in a computer.

Graphics printer

A printer, such as a laser, ink-jet, or dot-matrix impact printer, that can produce graphics formed pixel by pixel and not merely text characters. Nearly all printers presently used with personal computers are graphics printers; daisy-wheel printers are the exception.

Gre

Generic Routing Encapsulation. Tunneling protocol developed by Cisco that can encapsulate a wide variety of protocol packet types inside IP tunnels, creating a virtual point-to-point link to Cisco routers at remote points over an IP internetwork. By connecting multiprotocol subnetworks in a single-protocol backbone environment, IP tunneling using GRE allows network expansion across a single-protocol backbone environment.

Green PC

A computer system designed to conserve energy. For example, some computers shut off power to nonessential systems when no input has been detected for a certain amount of time, a condition known as sleep mode. Green PCs may also be distinguished by the use of minimal packaging materials and replaceable components, such as toner cartridges, that are recyclable.

Griefer

A player of an online game who harasses other players.

Ground

An electrical conductor that is neither negatively or positively charged.

Ground station

Collection of communications equipment designed to receive signals from (and usually transmit signals to) satellites. Also called a downlink station.

Group multicasting
A communication model for communication between groups of cooperating processes.

Groupware
Software that serves the group and makes the group as a whole more productive and efficient in group tasks. Example: Group Scheduling.

Guard band
Unused frequency band between two communications channels that provides separation of the channels to prevent mutual interference.

Guard condition
A Boolean expression that must be true in order for a transition to occur.

Guarded transition
A transition that fires only if a guard condition is true.

GUI component
A control, such as a button, that can be placed into an applet.

Guidance
The giving of direction, or otherwise influencing a person's or group's conduct and actions.

H channel

High-speed channel. Full-duplex ISDN primary rate channel operating at 384 Kbps.

Hacker

A person with technical expertise who experiments with computer systems to determine how to develop additional features. Hackers are occasionally requested by system administrators to try and "break into" systems via a network to test security. The term hacker is sometimes incorrectly used interchangeably with cracker. A hacker is called a "white hat" and a cracker a "black hat."

Half adder

A circuit that adds two 1-bit binary numbers and output a sum bit and a carry bit, but does not have a provision to accept a carry input from a previous adder stage. Two Half Adders can be combined to form a Full Adder.

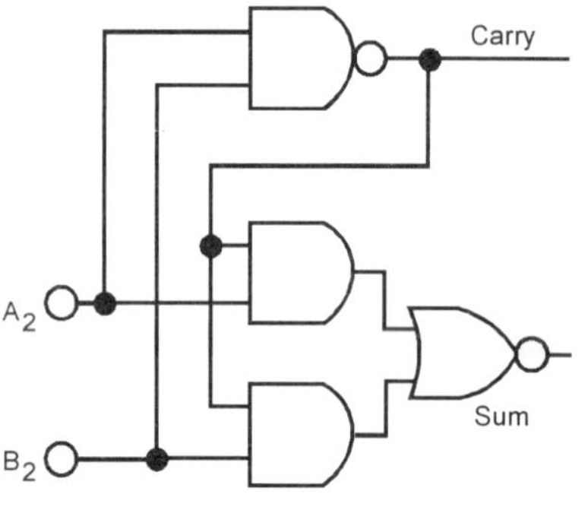

Half-duplex

Data flow in either direction, but not in both directions at the same time. There are a number of interface buses that only allow Half-Duplex operation, while some bus networks just add a redundant path in the opposite direction to allow communication in either direction at the same time. Operation in both directions at the same time is called Full-Duplex.

Half-duplex transmission

Two-way electronic communication that takes place in only one direction at a time.

Half-power point

A point on a waveform or radar beam that corresponds to half the power of the maximum power point.

Half-wave dipole

A style of Dipole Antenna.

Half-wave rectifier

A rectifier using only one-half of each cycle to change ac to pulsating dc. The direction of the diode or the winding of the transformer selects the polarity of the output across the load. Resistor Rs is not required but is used to limit the current through the diode. Refer to the Half-Wave Rectifier Circuit detail.

Half-wave voltage doubler

Two half-wave voltage rectifier circuits connected to double the input voltage.

Read more on Voltage Multiplier Circuits. A voltage doubler circuit that only operates on half of the input cycle.

Hall effect

An electric field that is produced when a current carrying conductor is placed in a magnetic field whose direction is perpendicular to both the direction of the current and the magnetic field.

Hall effect device

A Hall Effect Sensor component or device.

Halt

A command that stops the transfer of data on a bus, or stops the executions of commands by a processor.

Hamming code

An error-detecting and error-correcting binary code, used in data transmission, that can detect all single- and double-bit errors and correct all single-bit errors.

Hamming weight

The number of non-zero symbols in a symbol sequence.

Hand

(Have A Nice Day) Internet slang, often used ironically.

Handheld computer

A computer small enough to be held in one hand while being operated by the other hand. Handheld computers are commonly used in transportation and other field service industries. They are usually built to perform specific tasks. They often have restricted specialized keyboards rather than the standard QWERTY layout, smaller displays, input devices such as bar code readers, and communications devices for sending their data to a central computer; they rarely have disk drives. Their software is usually proprietary and stored in ROM.

Handling

Taking responsibility for and acting to deal with a person, activity, requirement, etc.

Hands-free

Not having to hold the telephone, but carry on a conversation using a microphone speaker facility.

Handshacking

How one device communicates with one or more other devices, at a predetermined speed. However the actual speed of the transfer could vary for every different transfer, because the transfer speed is defined as when both devices are ready.

Handshake

The interchange of signals between a 'talker' and a 'listener' to exchange data on a bus. During a Handshake a listener [slave] indicates ready for data, a talker [master] indicates data ready, the slave then indicates data received.

Handshaking

A procedure performed by modems, terminals, and computers to verify that communication has been correctly established.

Hang

To stop responding. A hung program or computer system does not respond to user input, but the screen looks as if everything is running normally. The program or system might be waiting for something, for example, information from a network, or it might have terminated abnormally. It might resume running normally on its own, or the user might need to terminate and restart the program or reboot the computer. A hung computer system is said to be locked up.

Hard copy

A printed copy of machine output in a visually readable form.

Hard disk

A device containing one or more inflexible platters coated with material in which data can be recorded magnetically, together with their read/write heads, the head-positioning mechanism, and the spindle motor in a sealed case that protects against outside contaminants. The protected environment allows the head to fly 10 to 25 millionths of an inch above the surface of a platter rotating typically at 3600 to 7200 rpm; therefore, much more data can be stored and accessed much more quickly than on a floppy disk. Most hard disks contain from two to eight platters. Also called hard disk drive.

Hard disk controller

The section of the hard disk that receives commands from a processor and than performs disk transfers.

Hard disk drive (HDD)

a non-volatile storage device that stores digitally encoded data on rapidly rotating rigid (i.e. hard) platters with magnetic surfaces.

Hard disk type

One or more numbers that inform a computer about the characteristics of a hard disk, such as the number of read/write heads and the number of cylinders the hard disk contains. The hard disk type numbers are usually marked on a label attached to the disk and must be input to the computer when the hard disk is installed, often by means of the computer's CMOS setup program.

Hard drive cache

A temporary storage area on a hard drive.

Hard project

A project that has a well defined physical product as its outcome as distinct from a soft project, the product of which is essentially intellectual.

Hard return

A character input by the user to indicate that the current line of text is to end and a new line is to beginning in word-processing programs that automatically break lines within the margins of a page, a hard return indicates the end of a paragraph. In text-entry programs that lack wordwrap, on the other hand, a hard return is required to end each line, and often two or more hard returns are needed to end a paragraph.

Hard tube

A high-vacuum electron tube modulator that uses a driver for pulse forming.

Hardware

Multiple physical components of a computer, upon which can be installed an operating system and a multitude of software to perform the operator's desired functions.

Hardware address

An address, fixed at the time of manufacturing, that identifies a network adapter such as an Ethernet card.

Hardware configuration item

A hardware component of a system, which is designated for configuration management to the integrity of the delivered product. It may exist at any level in the system hierarchy, since configuration management must be imposed down to the lowest level where item interchangeability is required. Each HWCI is to have (as appropriate) individual design reviews, individual qualification certification, individual Acceptance Reviews, and separate operator and maintenance manuals.

Hardware interrupt

A request for service from the central processing unit, generated either externally by a hardware device such as a disk drive or an input/output port or internally by the CPU itself. External hardware interrupts are used for such situations as a character received from a port and needing to be processed, a disk drive ready to transfer a block of data, or a tick of the system timer. Internal hardware interrupts occur when a program attempts an impossible action such as accessing an unavailable address or dividing by zero. Hardware interrupts are assigned levels of importance or priority. The highest priority is given to a type of interrupt called a nonmaskable interrupt—one that indicates a serious error, such as a memory failure, that must be serviced immediately.

Hardware project

A project in which the principal deliverable item is a physical product or functioning device of some sort.

Hardwired

Circuits that are permanently interconnected to perform a specific function, as distinct from circuits addressed by software in a program and, therefore, capable of performing a variety of functions, albeit more slowly. Also used to describe a non-switched connection between devices.

Harmonic

A frequency that is a whole-number multiple of a smaller base frequency. Of a sinusoidal wave, an integral multiple of the frequency of the wave. Harmonic percentages of a half sine wave; 2nd, 21.2%, 3rd, 0%, 4th 4.2%, 5th, 0% and 6th harmonic is 1.8%.

Harmonic distortion

A ratio of 100 times the sum of all the harmonics to the fundamental. In the output signal of a device, distortion caused by the presence of frequencies that are not present in the input signal, caused by nonlinearities within the device. The production of harmonic frequencies at the output of a nonlinear device when a sinusoidal signal is applied to the input.

Harness

An assembly of wires or cables, or wires and cables arranged so it may be installed or removed as a unit in the same electronic or electrical equipment. One or more insulated wires or cables, with or without helical twist; with or without common covering, jacket, or braid; with or without breakouts; assembled with two or more electrical termination devices; and so arranged that as a unit it can be assembled and handled as one assembly.

Hartley Oscillator

An oscillator that uses two series connected inductors in parallel [a tapped coil or split coil] with a capacitor. The feedback point for the

Hartley oscillator is between the two inductors as shown in the diagram. The oscillating frequency is determined by the LC circuit.

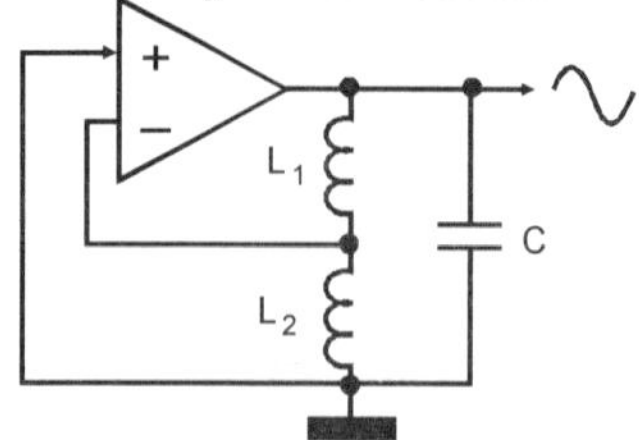

Hash

To be mapped to a numerical value by a transformation known as a hashing function. Hashing is used to convert an identifier or key, meaningful to a user, into a value for the location of the corresponding data in a structure, such as a table. For example, given the key MOUSE and a hashing function that added up the ASCII values of the characters, divided the total by 127, and took the remainder, MOUSE would hash to 12, and the data identified by MOUSE would be found among the items in entry 12 in the table.

Hashcode

a number derived from the contents of a data item which is used to store and locate the data.

Hay bridge

An AC bridge that uses capacitors and resistors to determine the value of an unknown inductor.

Hayes compatible

Hayes Microcomputer Products is one of the leading manufacturers of modems and has developed a language called the AT command set for controlling modems that has become the de facto standard. Any modem that recognizes Hayes modem commands is said to be Hayes-compatible. This is very useful because most communications programs use Hayes modem commands. Virtually all modems manufactured today are Hayes-compatible.

Hazard

A situation or substance that could cause injury or illness.

HBD3

Line code type used on E1 circuits.

HD audio

Intel® High Definition Audio is the audio architecture standard that replaces AC'97.

HD, HDD

(Hard Disk Drive) The main data storage unit in a computer.

HDCP

High-bandwidth Digital Content Protection is a copy protection scheme to prevent data from being copied or shared illegally.

HDLC

High-level Data Link Control is a group of protocols for transmitting data Packets between Point-to-Point nodes. Data is organized into a frame in HDLC. HDLC protocol resides with Layer 2 of the OSI model, the data link layer.

HDMI

HDMI (High-Definition Multimedia Interface) is a compact audio/video interface for transferring encrypted uncompressed digital audio/video data from a HDMI-compliant device ("the source" or "input") to a compatible digital audio device, computer monitor, video projector, and digital television.

HDTV

A method of transmitting and receiving television signals that produces a picture with much greater resolution and clarity than does standard television technology. International standards for HDTV are not yet established.

Headend

The end point of a broadband network. All stations transmit toward the headend; the headend then transmits toward the destination station.

Header

Data that includes information about the message being transmitted but is not the message itself (e.g. in email, the header might include the sender and recipient's email addresses).

Header

In a network packet or frame, a section of data that describes the data that immediately follows.

Heap

The RAM memory allocated by system software and system extensions to hold frequently used instructions and data not contained in ROM or firmware.

Heatsink

An object used to absorb heat from a processor

Hello

Interior routing protocol used principally by NSF net nodes. HELLO allows particular packet switches to discover minimal delay routes. Not to be confused with the Hello protocol.

Hello packet

Multicast packet that is used by routers for neighbor discovery and recovery. Hello packets also indicate that a client is still operating and network-ready.

Hello protocol

Protocol used by OSPF systems for establishing and maintaining neighbor relationships. Not to be confused with HELLO.

Help

1. Technical support staff who help solve users' problems with hardware or software systems or refer such problems to those who can solve them. Help desks are typically run by larger organizations, such as corporations or universities, or vendors to corporations, to assist users in the organization.
2. A software application for tracking problems with hardware and software and their solutions.

Help key

A key on the keyboard that the user can press to request help.

Helper address

Address configured on an interface to which broadcasts received on that interface will be sent.

Hepnet

High-Energy Physics Network. Research network that originated in the United States, but that has spread to most places involved in high-energy physics. Well-known sites include Argonne National Laboratory, Brookhaven National Laboratory, and the Stanford Linear Accelerator Center (SLAC).

Hertz (Hz)

A unit of measure of the frequency of cyclic wave form, equal to one cycle or period per second.

Heterogeneous network

Network consisting of dissimilar devices that run dissimilar protocols and in many cases support dissimilar functions or applications.

Hexadecimal

A numerical system with a base of 16 that is useful for expressing digital data. One hexadecimal digit represents for bits.

HFC

Hybrid fiber-coaxial (cable network). Older CATV systems were provisioned using only coaxial cable. Modern systems use fiber transport from the headend to an optical node located in the neighborhood to reduce system noise. Coaxial cable runs from the node to the subscriber. The fiber plant is generally a star configuration with all optical node fibers terminating at a headend. The coaxial cable part of the system is generally a trunk-and-branch configuration.

HFS

Hierarchical File System

Hierarchical coding structure

A coding system that can be represented as a multi-level tree structure in which every code except those at the top of the tree has a parent code.

Hierarchical file

A hierarchical file is one that contains information collected on multiple units of analysis where each unit of analysis is subordinate to another unit. For example, if the physical housing structure is one unit, and individual persons within the structure is another unit, the person records are subordinate (e.g. related to) the housing unit. An example would be the Current Population Survey Annual Demographic File which has household, family, and person units of analysis. Studies that include data for different units of analysis often link those units to each other so that, for instance, one can analyze the persons as they group in a structure. Such studies are sometimes referred to as having a relational structure.

Hierarchical file structure

A format for storing hierarchical files. Each unit of analysis has its own record structure or record type. Different units of analysis do not necessarily have the same number of bytes or characters as the records for other units of analysis. In order to give such a file a common physical record length , short logical records are typically "padded" with blanks so that they will all be the same physical record length. A hierarchical file can be also be stored in a rectangular file. For instance, the Survey of Income and Program Participation is distributed both ways; users can choose the format they prefer. Typically, the hierarchical file structure is more space-efficient but more difficult to use.

Hierarchical planning

A planning approach where each managerial level breaks planning tasks down into the activities that must be done at that level. Typically, upper-level planning establishes the objectives for the next lower-level manager's planning.

Hierarchical routing

Routing based on a hierarchical addressing system. For example, IP routing algorithms use IP addresses, which contain network numbers, subnet numbers, and host numbers.

High memory area

In DOS-based systems, the high memory area refers to the first 64K of extended memory.

High-Performance Computing and Communications (HPCC)

The term high-performance computing encompasses advanced computing, communications, and information technologies, including scientific workstations, supercomputer systems, high-speed networks, special purpose and experimental systems, the new generation of large scale parallel systems, and application and systems software with all components well integrated and linked over a high-speed network. The HPCC Acts legislation passed by the U.S. Congress in the early 1990s (also known as the "Dole Bills") established national networking objectives for the United States. See also National Research and Education Network.

Hint

In dynamic addressing, an address that a node will test for uniqueness first. The hint is either the last successful address the node used previously (the Macintosh keeps such a hint in PRAM) or a particular address that is specific to a particular model of device (the GatorBox always tries 128 first or LocalTalk networks).

HIPPI

High-Performance Parallel Interface. High-performance interface standard defined by ANSI. HIPPI is typically used to connect supercomputers to peripherals and other devices.

Hits

The number of matches a search engine returns based on the search topic.

Holddown

State into which a route is placed so that routers will neither advertise the route nor accept advertisements about the route for a specific length of time (the holddown period). Holddown is used to flush bad information about a route from all routers in the network. A route is typically placed in holddown when a link in that route fails.

Home page

A page on the World Wide Web. Confusingly "homepage" is used indiscriminately to describe several slightly different things : an amateur's hobby site; the front or main page of any website; or the page which your browser first goes to when you start it up.

Homologation

Conformity of a product or specification to international standards, such as ITU-t, CSA, TUV, UL, or VCCI. Enables portability across company and international boundaries.

Homomorphism

A mapping between two associations.

Hop

In routed networks, the passage of a packet through a router on the way to its destination.

Hop count

In AppleTalk packets, a 4-bit counter in the DDP header that is incremented each time a packet passes through a router on the way to its destination.

Hop distance

A unit of measure used to express the number or routers that a packet must pass through its way to its destination.

Host

In terminal emulation, the remote computer that is being controlled by the terminal emulation software.

Host adapter

A device for connecting a peripheral to the main computer, typically in the form of an expansion card. Also called controller, host bus adapter.

Host computer

In the context of networks, a computer that directly provides service to a user. In contrast to a network server, which provides services to a user through an intermediary host computer.

Host name

The domain name given to a computer. The following are all domain names: nic.ddmil, eff.org, and terminator.um.cc.umich.eau. The terms "host name" and "Fully Qualified Domain Name" are interchangeable in most contexts; host name is a more informal term.

Host node

SNA subarea node that contains an SSCP.

Host not responding

An error message issued by an Internet client indicating that the computer to which a request has been sent is refusing the connection or is otherwise unavailable to respond to the request.

Host number

Part of an IP address that designates which node on the subnetwork is being addressed. Also called a host address.

Hot docking

The process of attaching a laptop computer to a docking station while the computer is running, and automatically activating the docking station's video display and other functions.

Hot fix

Novell, Inc.'s term for the feature of their network file server operating system, Novell NetWare, which handles errors in disk write operations. The OS re-reads every block it writes to disk while it holds the data to be written in memory. In the case of an error, the data block is written to a spare area on the disk. The feature lost much of its importance with the widespread use of hard disk drives with built-in error correction and bad block re-mapping.

Hot insertion

The insertion of a device or card while there is power to the system. Many newer laptops allow for hot insertion of PCMCIA cards. High-end servers may also allow hot insertion to reduce downtimes.

Hotspot

A location where a computer can connect to a wireless network.

HPCC

High Performance Computing and Communications. U.S. government funded program advocating advances in computing, communications, and related fields. The HPCC is designed to ensure US. leadership in these fields through education, research and development, industry collaboration, and implementation of high-performance technology. The five components of the HPCC are ASTA, BRHR, HPCS, IITA, and NREN.

HPCS

High Performance Computing Systems. Component of the HPCC

program designed to ensure US. technological leadership in high-performance computing through research and development of computing systems and related software.

HPR

High Performance Routing. Second-generation routing algorithm for APPN. HPR provides a connectionless layer with nondisruptive routing of sessions around link failures, and a connection-oriented layer with end-to-end flow control, error control, and sequencing.

HSRP

Hot Standby Router Protocol. Provides high network availability and transparent network topology changes. HSRP creates a Hot Standby router group with a lead router that services all packets sent to the Hot Standby address. The lead router is monitored by other routers in the group, and if it fails, one of the standby routers inherits the lead position and the Hot Standby group address.

HSSI

High-Speed Serial Interface. Network standard for high-speed (up to 52 Mbps) serial connections over WAN links.

HTH

(Hope This Helps) Internet slang, often added at the end of an email or newsgroup post answering a question.

HTML

HyperText Markup Language, the coding language used to create hypertext documents for the World Wide Web. In HTML, a block of text can be surrounded with tags that indicate how it should appear (for example, in bold face or italics). Also, in HTML a word, a block of text, or an image can be linked to another file on the Web. HTML files are viewed with a World Wide Web browser.

HTPC

Home Theater PC is a device that combines the capabilities of a personal computer with a software application that supports video, photo, music playback and digital video recording.

HTTP

HyperText Transfer Protocol. Extremely fast protocol used for network file transfers in the WWW environment.

Hub

1. Generally, a term used to describe a device that serves as the center of a star-topology network.
2. Hardware of software devices that contains multiple independent but connected modules of network and internetwork equipment. Hubs can be active (where they repeat signals sent through them) or passive (where they do not repeat, but merely split, signals sent through them).
3. In Ethernet and IEEE 802.3, an Ethernet multiport repeater, sometimes referred to as a concentrator.

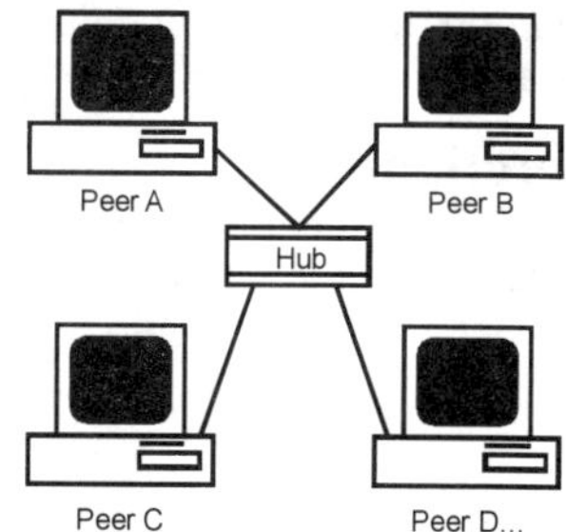

Hung

If a computer (or sometimes just a program) gets completely stuck and refuses to do anything, it has hung.

Hybrid

A device or system combining two types of mechanisms, circuits, or design approaches, each of which could of itself accomplish the total function but in a different and usually less effective manner. A hybrid computer combines digital and analog computers into one functioning system.

Hybrid circuit

A circuit in which fundamentally different types of components are used to perform similar functions, such as a stereo amplifier that uses both tubes and transistors.

Hybrid network

Internetwork made up of more than one type of network technology, including LANs and WANs.

Hygiene

Factors associated with the health and well-being of personnel. In project management, these factors more particularly refer to those elements such as pay and working conditions that tend to motivate or demotivate project team members.

Hypercard

A hypertext Multimedia package popular on Macintosh computers in the late 80's.

Hypercritical

A condition when an imposed date has been set such that the critical path leading to that point is too long to finish by that date. The critical path then becomes hypercritical and possesses negative float.

Hypercritical activities

Activities on the critical path with negative float. This can be achieved through the imposition of constraints such as target dates.

Hyperlink

A pointer that when chosen displays the item to which it points. It typically takes the form of a button or highlighted text that points to related text, picture, video, or audio. Hyperlinks allow non-linear exploration of media that contain them.

Hypermedia

Media (such as text, graphics, video, audio) that contains hyperlinks.

Hypertext

A way of presenting text so that you can click on a link within it, say a cross-reference, and instantly be transported to the relevant text, whether it is elsewhere in the current document or in another document entirely. The most obvious examples are World Wide Web pages.

Hyper-threading technology

Hyper-Threading Technology is technology proprietary to Intel that allows different parts of the CPU to work on different tasks simultaneously.

I

I/O

Input/Output. The part of a computer system or the activity that is primarily dedicated to the passing of information into or out of a central processing unit.

I/O bound

A computer or network activity whose speed is limited by the time necessary to perform I/O functions.

I/O controller hub

The chipset component that handles communication with components such as the hard drives and communicates with the CPU via the MCH.

IA32

Intel® architecture 32-bit is the 32-bit implementation of the x86 architecture

IA64

IA-64 often refers to Itanium® architecture. Intel® 64 architecture is the 64-bit implementation of the x86 architecture.

IAB

Internet Architecture Board. Board of internetwork researchers who discuss issues pertinent to Internet architecture. Responsible for appointing a variety of Internet-related groups such as the IANA, IESG, and IRSG. The IAB is appointed by the trustees of the ISOC.

IANA

Internet Assigned Numbers Authority. Organization operated under the auspices of the ISOC as a part of the IAB. IANA delegates authority for IP address-space allocation and domain-name assignment to the NIC and other organizations. IANA also maintains a database of assigned protocol identifiers used in the TCP/IP stack, including autonomous system numbers.

IANAL

(I Am Not A Lawyer) Internet slang. Amazing how often this one comes up.

IBM

(International Business Machines) The company that designed and built the first PCs, and still a giant of the industry. Standard PCs were originally referred to as “IBM compatible”, although IBM no longer controls the PC standard.

IBM AT

A class of personal computers introduced in 1984 and conforming to IBM’s PC/AT (Advanced Technology) specification. The first AT was based on the Intel 80286 processor and dramatically outperformed its predecessor, the XT, in speed.

IBM PC

Short for IBM Personal Computer. A class of personal computers introduced in 1981 and conforming to IBM's PC specification. The first PC was based on the Intel 8088 processor. For a number of years, the IBM PC was the de facto standard in the computing industry for PCs, and clones, or PCs that conformed to the IBM specification, have been called PC-compatible.

Icalendar

The iCalendar standard refers to the format used to store calendar type information (including events, to-do items, and journal entries) on the Internet. iCalendar data can be found on some World-Wide-Web pages or attached to e-mail messages.

ICD

International Code Designator. One of two ATM address formats developed by the ATM forum for use by private networks. Adapted from the subnetwork model of addressing in which the ATM layer is responsible for mapping network layer addresses to ATM addresses.

ICH

I/O controller hub

ICMP

Internet Control Message Protocol. Network layer Internet protocol that reports errors and provides other information relevant to IP packet processing. Documented in RFC 792.

Icon

Small pictogram either representing a file, or providing shortcuts for carrying out common tasks such as saving and printing inside anapplication.

Iconic interface

A user interface that is based on icons rather than on typed commands. See also graphical user interface, icon.

ID-10-T

clueless user; everybody giving a hard time to (computer) administrators.

IDE

(Integrated Drive Electronics) A type of PC hard disk, now obsolete, the foreunner of EIDE.

IDE

It stands for Integrated Development Environment. IDE is a programming system that combines several tools of programming to provide an integrated platform for programming. For instance, Visual Basic provides an IDE.

Idempotent law

In Boolean algebra, combining a quantity with itself either by logical addition or logical multiplication will result in a logical sum or product that is the equivalent of the quantity (for example, A + A = A; A x A = A).

Idempotent operation

an operation that can be performed repeatedly with the same effect as if it had been performed exactly once.

Identifier

A series of letters, digits, and underscores used to name program units such as classes, methods, and variables.

Identity

a distinguishing characteristic of an object that denotes a separate existence of the object even though the object may have the same data values as another object.

Identity comparator

A circuit that compares to numbers and provides an output to indicate if the numbers are equal or unequal, as in a 74521 TTL 8-bit Identity Comparator.

Identity law

In Boolean algebra, the law which states that any expression is equal to itself.

Identify opportunity

A pre-project activity. One that precedes the concept phase in the project life cycle and may lead to the initiation of a project.

IDI

Initial domain identifier. In OSI, the portion of the NSAP that specifies the domain.

Idle-channel noise

Noise that is present in a communications channel when no signals are applied. Note: The channel conditions and terminations must be stated for idle-channel noise measurements to be meaningful.

Idler frequency

In a parametric amplifier, the difference between the input signal and the pump signal frequency. Also called the Lower-Sideband Frequency.

IDP

Initial domain part. The part of a CLNS address that contains an authority and format identifier and a domain identifier.

IDPR

Interdomain Policy Routing. Interdomain routing protocol that dynamically exchanges policies between autonomous systems. IDPR encapsulates interautonomous system traffic and routes it according to the policies of each autonomous system along the path. IDPR is currently an IETF proposal.

IDRP

IS-IS Interdomain Routing Protocol. OSI protocol that specifies how routers communicate with routers in different domains.

IE

Acronym for information engineering. A methodology for developing and maintaining information-processing systems, including computer systems and networks, within an organization.

IE

(Internet Explorer) Microsoft's web browser, included free in Windows. If followed by a number (IE9, IE8 etc), it refers to a particular version of that browser.

IEC

International Electrotechnical Commission. Industry group that writes and distributes standards for electrical products and components.

IEEE

The Institute or Electrical and Electronic Engineers, a non-profit organization that, among many other activities, endeavors to coordinate, synthesize and promote data networking standards.

IEEE 802.1

IEEE specification that describes an algorithm that prevents bridging loops by creating a spanning tree. The algorithm was invented by Digital Equipment Corporation. The Digital algorithm and the IEEE 802.1 algorithm are not exactly the same, nor are they compatible.

IEEE 802.12

IEEE LAN standard that specifies the physical layer and the MAC sublayer of the data link layer. IEEE 802.12 uses the demand priority media-access scheme at 100 Mbps over a variety of physical media.

IEEE 802.2

The committee of the IEEE charged with the responsibility of coordinating standards at the Data Link Layer. The committee also oversees the work of many sub-committees that govern individual Data Link standards such as the 802.3 standard.

IEEE 802.3

IEEE LAN protocol that specifies an implementation of the physical layer and the MAC sublayer of the data link layer. IEEE 802.3 uses CSMA/CD access at a variety of speeds over a variety of physical media. Extensions to the IEEE 802.3 standard specify implementations for Fast Ethernet. Physical variations of the original IEEE 802.3 specifications include 10Base2, 10Base5, 10BaseF, 10BaseT, and 10Broad36. Physical variations for fast ethernet include 100BaseT, 100BaseT4, and 100BaseX.

IEEE 802.4

IEEE LAN protocol that specifies an implementation of the physical layer and the MAC sublayer of the data link layer. IEEE 802.4 uses token-passing access over a bus topology and is based on the token bus LAN architecture.

IEEE 802.5

IEEE LAN protocol that specifies an implementation of the physical layer and MAC sublayer of the data link layer. IEEE 802.5 uses token passing access at 4 or 16 Mbps over STP cabling and is similar to IBM Token Ring.

IEEE 802.6

IEEE MAN specification based on DQDB technology. IEEE 802.6 supports data rates of 1.5 to 155 Mbps.

IEEE-1284

A personal Computer interface that defined a parallel printer bus specification at 1MBps. IEEE-1284 defines a Point-To-Point asynchronous bi-directional interface. Devices may be either 1284 compatible {the older parallel port devices} or 1284 compliant. The maximum length for a printer cable is 25 feet, 32 feet maximum. Centronics parallel cables run out to 12 feet. The IEEE1284 cable replaced the 'Centronics' cable which is obsolete.

IESG

Internet Engineering Steering Group. Organization, appointed by the IAB, that manages the operation of the IETF.

IETF

Internet Engineering Task Force. Task force consisting of over 80 working groups responsible for developing Internet standards. The IETF operates under the auspices of ISOC.

IF amplifier

Usually a narrow-bandwidth IF amplifier that is tuned to one of the output frequencies produced by the mixer.

IF bandwidth

The range of frequencies centered around the IF frequency, limited by the 3dB amplitude points.

IF selectivity

The ability of the IF stages to accept the signal from one station while rejecting a signal from adjacent stations.

IF statement

The if statement conditionally executes a statement based upon the value of a boolean condition. The if part is executed if the condition is true, the else part, if present, is executed if the condition is false.

IGFET

Insulated Gate Field-Effect Transistor. Any FET that has an insulated gate.

IGMP

Internet Group Management Protocol Used by IP hosts to report their multicast group memberships to an adjacent multicast router.

IGP

Interior Gateway Protocol. Internet protocol used to exchange routing information within an autonomous system. Examples of common Internet IGPs include IGRP, OSPF, and RIP.

IGRP

Interior Gateway Routing Protocol. IGP developed by Cisco to address the problems associated with routing in large, heterogeneous networks.

IIH

IS-IS Hello. Message sent by all IS-IS systems to maintain adjacencies.

IIRC

(If I Recall Correctly) Internet slang.

IITA

Information Infrastructure Technology and Applications. Component of the HPCC program intended to ensure U.S. leadership in the development of advanced information technologies.

ILMI

Interim Local Management Interface. Specification developed by the ATM Forum for incorporating network-management capabilities in the ATM UNI.

IM

(Instant Messenging) A program that allows you to "chat" live via keyboard over the internet. Both parties must be running the same IM software - there are several different brands, mostly incompatible with each other.

Image

Some form of representation of a person or thing. This includes hardcopy such as pictures and printed graphics, electronic imaging where these potential hardcopies are committed to electronic media, and notional images such as the impression portrayed by the culture and behavior of an organization.

Image colour matching

The process of image output correction to match the same colours as were scanned or input.

Image editor

An application program that allows users to modify the appearance of a bitmapped image, such as scanned photos, by using filters and other functions. Creation of new images is generally accomplished in a paint or drawing program.

Image frequency

An undesired frequency capable of producing the desired frequency through heterodyning.

Image map

An image that contains more than one hyperlink on a Web page. Clicking on different parts of the image links the user to other resources on another part of the Web page, a different Web page, or a file. Often an image map, which can be a photograph, drawing, or a composite of several different drawings or photographs, is used as a map to the resources found on a particular Web site. Image maps are created with CGI scripts. Also called clickable maps.

Image rejection

The ability of a tuner to reject a signal which is the sum or difference of the tuners oscillator and IF signals.

IMP

Interface message processor. Old name for ARPANET packet switches. An IMP is now referred to as a PSN (packet-switch node).

Impedance

The total opposition offered to the flow of an alternating current. It may consist of any combination of resistance, inductive reactance, and capacitive reactance. The total passive opposition offered to the flow of electric current. The symbol for impedance is Z. Impedance is a function of frequency, except in the case of purely resistive networks.

Impedance bridge

A bridge circuit used for measuring resistance and reactance.

Impedance matching

The connection of an additional impedance to an existing one in order to accomplish a specific effect, such as to balance a circuit or to reduce reflection in a transmission line. The matching of impedances from one circuit to another to insure optimum power transfer.

Implementation

A stage in the development cycle in which a design is realized in an executable form.

Implementation

The physical manifestation of a network standard or design.

Implosion

The inward bursting of a CRT because of high vacuum. The opposite of explosion.

Import

The process of bringing (importing) data into an application which has been exported from another application.

Improper fraction

a fraction in which the numerator is larger than the denominator.

Impulse

A short surge of electrical, magnetic, or electromagnetic energy. A unidirectional voltage that rises rapidly and than decays to zero at a slower rate.

Impulse noise

Noise consisting of random occurrences of energy spikes having random amplitude and and spectral content. Note: Impulse noise in a data channel can be a definitive cause of data transmission errors. Noise generated in discrete energy bursts which has a characteristic wave shape.

Impulse waveform

A short duration pulse. The pulse duration is defined from the peak duration to 50 percent of peak.

In-band signaling

Transmission within a frequency range normally used for information transmission.

Inbox

The mailbox that holds incoming e-mail.

Incandescent

The process of emitting light by being heated to a high temperature, as in passing current through a wire until it heats up [light bulb].

Incandescent light bulb

An incandescent lamp or incandescent light makes light by heating a metal filament wire to a high temperature until it glows. Note that an incandescent bulb output light in a particular light spectrum. A lamp or bulb that generates light by incandescence.

Incentive

A contribution to motivation and motivating.

Incentive scheme

A formal program of incentives, typically associated with pay scales and conditions of employment.

Inception

The first phase of the Unified Process, in which the seed idea, request for proposal, for the previous generation is brought to the point of being (at least internally) funded to enter the elaboration phase.

Incident wave

The wave that strikes the surface of a medium. The wave that travels from the sending end to the receiving end of a transmission line.

In-circuit meter

A meter permanently installed in a circuit; used to monitor circuit operation.

Incoherent

Refers to radiation on a broad band of frequencies.

Incremental backup

Any files that have changed since the last full or incremental backup, are duplicated.

Index

A list of the messages contained in a conference or a mail folder. Indexes generally show the date of the message, its title (or subject), the name of the user who wrote it, and an indication (with a "*" marker) of whether you have read that message.

Inf

A text file that contains all the information needed in order to install a piece of software or a driver that controls a hardware device.

Information

Data that has been processed and is meaningful.

Information explosion

1. The current period in human history, in which the possession and dissemination of information has supplanted mechanization or industrialization as a driving force in society.
2. The rapid growth in the amount of information available today. Also called information revolution.

Information hiding

A technique by which the structure and precise usage of information and data is concealed. The information is private to its owning objects and accessible to all other objects only by sending a message to the owner. This is the basis of encapsulation.

Information processing

The acquisition, storage, manipulation, and presentation of data, particularly by electronic means.

Information retrieval

The process of finding, organizing, and displaying information, particularly by electronic means.

Information science

The study of how information is collected, organized, handled, and communicated.

Information server

A computer on the Internet which acts as a library of documents and files that users can download.

Information superhighway

A term popularized by Vice President Al Gore. According to his vision, it is a high-speed network of computers that will serve thousands of users simultaneously, transmitting E-mail, multimedia files, voice, and video.

Infrared

1. A portion of electromagnetic spectrum situated between visible light and microwaves.
2. A means of short distance wireless networking that depends on an unobstructed line of sight path.

Infrared communications

A device with an infrared port can communicate with other devices at a distance by beaming infrared light signals. Two incompatible protocols are used for infrared communications: IrDA and ASK. Many devices support both.

Infrared data association

The industry organization of computer, component, and telecommunications vendors who have established the standards for infrared communication between computers and peripheral devices such as printers.

Infrastructure network

Wi-Fi network centered around an access point (AP) or broadband Wi-Fi router. In this environment, the AP not only provides communication with the wired network, but also mediates Wi-Fi network traffic in the immediate neighborhood.

Inherently concurrent

two objects that can receive events at the same time without interacting.

Inheritance

The ability of hierarchically-arranged objects to acquire attributes and behaviors of objects above them without duplicating the code.

Init

Archaic. A Macintosh System Extension.

Initial graphics exchange specification

A standard file format for computer graphics, supported by the American National Standards Institute (ANSI), that is particularly suitable for describing models created with computer-aided design (CAD) programs. It includes a wide variety of basic geometric forms (primitives) and, in keeping with CAD objectives, offers methods for describing and annotating drawings and engineering diagrams.

Initialization

The entry of a set of process parameters (performed by a human or automatically loaded from a file) that are necessary to begin a software process.

Initialize

To set a starting value for a variable.

Inkjet

A very popular colour printer technology, which works by squirting tiny jets of ink onto paper with great precision.

Inkjet printer

Printer that prints hard copies by spraying ink from a matrix of tiny jets.

Inner class

A class whose definition is nested inside another class's definition.

INOC

Internet Network Operations Center. BBN group that in the early days of the Internet monitored and controlled the Internet core gateways (routers). INOC no longer exists in this form.

Input

As a verb, to enter information, instructions, text, etc. , in a computer system or program. As a noun, the data so entered. Input devices include the keyboard and OCR reader.

Input device

Any peripheral piece of computer hardware equipment) used to provide data and control signals to an information processing system.

Input/output

The communication between an information processing system (such as a computer), and the outside world possibly a human, or another information processing system.

Insertion point

The flashing vertical bar that indicates where the text will be entered; the current position.

Install

To transfer a program or programs from CD ROM or DVD onto a PC's hard disk. Most programs need to be installed before they can be used, though a few can be run directly from the floppy or CD.

Instance

A particular occurrence of an object defined by a class. All instances of a class share the behavior implemented and inherited by the class. Each instance has its own private set of the instance variables implemented and inherited by the class.

Instantiation

The act of creating an instance of a class.

Instantiation

The process of creating instances from classes.

Instruction

A statement to the computer that specifies an operation to be performed and the values and locations of the data to be processed.

Insulator

A material that is highly resistant to electrical and/or thermal conduction.

Insured burst

The largest burst of data above the insured rate that will be temporarily allowed on a PVC and not tagged by the traffic policing function for dropping in the case of network congestion. The insured burst is specified in bytes or cells.

Insured rate

The long-term data throughput, in bits or cells per second, that an ATM network commits to support under normal network conditions. The insured rate is 100 percent allocated; the entire amount is deducted from the total trunk bandwidth along the path of the circuit.

Insured traffic

Traffic within the insured rate specified for the PVC. This traffic should not be dropped by the network under normal network conditions.

Integrate

The process of combining data from multiple applications

Integrated circuit

A semiconductor device that includes many transistors and electrical circuits.

Integrated graphics

The graphics controller is built into the chipset.

Integrated IS-IS

Routing protocol based on the OSI routing protocol IS-IS but with support for IP and other protocols. Integrated IS-IS implementations send only one set of routing updates, making it more efficient than two separate implementations. Formerly referred to as Dual IS-IS.

Integrity

In networking, a desirable condition where the information received is exactly equal to the information sent.

Intel

The Intel Corporation is the leading manufacturer of processor chips for PCs, most famously the Pentium.

Intel® 64

Intel® Extended Memory 64 Technology

Intelligence

The ability of a system to use general information to respond appropriately to specific events.

Intentions list

a list recorded by the server that contains all the names and values that are altered by a transaction.

Interactive

Pertaining to an application in which each entry evokes a response from a system or program, as in an inquiry system, for example, an airline reservation system. An interactive system may also be conversational, implying continuous dialog between the user and the system.

Interarea routing

Term used to describe routing between two or more logical areas.

Interface

1. Connection between two systems or devices.
2. In routing terminology, a network connection.
3. In telephony, a shared boundary defined by common physical interconnection characteristics, signal characteristics, and meanings of interchanged signals.

4. The boundary between adjacent layers of the OSI model.

Interference

Anything that alters or disrupts a message as it travels between the sender and the receiver.

Interleaved mode

This mode is enabled when the installed memory capacities of both DIMM channels are equal. Also known as dual-channel mode.

Internal client

Other workers within the same organisation.

Internal line

Telephone access inside the organisation or company.

Internet

A concatenation of many individual TCP/IP campus, state, regional, and national networks (such as CSUNET, SUPERNET, WESTNET, NSFNET, ARPANET) into one single logical network all sharing a common addressing scheme. The global "network of networks" that connects huge corporations, small businesses, universities, and individuals. Every Internet user can send E-Mail to every other Internet user. Most Internet users can also read and post Netnews messages. In addition, many Internet users have access to more advanced services for information search and retrieval, such as Gopher, FTP, WWW, and WAIS.

Internet address

An address that identifies a communication entity on an internet.

Internet protocol

Any protocol that is part of the TCP/IP protocol stack.

Internet relay chat (irc)

A world-wide "party line" protocol that allows users to converse with each other in real time. IRC is structured as a network of servers, each of which accepts connections from client programs, one per user. Some schools and organizations have disabled IRC on their computers and networks because of congestion problems or organizational policies about appropriate use. IRC garnered world-wide attention during the Gulf War, when citizens on their computers in Tel Aviv during the bombing raids were describing the events as they happened over IRC to listeners around the world.

Internet research steering group

The governing body of the Internet Research Task Force (IRTF).

Internet research task force

A volunteer organization that makes long-term recommendations concerning the Internet to the Internet Architecture Board.

Internet router

A router that uses the rules of one or more Network Layer protocols to forward packets between networks.

Internet security

A broad topic dealing with all aspects of data authentication, privacy, integrity, and verification for transactions over the Internet. For example, credit card purchases made via a World Wide Web browser require attention to Internet security issues to help ensure that the credit card number is not intercepted by an intruder or copied from the server where the number is stored, and to verify that the credit card number is actually sent by the person who claims to be sending it.

Internet service provider (ISP)

Subscribers obtain access to the Internet from their homes, small businesses or corporate networks by paying these providers for service.

Internet society

An international organization, comprising individuals, companies, foundations, and government agencies, that promotes the use, maintenance, and development of the Internet. The Internet Architecture Board (IAB) is a body within the Internet Society. In addition, the Internet Society publishes the Internet Society News and produces the annual INET conference.

Internetwork

Collection of networks interconnected by routers and other devices that functions generally) as a single network. Sometimes called an internet, which is not to be confused with the Internet.

Internetworking

General term used to refer to the industry that has arisen around the problem of connecting networks together. The term can refer to products, procedures, and technologies.

Interoperability

Ability of computing equipment manufactured by different vendors to communicate with one another successfully over the network.

Interpretation

What the receiver understands from the communication and what they get from it.

Interrupt

A suspension of a process, such as the execution of a computer program, caused by an event external to the computer and performed in such a way that the process can be resumed. Events of this kind include sensors monitoring laboratory equipment or a user pressing an interrupt key.

Intra-area Routing

Term used to describe routing within a logical area.

Intranet

A network designed for information processing within a company or organization. Its uses include such services as document distribution, software distribution, access to databases, and training. An intranet is so called because it usually employs applications associated with the Internet, such as Web pages, Web browsers, FTP sites, e-mail, newsgroups, and mailing lists, accessible only to those within the organization.

Intraware

Groupware or middleware for use on a company's private intranet. Intraware packages typically contain e-mail, database, workflow, and browser applications.

Intruder

An unauthorized user or unauthorized program, generally considered to have malicious intent, on a computer or computer network.

Invariant

A statement about some condition or relationship that must always be true.

Inventory

A list of assets.

Inverse ARP

Inverse Address Resolution Protocol. Method of building dynamic routes in a network. Allows an access server to discover the network address of a device associated with a virtual circuit.

Invocation

An access to an encapsulated resource.

IOPS

IOPS (Input/Output Operations Per Second, pronounced eye-ops) is a common performance measurement used to benchmark computer storage devices like hard disk drives (HDD), solid state drives (SSD), and storage area networks (SAN). As with any benchmark, IOPS numbers published by storage device manufacturers do not guarantee real-world application performance.

IP

Internet Protocol. The Network Layer protocol in the TCP/IP stack offering a connectionless internetwork service. IP provides features for addressing, type-of-service. IP provides features for addressing, type-of-service specification, fragmentation and reassembly, and security.

IP address

Short for Internet Protocol address. A 32-bit (4-byte) binary number that uniquely identifies a host (computer) connected to the Internet to other Internet hosts, for the purposes of communication through the transfer of packets. An IP address is expressed in "dotted quad" format, consisting of the decimal values of its four bytes, separated with periods; for example, 127.0.0.1. The first one, two, or three bytes of the IP address, assigned by InterNIC Registration Services, identify the network the host is connected to; the remaining bits identify the host itself. The 32 bits of all 4 bytes together can signify almost 232, or roughly 4 billion, hosts. (A few small ranges within that set of numbers are not used.)

IP multicast

Routing technique that allows IP traffic to be propagated from one source to a number of destinations or from many sources to many destinations. Rather than sending one packet to each destination, one packet is sent to a multicast group identified by a single IP destination group address.

Ipad

A popular tablet computer from Apple.

Iphone

An extremely popular smartphone from Apple.

IPNG

Acronym for Internet Protocol next generation. A version of Internet Protocol (IP) developed by the Internet Engineering Task Force (IETF). Improvements over the original Internet Protocol include improved security features and an increased IP address size of 16 bytes.

Ipod

The Apple Corporation's massively successful portable music player.

IPSO

IP Security Option. US. government specification that defines an optional field in the IP packet header that defines hierarchical packet security levels on a per interface basis.

IPX

Internetwork Packet Exchange. A protocol family that is proprietary to the Novell Netware system.

IPXWAN

Protocol that negotiates end-to-end options for new links. When a link comes up, the first IPX packets sent across are IPXWAN packets negotiating the options for the link. When the IPXWAN options have been successfully determined, normal IPX transmission begins.

IRC

Internet Relay Chat, or just Chat. An on-line group discussion.

IRDA

The Infrared Data Association (IrDA) is a voluntary organization of various manufacturers working together to ensure that the infrared communications between different computers, PDAs, printers, digital cameras, remote controls, etc. are all compatible with each other regardless of brand. The term is also often used to designate an IrDA compliant infrared communications port on a device. Informally, a device able to communicate via IrDA compliant infrared is sometimes simply said to "have IrDA". There is also an earlier, incompatible, and usually slower type of infrared communications still in use called ASK.

IRDP

ICMP Router Discover Protocol. Enables a host to determine the address of a router that it can use as a default gateway. Similar to ES-IS, but used with IP.

Irix

The variant of UNIX designed by Silicon Graphics, Inc. IRIX machines are known for their graphics capabilities and were initially optimized for multimedia applications.

IRN

Intermediate routing node. In SNA, a subarea node with intermediate routing capability.

IRQ

Acronym for interrupt request. One of a set of possible hardware interrupts, identified by a number, on a Wintel computer. The number of the IRQ determines which interrupt handler will be used. In the AT bus, ISA, and EISA, 15 IRQs are available; in Micro Channel Architecture, 255 IRQs are available; each device's IRQ is hardwired or set by a jumper or DIP switch. The VL bus and the PCI local bus have their own interrupt systems, which they translate to IRQ numbers.

Irrational number

a decimal that is nonterminating and nonrepeating.

IRSG

Internet Research Steering Group. Group that is part of the IAB and oversees the activities of the IRTF.

IRTF

Internet Research Task Force. Community of network experts that consider Internet-related research topics. The IRTF is governed by the IRSG and is considered a subsidiary of the IAB.

IS

Intermediate system. Routing node in an OSI network.

ISA

Industry-Standard Architecture. 16-bit bus used for Intel-based personal computers.

ISAPI

Acronym for Internet Server Application Programming Interface.

An easy-to-use, high-performance interface for back-end applications for Microsoft's Internet Information Server (IIS). ISAPI has its own dynamic-link library, which offers significant performance advantages over the CGI (Common Gateway Interface) specification.

Isarithmic flow control

Flow control technique in which permits travel through the network. Possession of these permits grants the right to transmit. Isarithmic flow control is not commonly implemented.

ISDN

Integrated Services Digital Network. An international communications standard for a common interface to digital networks that allows the integration of voice and data on a common transport mechanism. Proposed by Bellcore for transmission of data, voice and higher-bandwidth technologies over phone lines.

IS-IS

Intermediate System to Intermediate System. A dynamic routing protocol for IP.

ISO

International organization that is responsible for a wide range of standards, including those relevant to networking. ISO developed the OSI reference model, a popular networking reference model.

ISO 3309

HDLC procedures developed by ISO. ISO 3309:1979 specifies the HDLC frame structure for use in synchronous environments. ISO 3309:1984 specifies proposed modifications to allow the use of HDLC in asynchronous environments as well.

ISO 9000

Set of international quality-management standards defined by ISO. The standards, which are not specific to any country, industry, or product, allow companies to demonstrate that they have specific processes in place to maintain an efficient quality system.

ISOC

Internet Society. International nonprofit organization, founded in 1992, that coordinates the evolution and use of the Internet. In addition, ISOC delegates authority to other groups related to the Internet, such as the IAB. ISOC is headquartered in Reston, Virginia, U.S.A.

Isochronous transmission

Asynchronous transmission over a synchronous data link. Isochronous signals require a constant bit rate for reliable transport.

ISODE

ISO development environment. Large set of libraries and utilities used to develop upper-layer OSI protocols and applications.

ISP

Acronym for Internet service provider. A business that supplies Internet connectivity services to individuals, businesses, and other organizations. Some ISPs are large national or multinational corporations that offer access in many locations, while others are limited to a single city or region Also called access provider, service provider.

ISR

Intermediate Session Routing. Initial routing algorithm used in APPN. ISR provides node-to-node connection-oriented routing. Network outages cause sessions to fail because ISR cannot provide nondisruptive rerouting around a failure. ISR has been replaced by HPR.

ISSI

Inter-Switching System Interface. Standard interface between SMDS switches.

ISTM

(It Seems To Me) Internet slang.

ISTR

(I Seem To Recall) Internet slang.

IT

(Information Technology) What computers are all about - using technology to manage information. The computer industry is often called the IT industry, and computer departments often refer to themselves as the IT department.

Italics

A type style with slightly slanted characters, used for emphasis. Best used to set off quotes, special phrases, and foreign words, italic letters have a redesigned structure that allows them to slant to the right. The first italic type was designed by Aldus Manutius in AD 1501 and was based on the handwriting style of that time. Furthermore, lowercase letters were in italics while capital letters were Roman (or vertical stance).

Itunes

The Apple Corporation's online music store, where you can download millions of music tracks to an iPod or computer - for a fee, of course. As with many Apple products, it is only compatible with Apple hardware and software.

ITU-T

International Telecommunication Union Telecommunication Standardization Sector. International body that develops worldwide standards for telecommunications technologies. The ITU-T carries out the functions of the former CCITT.

J

Jabber

A condition wherein a station transmits for a period of time longer than the maximum permissible packet length, usually due to a fault condition. In local area networks, transmission by a data station beyond the time interval allowed by the protocol.

Jack

A socket. A receptacle. The fixed portion of a two connector system. The female end of a mating connector which accepts a Plug. An example Banana Jack, or panel-mount Test Jack is shown in the graphic.

Jack retasking

The technology that allows audio jack functionality to be reassigned depending on the type of device that is connected.

Jack screw

A threaded jack. A female post used to accept a bolt or other threaded part. A locking device specifically designed to secure engaged electrical connectors. Its mating end is either internally or externally threaded.

Jack sensing

The technology that allows an audio controller to detect that a device has been connected to an audio jack.

Jacket

The outermost layer of insulating material of a cable or harness. The outer sheath which protects a cable. The outer sheath or covering material,such as natural or synthetic rubber, lead sheath,steel tape, or a thermoplastic compound, applied over a single-insulated conductor or over an assembly of insulated conductors for protection against crushing,cutting,and abrasion of the conductors and their insulation.

Jacketed cable

A bundle of insulated wires encased in a common sheath.

Jam nut

A jam nut is a low profile type of nut, typically half as tall as a standard nut. It is commonly used as a type of locknut, where it is "jammed" up against a standard nut to lock the two in place. It is also used in situations where a standard nut would not fit.

JAN

Joint Army Navy specification. There are five quality levels, from the lowest level to the highest level are: JAN, JANTX, JANTXV, JANJ, and JANS. Eight radiation hardness assurance (RHA) levels are provided for the JANTXV and JANS quality levels. JANKC is intended for space applications and JANHC is intended for standard military applications.

Janet

Joint Academic Network. X.25 WAN connecting university and research institutions in the United Kingdom.

Java

A platform independent programming language, developed by Sun Microsystems. Java Applications are compiled and stored on a server and downloaded to be run on local "Java Virtual Machines" embedded into the client software.

Java applet

A Java class that is loaded and run by an already-running Java application such as a Web browser or an applet viewer. Java applets can be downloaded and run by any Web browser capable of interpreting Java, such as Internet Explorer, Netscape Navigator, and HotJava. Java applets are frequently used to add multimedia effects and interactivity to Web pages, such as background music, real-time video displays, animations, calculators, and interactive games. Applets can be activated automatically when a user views a page, or they may require some action on the part of the user, such as clicking on an icon in the Web page.

Java chip

An implementation on a single integrated circuit of the virtual machine specified for execution of the Java programming language. Such chips, which are being developed by Sun Microsystems, Inc., could be used in very small devices and as controllers for appliances.

Java compliant browser

A Web browser with support for the Java programming language built into it. Most current Web browsers are Java-compliant.

Java management application programming interface

A set of application programming interface specifications, proposed by Sun Microsystems, Inc., to enable the Java language to be used for network management.

Javascript

A set of program instructions, vaguely similar to Java but not actually related, written straight into the HTML of a webpage instead of as an applet.

Javascript/ECMA script

A programming language used almost exclusively to manipulate content on a web page. Common Java script functions include validating forms on a web page, creating dynamic page navigation menus, and image rollovers.

JDK

Java Development Kit — the software development kit for creating Java programs.

Jedec

Joint Electron Devices Engineering Council (JEDEC) - an independent semiconductor engineering trade organization and standardization body.

JFC

Java Foundation Classes — classes for building graphical user interfaces in Java. The JFC consists of Swing, Java 2D, Accessibility, Drag & Drop, and Application Services.

JFET

Junction FET [Field Effect Transistor], a voltage controlled transistor and not current controlled. A transistor in which the conduction is due entirely to the flow of majority carriers through a conduction channel controlled by an electric field arising from a voltage applied between the gate and source terminals. [FET Manufacturers] and vendors. An N-Channel FET is shown to the right.

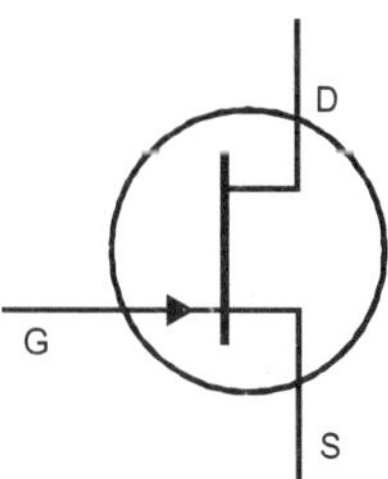

Jitter

Jitter is the difference [deviation] between the expected occurrence of a signal edge and the time the edge actually occurs [phase variation]. Jitter may also be expressed as the movement of a signal edge from its ideal position in time [the expected position]. Abrupt and unwanted variations of one or more signal characteristics, such as the interval between successive pulses, the amplitude of successive cycles, or the frequency or phase of successive cycles.

Jitter tolerance

The amount of jitter that a system could tolerate before errors occur due to jitter.

JK flip flop

A style of flip flop that has a J input and a K input, and also may have a Set [S] and Reset [R] input.

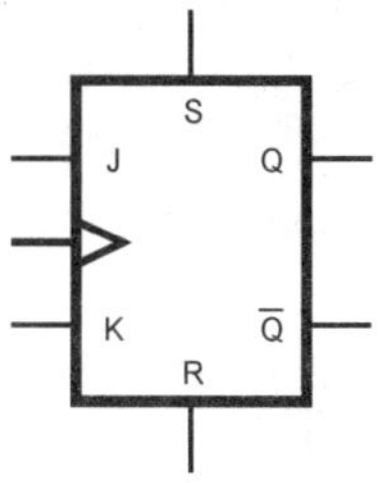

No change occurs when J and K are low. When the K is low the output is low and when the J is low the output goes high. When both J and K are high the output toggles. Truth Table to right. Examples ICs; 7473, 7476, 74107, 7470.

Job

A set of data that defines a unit of work for a computer; it usually includes all necessary computer programs, linkages, files and instructions to the operating system.

Joe job, joe-job

Spam email apparently promoting a website that actually has nothing to do with it, intended to get the owner of the website in trouble.

Johnson counter

A style of ring counter that recycles base on the inverted output being feed back to the input.

Join class

A class with more than one superclass.

Joule

The work done by a force of one newton acting through a distance of one meter.

Joystick

A pointing device used mainly but not exclusively for computer games. A joystick has a base, on which control buttons can be mounted, and a vertical stem, which the user can move in any direction to control the movement of an object on the screen; the stem may also have control buttons. The buttons activate various software features, generally producing on-screen events. A joystick is usually used as a relative pointing device, moving an object on the screen when the stem is moved and stopping the movement when the stem is released. In industrial control applications, the joystick can also be used as an absolute pointing device, with each position of the stem mapped to a specific location on the screen.

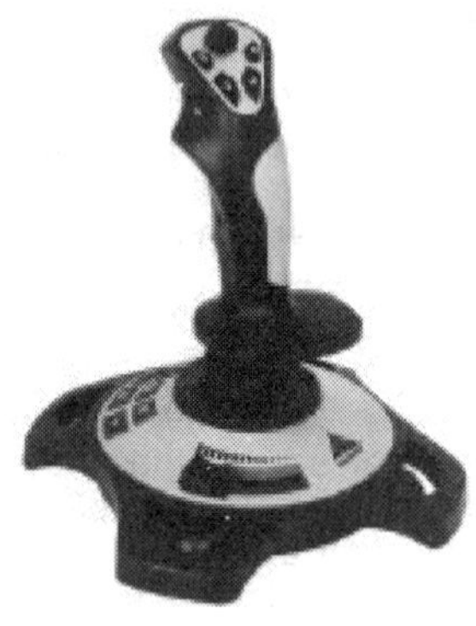

JPEG

Joint Photographic Experts Group. The ISO proposed standard for compression of digital data, especially 24-bit color images. It is lossy in that it reduces the file size at the expense of image quality. PostScript Level 2 color printers are supposed to be able to receive, decompress and print JPEG compressed images. Uses quantization and Huffman encoding.

JRE

Java Runtime Environment.

JSP

Java Server Pages; a Java-based scripting language that is parsed on a server, but is transmitted to a web browswer as HTML.

JTAG

Joint Test Action Group. IEEE Std 1149.1-1990, Test Access Port and Boundary-Scan Architecture (3) The JTAG interface is a serial bus with four signals: Test Clock (TCK), Test Mode Select (TMS), Test Data Input (TDI), and Test Data Output (TDO).

Julian calendar

The calendar introduced by Julius Caesar in 46 B.C. to replace the lunar calendar. The Julian calendar provided for a year of 365 days with a leap year every 4 years, or an average year length of 365.25 days. Because the solar year is slightly shorter, the Julian calendar gradually moved out of phase with the seasons and was superseded by the Gregorian calendar, introduced by Pope Gregory XIII.

Jumper

A short length of wire used to complete a circuit. A small plastic case with two female receptacles [shunt] used to short two adjacent contacts or pins, normally on 0.1 inch centers. The term may also describe a Zero Ohm Resistor. A jumper is usually used with a 2-pin header. Header Manufacturers. The graphic shows two male board headers, with jumpers or shunts installed on three pairs of the pins.

Junction

The connection between two or more conductors. The contact between two dissimilar metals or materials, as in a thermocouple. A region of transition between semiconductor layers, such as a p/n junction, which goes from a region that has a high concentration of acceptors (p-type) to one that has a high concentration of donors (n-type).

Junction box

A box with a cover that serves the purpose of joining different runs of wire or cable and provides space for the connection and branching of the enclosed conductors. An enclosure of other than cast metal designed to house, mount, and protect, but does not include wiring connections or electrical devices such as terminals, terminal boards, switches, jacks, fuse-holders, connectors, or circuit breakers.

Junction diode

A two-terminal device containing a single crystal of semi-conducting material that ranges from P-type at one terminal to N-type at the other. Also refer to Diode Manufacturers. A semiconductor device with a junction and a built-in potential that passes current better in one direction than the other. All solar cells are junction diodes.

Junction transistor

A bipolar transistor constructed from interacting PN junctions. The term is used to distinguish junction transistors from other types, such as field-effect and point-contact.

Junet

Japan UNIX Network. Nationwide, noncommercial network in Japan, designed to promote communication between Japanese and other researchers.

Just-a-Bunch-Of-Disks

[JBOD] A collection of hard disk drives connected in a Redundant Array of Independent Disks [RAID]. A group of disks that are used in a system that may be used separately or together.

Justification

Paragraph alignment - left, centre, right or fully justified.

Justify

In word processing, to print a document with even (straight, non-ragged) right and left margins.

JVM

Java Virtual Machine — The part of the JRE that interprets bytecodes.

Jvncnet

John von Neumann Computer Network. Regional network, owned and operated by Global Enterprise Services, Inc., composed of T1 and slower serial links providing midlevel networking services to sites in the Northeastern United States.

K band

An out-dated reference to a band of frequencies ranging between 18GHz and 27GHz. Older documents place the frequency range at 10,900MHz to 36,000MHz. The actual frequency range may differ between different organizations. .

Kalman filter

A computational algorithm that processes measurements to deduce an optimum estimate of the past, present, or future state of a linear system by using a time sequence of measurements of the system behavior, plus a statistical model that characterizes the system and measurement errors, plus initial condition information.

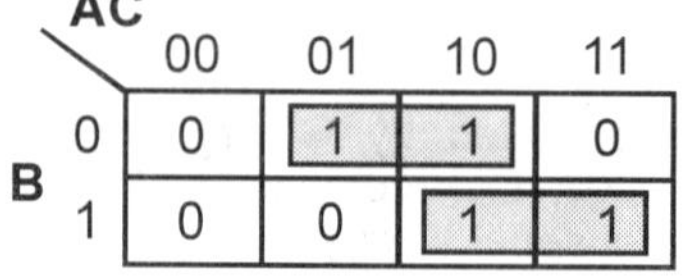

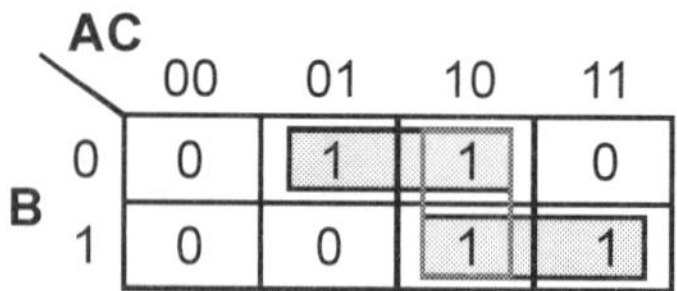

Karnaugh map

A graphical method of representing a Boolean function. A True Table displayed so that a circuit reduction can take place.

Karn's algorithm

Algorithm that improves round-trip time estimations by helping transport layer protocols distinguish between good and bad round-trip time samples.

KB

A unit of memory storage that is equal to 1,024 bytes.

KB

Kilobyte

KB

Kilobit

KBPS

(KiloBits Per Second) A measure of speed of information flow, usually over a modem. A Kilobit is a thousand bits.

KBPS

A unit of measure used to describe the rate of data transmission equal to 1000 bits per second.

Kbyte

A unit of measure used to describe an amount of information equal to 1024 (210) bytes.

KC

Kilocycle. The term is obsolete, use kHz.

KDE

The K desktop environment is a popular free window manager (and much more — as its name touts, it is more of a desktop environment) that runs under X-Windows.

Keep-alive interval

Period of time between each keep alive message sent by a network device.

Keep-alive message

Message sent by one network device to inform another network device that the virtual circuit between the two is still alive.

Keep-alive voltage

DC voltage applied to a tr gap electrode to produce a glow discharge that allows the tube to ionize faster when the transmitter fires.

Keep-out

A clearance zone or area on a printed wiring board not to be used. .

Kelvin

A unit of temperature equal to 0.010 Celsius.

Kermit

Very slow telecom data-transfer protocol developed at Columbia, and used primarily in VAX environments, although widely ported. Like any other telecom data-transfer protocol it's purpose is to break a data stream into blocks, and provide flow-control, error detection, and re-transmission on the transfer of the blocks. Much less efficient than Xmodem, Ymodem, or Zmodem.

Kernal

It is a program called when a computer system is started. Kernel is responsible for setting up system calls in order to manage hardware and system services, and allocate resources to applications.

Key

An identifier in a database or file. A primary key is a unique identifier. A secondary key is typically not unique. A key may be used to specify data in a query. Example: Tag number to specify a car in a database of automobile registration information

Key clicks

Interference in the form of clicks or thumps caused by the sudden application or removal of power.

Key switch

A style of switch that requires a key to actuate the switch. .

Keyboard

A keyboard on a computer is almost identical to a keyboard on a typewriter. Computer keyboards will typically have extra keys, however. Some of these keys (common examples include Control, Alt, and Meta) are meant to be used in conjunction with other keys just like shift on a regular typewriter. Other keys (common examples include Insert, Delete, Home, End, Help,function keys,etc.) are meant to be used independently and often perform editing tasks. Keyboards on different platforms will often look slightly different and have somewhat different collections of keys. Some keyboards even have independent shift lock and caps lock keys. Smaller keyboards with only math-related keys are typically called "keypads".

Keyboard buffer

A small amount of system memory that stores the most recently typed characters. This buffer is used to store typed characters that have not yet been processed. Also called type-ahead buffer.

Keyboard controller

A microprocessor installed in a keyboard whose primary function is to wait for and report on keystrokes.

Keyboard layout

The key arrangement used for a particular keyboard, including such factors as the number of keys (101 is the current standard) and the configuration of the keys (QWERTY is the United States standard). Some proprietary systems use different layouts, and many allow you to map the keys to characters according to your preferences.

Keycap

A plastic covering or cap placed over a switch lever so that an operator presses or touches the keycap to actuate a switch. In many cases a keycap may show an indication [printed character] of what the switch performs when pressed, as in the letters on a key-board.

Key-click filters

Filters used in keying systems to prevent key-click interference.

Keyed-oscillator transmitter

A transmitter in which one stage is used to produce the RF pulse.

Keyer

A device that changes dc pulses to mark and space modulation for teletypewriter transmissions. A synchronizer. This term is obsolete.

Keying relays

Relays used in radio transmitters where the ordinary hand key cannot accommodate the plate current without excessive arcing. .

Keystone

A shape, and term used to refer to a D style connector. The graphic to the right shows the basic shape of a keystone connector shell used with D-sub connectors. No dimensions are provided because the connector could be any size as long as it retains the same basic shape.

Keystroke

The act of pressing a key on a keyboard to enter a character or initiate a command in a program. The efficiency and ease of use of certain applications is often measured in terms of how many keystrokes it takes to perform common operations.

Keyword

A word with a special, predefined meaning in Java language.

Kickback

The voltage developed across an inductor when the current through the inductor is removed and the magnetic field across the inductor collapses.

Killer app

(Killer application) A program that is so obviously massively useful to someone that they will rush out and buy it immediately, and a computer to run it on.

Kilo

A prefix meaning one thousand, 10^3.

Kilobyte

Unit of measurement for pieces of information : actually 1024 Bytes (characters), but in practice almost always rounded down to 1000. Often written as just K, eg 250 K is 250 Kilobytes (250,000 bytes/characters - well not exactly, but close enough).

Kilobyte (K)

1,024 bytes, often used to mean 1,000 bytes.

Kilowatt-hour

[kWh] One thousand watts acting over a period of 1 hour. The kWh is a unit of energy. 1 kWh=3600 kJ.

Kinetic energy

Energy that a body possesses by virtue of its motion.

Kirchhoff's laws

The algebraic sum of the current flowing toward any point in a circuit and the current flowing away from it is zero. The algebraic sum of the products of the current and resistance in each of the conductors in any closed path in a network is equal to the algebraic sum of the electromotive forces in the path.

Kludge

A word used to describe a solution to a problem that lacks elegance or that contains components for a purpose significantly different that their original design purpose.

Klystron power amplifier

A multi-cavity microwave electron tube that uses velocity modulation. .

Knee of the Curve

The point of maximum curvature of a magnetization curve.

Knife switch

A style of switch that uses a movable thin metal element that is sandwiched between to metal contacts. A switch using hinged blades for contacts which enter or embrace fixed contact clips. Includes switches which have a movable blade which swivels to permit contact with each of several fixed contact clips.

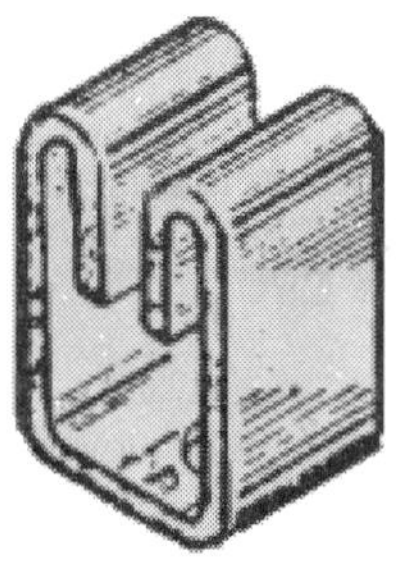

Knob

A hand grippable component attached to a shaft to allow the shaft to be turned. Also refer to Knob and Dial Manufacturers.

Knurled knob

A handle, knob or dial which has had a either a diamond-shaped [criss-cross] pattern, small ridges or grooves applied to the surface of the knob to aid in gripping the part or provide a texture to the part.

L band

An out dated term used to describe a range of frequencies between 1 and 2GHz.

L1 cache

The smallest and fastest level of CPU cache, this is the first level of cache used by the CPU.

L2 cache

Slightly larger and slower than L1 cache, this is the second level of cache used by the CPU.

L3 cache

Slightly larger and slower than L2 cache, this is the third level of cache used by the CPU.

Label swapping

Routing algorithm used by APPN in which each router that a message passes through on its way to its destination independently determines the best path to the next router.

Labeled tape

A labeled tape has machine readable "labels" indicating the file name and other information about each file on the tape. Tapes can be "labeled" or "unlabeled." Labels can be "standard IBM" or "ANSI."

Ladder activity

A type of activity identified in network scheduling. An arrangement in which two or more series of activities progress concurrently but in lockstep because of dependent links between the same rungs of each ladder.

Ladder attenuator

An attenuator circuit that uses a series of components to produce known ratios of values.

Ladder diagram

A method of showing circuit interconnection using relay contacts, used in industrial engineering. It's the same term as Ladder Logic.

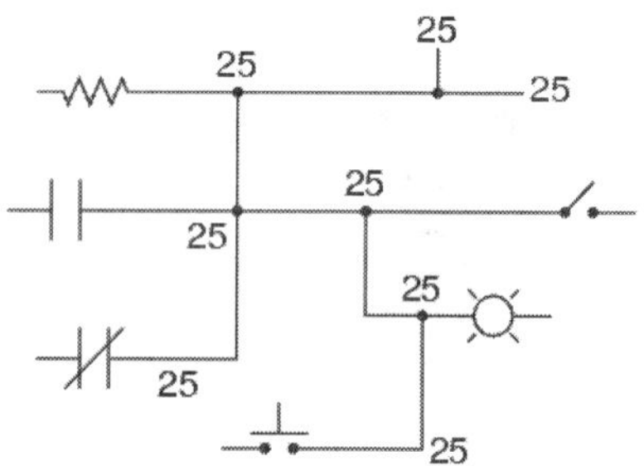

Ladder filter

A type of Passive Filter.

Lag

The relative time delay between two successive events. The amount one wave is behind another in time; expressed in electrical degrees. Also refer to Phase [Angle]. The difference in time between when a circuit or system transmits a signal and when the far end receives the signal.

Lag duration

A duration by which a given task must be completed before the succeeding activity can begin.

Lagging current

The difference in phase between a current and the voltage that produced it.

Lagging load

An inductive load that causes the current to lag behind the voltage in phase. A load that is primarily reactive, rather than capacitive.

Laminate

A product made by bonding two or more layers together, usually of different materials, under heat and pressure to form a single structure. The term used to describe the Fabrication of a Printed Circuit Board [PCB].

Laminated core

A core built up from thin sheets of metal insulated from each other and used in transformers. .

Lamp driver

An IC designed to supply the current required by a lamp or other device. .

LAN

Acronym for local area network. A group of computers and other devices dispersed over a relatively limited area and connected by a communications link that enables any device to interact with any other on the network. LANs commonly include microcomputers and shared resources such as laser printers and large hard disks. The devices on a LAN are known as nodes, and the nodes are connected by cables through which messages are transmitted.

LAN e-mail system

An e-mail system in which the UA runs on LAN-attached workstations.

LAN manager

A local area network technology developed by Microsoft Corporation and distributed by Microsoft, IBM (as IBM LAN Server), and other original equipment manufacturers. LAN Manager connects computers running the MS-DOS, OS/2, or UNIX operating system and allows users to share files and system resources and to run distributed applications using a client/ server architecture.

LAN server

A general term used to describe a device that manages and allows the use of more than one kind of resource such as storage or file services, print services, communication services, data base services, etc.

LAN switch

High-speed switch that forwards packets between data-link segments. Most LAN switches forward traffic based on MAC addresses. This variety of LAN switch is sometimes called a frame switch. LAN switches are often categorized according to the method they use to forward traffic: cut-through packet switching or store-and-forward packet switching. Multilayer switches are an intelligent subset of LAN switches.

Lands

A metallic contact area. Conductors or runs on Printed Circuit Boards [PCB's]. However copper runs are normally called Traces, while copper pads are referred to as lands.

PWB Lands

Landscape

The orientation of the document when printed; wider than it is long.

Lane

LAN emulation. Technology that allows an ATM network to function as a LAN backbone. The ATM network must provide multicast and broadcast support, address mapping (MAC-to-ATM), SVC management, and a usable packet format. LANE also defines Ethernet and Token Ring ELANs.

Language

Computer programs can be written in a variety of different languages. Different languages are optimized for different tasks. Common languages include Java, C, C++, ForTran, Pascal, Lisp, and BASIC. Some people classify languages into two categories, higher-level and lower-level. These people would consider assembly language and machine language lower-level languages and all other languages higher-level. In general, higher-level languages can be either interpreted or compiled; many languages allow both, but some are restricted to one or the other. Many people do not consider machine language and assembly language at all when talking about programming languages.

Lanyard

A cord attached to a connector dust cap to insure that the cap stays attached to the connector while disconnected.

LAP

Link Access Protocol. Any protocol of the Data Link Layer, such as EtherTalk.

Lap splice

A joint formed by the connecting of two or more conductors. The Lap splice is one of a number of different styles of wire splices.

Wire Lap Splice

Lap winding

An armature winding in which opposite ends of each coil are connected to adjoining segments of the commutator so that the windings overlap.

LAPB

Link Access Procedure, Balanced. Data link layer protocol in the X.25 protocol stack. LAPB is a bit-oriented protocol derived from HDLC.

LAPD

Link Access Procedure on the D channel. ISDN data link layer protocol for the D channel. LAPD was derived from the LAPB protocol and is designed primarily to satisfy the signaling requirements of ISDN basic access. Defined by ITU-T Recommendations Q.920 and Q.921.

LAPM

Link Access Procedure for Modems. ARQ used by modems implementing the V.42 protocol for error correction.

Laptop

A small, portable personal computer that runs on either batteries or AC power, designed for use during travel. Laptops have flat LCD or plasma screens and small keyboards. Most can run the same software as their desktop counterparts and can accept similar peripherals, such as sound cards, internal or external modems, and floppy disks and CD-ROM drives.

Some laptops are designed to be plugged into a docking station, effectively making them desktop computers. Most have connectors for plugging in external keyboards and full-sized monitors. Older laptops weighed as much as 15 pounds; current laptops can weigh as little as 5 pounds, without peripherals such as floppy disk or CD-ROM drives. While notebook is the current term for ultralight portable computers, these machines are also commonly referred to as laptops.

Laser

Light amplification by simulated emission of radiation. Analog transmission device in which a suitable active material is excited by an external stimulus to produce a narrow beam of coherent light that can be modulated into pulses to carry data. Networks based on laser technology are sometimes run over SONET.

Laser printer

A high speed printer intended mainly for office use, usually better for text than graphics, especially in colour.

Laserdisc

Large, metallic-looking records about the size of 33 RPM albums (12 inches in diameter), sometimes called videodiscs. Laserdiscs can store a vast amount of information in text, sound, and images. To play a laserdisc, you need a laserdisc player and either a computer monitor or television set. Laserdiscs come in two formats. CLV (constant linear velocity) is accessed by time and CAV (constant angular velocity) is accessed by frame number.

Laserwriter

Any of a group of laser printers that uses PostScript as an imaging language and can communicate using AppleTalk protocols.

LAT

Local Area Transport. DECnet's method for communication between terminals and terminal servers. LAT cannot be routed.

Latch

A circuit designed to store information. A component or circuit that maintains its assumed condition until reset by an external signal. The output of a latch will change when the clock goes high but will not latch until the clock goes low. Latches are considered bad design practice in VHDL because they are unusable in synchronous logic circuits. .

Latching switch

A switch that remains in a preselected position whenever the actuating voltage is removed or interrupted, and holds that preselected position until a voltage is applied to another position. A mechanical switch that remains in its present position until pushed again.

Latch-up

A unintended condition occurring in an IC by the application of an improper voltage. A circuit condition when the collector voltage of a transistor does not return to the supply voltage as the transistor is switched from saturation to cut-off, remaining in its avalanche region.

Latency

In data transmission, the delay in transmission time that occurs while information remains in a device's buffered memory (such as a bridge or router) before it can be sent along its path.

Lattice filter

A filter arranged in a bridge network.

Law of Magnetism

Like poles repel; unlike poles attract.

Layer

A term used to describe a group of communication functions and the protocols implemented to perform them as defined by a network standards organization, most often referring to a group of functions as described by the OSI 7-Layer Model designated by the ISO.

LBA

Logical Block Addressing. A common scheme used for specifying the location of blocks of data stored on computer storage devices.

LC capacitor-input filter

This is the most common type of filter. It is used in a power supply where output current is low and load current is relatively constant.

LC choke-input filter

This filter is used in power supplies where voltage regulation is important and where the output current is relatively high and subject to varying load conditions. .

LC circuit

A circuit comprising a capacitor and inductor. A tuned circuit. A Filter. A frequency dependent network used to form a resonant circuit when both the inductance reactance and capacitance reactance are equal.

LCD

Abbreviation of liquid crystal display, a type of display used in digital watches and many portable computers.

LCD displays utilize two sheets of polarizing material with a liquid crystal solution between them. An electric current passed through the liquid causes the crystals to align so that light cannot pass through them. Each crystal, therefore, is like a shutter, either allowing light to pass through or blocking the light. Monochrome LCD images usually appear as blue or dark gray images on top of a grayish-white background.
Color LCD displays use two basic techniques for producing color: Passive matrix is the less expensive of the two technologies. The other technology, called thin film transistor (TFT) or active-matrix, produces color images that are as sharp as traditional CRT displays, but the technology is expensive. Recent passive-matrix displays using new CSTN and DSTN technologies produce sharp colors rivaling active-matrix displays.

LCI

Logical channel identifier.

LCN

Logical channel number.

Leaders

Used between text and tab stops such as dots, dashes, lines or symbols.

Lead-free

Part of the Restriction of Hazardous Substances Directive* (also known as RoHS) in the European Union that restricts the use of certain hazardous substances when manufacturing specific electronic or electrical equipment

Leaf internetwork

In a star topology, an internetwork whose sole access to other internetworks in the star is through a core router.

Learning bridge

Bridge that performs MAC address learning to reduce traffic on the network. Learning bridges manage a database of MAC addresses and the interfaces associated with each address.

Leased line

Transmission line reserved by a communications carrier for the private use of a customer. A leased line is a type of dedicated line.

LEC

LAN Emulation Client. Entity in an end system that performs data forwarding, address resolution, and other control functions for a single ES within a single ELAN. A LEC also provides a standard LAN service interface to any higher-layer entity that interfaces to the LEC. Each LEC is identified by a unique ATM address, and is associated with one or more MAC addresses reachable through that ATM address.

LECS

LAN Emulation Configuration Server. Entity that assigns individual LANE clients to particular ELANs by directing them to the LES that corresponds to the ELAN. There is logically one LECS per administrative domain, and this serves all ELANs within that domain.

LED

Light emitting diode. Semiconductor device that emits light produced by converting electrical energy. Status lights on hardware devices are typically LEDs.

Leet

Leet, or "1337", (from *elite*) is someone who is unnaturally adept at a certain trait or ability. Originally used as a slightly *infra dig*expression in the hacker community. Later usage centered around video games players.

Left align

All text aligns to the left hand side of the document

LEN node

Low-entry networking node. In SNA, a PU 2.1 the supports LU protocols, but whose CP cannot communicate with other nodes. Because there is no CP-to-CP session between a LEN node and its NN, the LEN node must have a statically defined image of the APPN network.

LES

LAN Emulation Server. Entity that implements the control function for a particular ELAN. There is only one logical LES per ELAN, and it is identified by a unique ATM address.

Level 1 router

Device that routes traffic within a single DECnet or OSI area.

Level 2 router

Device that routes traffic between DECnet or OSI areas. All Level 2 routers must form a contiguous network.

LFP

Local Flat Panel refers to a flat panel display on a notebook computer

Library

A collection of useful algorithms.

Limited resource resource link

Defined by a device operator to remain active only when being used.

Line

In communications, a wire connecting a terminal to a computer; also a unit of text.

Line code type

One of a number of coding schemes used on serial lines to maintain data integrity and reliability. The line code type used is determined by the carrier service provider.

Line conditioning

Use of equipment on leased voice-grade channels to improve analog characteristics, thereby allowing higher transmission rates.

Line driver

Inexpensive amplifier and signal converter that conditions digital signals to ensure reliable transmissions over extended distances.

Line editor

An editor where the text is considered to be a series of lines separated by end-of-line markers and in which alterations are made to individual lines or groups of lines through editor commands.

Line of Sight

Characteristic of certain transmission systems, such as laser, microwave, and infrared systems, in which no obstructions in a direct path between transmitter and receiver can exist.

Line printer

A computer output device in which an entire line of print is composed and determined within the printer prior to printing. The line is printed as a unit and there is no movement of a print head.

Line turnaround

Time required to change data transmission direction on a telephone line.

Linear efficiency

A measure of algorithm efficiency in which the run time is is proportionate to the number of elements being processed; O(n).

Linear function

A function whose control flow contains no loops.

Linear list

A dynamic data structure in which each element except the last has a unique successor.

Linear loop

A loop that contains no other loops, and whose control variable is modified only via additive operations (addition or subtraction); A loop whose execution is directly a function of the number of elements being processed.

Link

Network communications channel consisting of a circuit or transmission path and all related equipment between a sender and a receiver. Most often used to refer to a WAN connection. Sometimes referred to as a line or a transmission link.

Link attribute

A named data value held by each link in an association.

Link state routing

A routing protocol that takes link loading and bandwidth when selecting between alternate routes. Example: OSPF.

Link state routing algorithm algorithm

Routing algorithm in which each router broadcasts or multicasts information regarding the cost of reaching each of its neighbors to all nodes in the internetwork. Link state algorithms create a consistent view of the network and are therefore not prone to routing loops, but they achieve this at the cost of relatively greater computational difficulty and more widespread traffic (compared with distance vector routing algorithms).

Linux

A rival PC operating system to Microsoft Windows, but unlike Windows it is “open source”, which means that anyone can create their own version of it without having to pay royalties, and requires a much less powerful computer. Initially required a lot of technical knowledge, but is rapidly being made much more user-friendly.

Listserv

A server that manages named lists of recipients and files and access-controls for them. Accepts commands by interactive message or electronic mail. A note sent to a list name is resent to each recipient in the list. Will send a copy of a file on command.

Little-endian

Method of storing or transmitting data in which the least significant bit or byte is presented first.

LLC

Logical Link Control.

LLC2

Logical Link Control, type2. Connection-oriented OSI LLC-sublayer protocol.

Lm/x

LAN Manager for INIX. Monitors LAN devices in UNIX environments.

LMAO

(Laughing My Ass Off) Internet slang.

LMI

Local Management Interface. Set of enhancements to the basic Frame Relay specification. LMI includes support for a keepalive mechanism, which verifies that data is flowing; a multicast mechanism, which provides the network server with its local DLCI and the multicast DLCI; global addressing, which gives DLCIs global rather than local significance in Frame Relay networks; and a status mechanism, which provides an on-going status report on the 'DLC Is known to the switch. Known as LMT in ANSI terminology.

LNM

LAN Network Manager. SRB and Token Ring management package provided by IBM. Typically running on a PC, it monitors SRB and Token Ring devices and can pass alerts up in NetView.

Load

To transfer a program held on some external storage medium (such as magnetic tape or disk) into the main memory of the machine in a form suitable for execution.

Load balancing

In routing, the ability of a router to distribute traffic over all its network ports that are the same distance from the destination address. Good load-balancing algorithms use both line speed and reliability information. Load balancing increases the utilization of network segments, thus increasing effective network bandwidth.

Local acknowledgment

Method whereby an intermediate network node, such as a router, responds to acknowledgments for a remote end host. Use of local acknowledgments reduces network overhead and, therefore, the risk of time-outs. Also known as local termination.

Local area network (LAN)

A network in which PCs and/or personal workstations in close proximity share resources.

Local bridge

Bridge that directly interconnects networks in the same geographic area.

Local explorer packet

Generated by an end system in an SRB network to find a host connected to the local ring. If the local explorer packet fails to find a local host, the end system produces either a spanning explorer packet or an all-routes explorer packet.

Local loop

Line from the premises of a telephone subscriber to the telephone company CO.

Local printer

A printer directly attached to the server computer.

Local traffic

Filtering process by which a bridge filters out (drops) frames whose source and destination MAC addresses are located on the same interface on the bridge, thus preventing unnecessary traffic from being forwarded across the bridge. Defined in the IEEE 802.1 standard.

Localtalk

A Data Link Layer protocol defined in Inside AppleTalk by Apple Computer that covers the transmission of data on twisted pair wire using CSMA/CA at 230.4 Kilobits per second.

Location transparency

A type of transparency that enables information objects to be accessed without knowledge of their location.

Lock manager

A module in a server program that is responsible for granting locks and maintaining a table of locks for the server's data items.

Lockup, locked up

An event which causes a computer to get stuck and refuse to do anything is a lockup. The computer is then said to be hung or locked up.

Logarithmic efficiency

A measure of algorithm efficiency in which the run time is proportionate to the log of the number of elements being processed; $O(\log_2 n)$.

Logarithmic loop

A loop which contains no other loops, and whose control variable is modified via multiplicative operations (multiplication or division).

Logic bomb

Virus that activates when it detects a certain condition, e.g., a certain date

Logic gates

Circuits that take one or more input signals and send out a single output signal.

Logical channel

Nondedicated, packet-switched communications path between two or more network nodes. Packet switching allows many logical channels to exist simultaneously on a single physical channel.

Logical clock

A incrementing counter used to timestamp events.

Logical record

All the data for a given unit of analysis. It is distinguished from a physical record because it may take several physical records to store all the data for a given unit of analysis. For instance, in Card Image data, a "card" is a physical record and it usually takes several "cards" to store all the information for a single case or unit of analysis.

Logical record length

Abbreviated LRECL A file storage format in which the length of a logical record is equal to the length of a physical record (which is constant). Thus, when the data for each case or unit of analysis is stored in a single physical record, the file structure is called "logical record length." Typically, logical record length format is more space-efficient than card image. The length, in bytes (i.e., columns), of a logical and physical record in a logical record length formatted file.

Login

A formal procedure where a computing device initiates a sustained connection to another computing device for the purpose of using a resource managed by the computer.

Login ID

Same as account name or user ID.

Login or logon

The opening sequence of key strokes used via computer screen instructions to connect to a system or begin operations on a computer.

Logoff

Leave a network system, usually by typing "bye" or "q" for quit. Sometimes called "logout."

Logout

A Formal procedure where a computing device severs its connection to another computing device.

LOL

(Laughing Out Loud) Internet slang.

Longitudinal study

In survey research, a study in which the same group of individuals is interviewed at intervals over a period of time. Note that some cross sectional studies are done regularly (for instance, the General Social Survey and the Current Population Survey (Annual Demographic File) are conducted once a year), but different individuals are surveyed each time. Such a study is not a true longitudinal study.

Loop

Route where packets never reach their destination, but simply cycle repeatedly through a constant series of network nodes.

Loopback packet

A test packet sent by a network adapter with a destination address equal to the adapter's own hardware address. The purpose of this test is typically to establish that the adapter is connected to a network that is functional enough to support a data transmission.

Loopback test

A test packet sent by a network adapter with a destination address equal to the adapter's own hardware address. The purpose of this test is typically to establish that the adapter is connected to a network that is functional enough to support a data transmission.

Loosely synchronized group

A group of servers in which a primary server is used until it fails, then a secondary server takes over.

Loss

The aggregate attenuation of a signal due to interaction with its environment.

Lossy

Characteristic of a network that is prone to lose packets when it becomes highly loaded.

Low-level language

A language that is machine dependent or that offers few control instructions and data types. Each statement in a program written in a low-level language usually corresponds to one machine instruction.

LPD

Line Printer Daemon. Protocol used to send print jobs between UNIX systems.

LPR

Line Printer Remote. A protocol that allows one system to send a file to another system to be queued to a device to which the receiving system has access.

LPT

Logical device name for a line printer, a name reserved by the MS-DOS operating system for up to three parallel printer ports designated LPT1, LPT2, and LPT3. The first port, LPT1, is usually the same as the primary MS-DOS hard-copy output device PRN (the logical device name for the printer). The letters LPT were originally used to stand for line print terminal.

LSA

Link State Advertisement. Broadcast packet used by link-state protocols that contains information about neighbors and path costs. LSAs are used by the receiving routers to maintain their routing tables. Sometimes called a link-state packet (LSP).

LSP

Link State Packet. A packet broadcast by a link state router listing the router's neighbors.

LU

Logical Unit.

LU6.2

An SNA communications protocol that establishes a peer-to-peer session between two processes.

LVDS

Low-Voltage Differential Signaling is an electrical digital signaling system that can run at very high speeds over inexpensive twisted-pair copper cables; used to transport video data from graphics adapters to computer monitors, particularly flat panels in notebook computers.

LYNX

A text-based World-Wide Web browser. Because it does not employ a graphics capability, it allows slower computers (or computers using a modem) to access the Internet with ease.

LZW compression

A compression algorithm that makes use of repeating strings of data in its compression of character streams into code streams. It is also the basis of GIF compression.

Mac

Media Access Control. The method whereby a computing device takes control of the transmission media for the purpose of sending an information packet.

Mac address

Standardized data link layer address that is required for every port or device that connects to a LAN. Other devices in the network use these addresses to locate specific ports in the network and to create and update routing tables and data structures. MAC addresses are 6 bytes long and are controlled by the IEEE. Also known as a hardware address, a MAC-layer address, or a physical address.

MAC address learning

Service that characterizes a learning bridge, in which the source MAC address of each received packet is stored so that future packets destined for that address can be forwarded only to the bridge interface on which that address is located. Packets destined for unrecognized addresses are forwarded out every bridge interface. This scheme helps minimize traffic on the attached LANs. MAC address learning is defined in the IEEE 802.1 standard.

Mac clone

A computer licensed and built to run the Macintosh operating system. Power Computing was named as the first licensee of the Macintosh OS in December 1994.

MAC layer

Media Access Control sub layer in the network stack.

Mac OS

Mac OS is the OS used on Macintosh computers. There are two distinctively different versions of it; everything prior to version 10 (sometimes called Mac OS Classic) and everything version 10 or later (called Mac OS X).

Mac OS classic

The OS created by Apple and originally used by Macs is frequently (albeit slightly incorrectly) referred to as Mac OS Classic (officially Mac OS Classic is this original OS running under the modern Mac OS X in emulation. Mac OS combines the functionality of both an OS and a window manager and is often considered to be the easiest OS to use. It is partially multitasking but will still sometimes crash when dealing with a buggy program. It is probably the second most popular OS, next only to Windows 'XP (although it is quickly losing ground to Mac OS X) and has excellent driver support and boasts a fair selection of games. Mac OS will run on PowerPC and 68xx based machines.

Machine language

A language that need not be modified, translated, or interpreted before it can be used by the processor for which it was designed.

Macintosh

A popular series of personal computers Introduced by the Apple Computer Corporation in January 1984. The Macintosh was one of the earliest personal computers to incorporate a graphical user interface and the first to use 3.5-inch floppy disks. It was also the first to use the 32-bit Motorola 68000 microprocessor. Despite its user-friendly features, the Macintosh has lost market share during the 1990s, losing ground to PC-compatible computers, but still enjoys widespread use in desktop publishing and graphics-related applications. Also called Mac.

MACIP

Network layer protocol that encapsulates IP packets in DDS or transmission over AppleTalk. MacIP also provides proxy ARP services.

Macro

A single computer instruction that stands for a given sequence of instructions.

Macro virus

Makes use of the built in programming languages in Microsoft Word and Excel (VBA). A macro that duplicate itself into other documents and spread just like any other virus once the file has been opened.

Magic-t junction

A hybrid style of waveguide combination of H-type and E-type T-junctions.

Magnet wire

Wire coated with an enamel insulation and used in coils, relays, transformers, motor windings, and so forth. Also refer to MIL J-W-1177; Wire, Magnet, Electrical, General Specification. A single solid insulated electrical conductor or various cross-sectional configurations. It must be specifically designed for use in electromagnetic circuits.

Magnetic amplifier

An electromagnetic device that uses one or more saturable reactors to obtain a large power gain. This device is used in servosystems requiring large amounts of power to move heavy loads.

Magnetic circuit

The complete closed path taken by magnetic flux.

Magnetic disk

A flat circular plate with a magnetizable surface layer used for storage of data.

Magnetic field

The region in which the magnetic forces created by a permanent magnet or by a current-carrying conductor or coil can be detected. The field that is produced when current flows through a conductor or antenna.

Magnetic flux

The magnetic field or induction in a material.

Magnetic head

A device that records, reads or erases data on a magnetic tape.

Magnetic induction

Generating a voltage in a circuit by the creation of relative motion between a magnetic field and the circuit. The relative motion can be the result of physical movement or the rise and fall of a magnetic field created by a changing current.

Magnetic lines of force

Imaginary lines used for convenience to designate the direction in which magnetic forces are acting as a result of magnetomotive force.

Magnetic microphone

A microphone in which the sound waves vibrate a moving armature. The armature consists of a coil wound on the armature and located between the pole pieces of a permanent magnet. The armature is mechanically linked to the diaphragm.

Magnetic poles

The section of a magnet where the flux lines are concentrated; also where they enter and leave the magnet.

Magnetic tape

A tape with a magnetizable surface layer on which data can be stored by magnetic recording.

Magnetic trip element

A circuit breaker trip element that uses the increasing magnetic attraction of a coil with increased current to open the circuit.

Magnetism

The property possessed by certain materials by which these materials can exert mechanical force on neighboring masses of magnetic materials and can cause currents to be induced in conducting bodies moving relative to the magnetized bodies.

Magneto-optic disc

An erasable or semi-erasable storage disc, similar to a CD-ROM disc and of very high capacity, in which a laser beam is used to heat the recording surface to a point at which tiny regions on the surface can be magnetically aligned to store bits of data.

Magneto-optical recording

A type of recording technology used with optical discs in which a laser beam heats a small portion of the magnetic material covering the disc. The heating enables a weak magnetic field to change the orientation of the portion, thus recording onto the disc. This technique can also be used to erase the disc, making the disc rewritable.

Magnetron oscillator

An electron tube that provides a high power output. Theory of operation is based on interaction of electrons with the crossed electric and magnetic fields in a resonant cavity.

Magnitude comparator

A circuit that compares one value with another. In digital logic a circuit that compares two binary numbers. .

Mail

A RiceMail UA that can send mail and operate on incoming messages.

Mail merge

To attach a data file or database to one main word document, enabling multiple copies to be printed.

Mail gateway

A computer that connects two or more (possibly dissimilar) electronic mail systems and transfers messages between them. Sometimes the mapping and translation can be quite complex, and it generally requires a store-and-forward scheme whereby the message is received from one system completely before it is transmitted to the next system, after suitable translations. Some mail gateways also have the capability of selecting which messages will be allowed through, either on political or technical grounds.

Mail server

A program that distributes files or information in response to requests sent via e-mail. Internet examples include Almanac and netlib. Mail servers have also been used in BITNET to provide FTP-like services. See also email, File Transfer Protocol.

Mailbox

A file of e-mail messages on which a UA can operate as if they were incoming messages (read, reply, forward, delete, etc).

Mailer

A BITNET MTA for VM/CMS that natively supports domain names and routing through gateways. It is supplied without charge to BITNET members by Princeton University.

Mailing list

An automated software program that distributes your message to a large group of people via e-mail. Also known as a listserver or listprocessor.

Main lobe

Of an antenna radiation pattern, the lobe containing the maximum power.

Main memory

Usually the fastest storage device of a computer and the one from which instructions are executed.

Mainframe

The cabinet that houses the central processing unit and main memory of a computer system, separate from peripheral devices such as card readers, printers, disk drives, etc. and device controllers. The term has come to be applied to the computer itself in the case of large systems. A large computer system; the IBM ES9000.

Mainframe computer

A high-level computer designed for the most intensive computational tasks. Mainframe computers are often shared by multiple users connected to the computer by terminals.

Mainframe, minicomputer, micro-computer

Three sizes of computers. Big corporations use mainframes and large school systems might use a mid-range computer, sometimes called a minicomputer, as a file server and administrative tool. The correct term for microcomputer is personal computer or PC.

Make-before-break

A switch that makes the new connection before it breaks the previous connection.

Male connector

A type of connector that has pins for insertion into receptacles. Male connector part numbers often include an M (male) or P (plug). For example, a male DB-25 connector might be labeled DB-25M or DB-25P.

Man

Metropolitan-area network. Network that spans a metropolitan area. Generally, a MAN spans a larger geographic area than a LAN, but a smaller geographic area that a WAN.

Managed object

In network management, a network device that can be managed by a network management protocol.

Management

Management of OSI networks. Accounting management subsystems are responsible for collecting network data relating to resource usage.

Management services

SNA functions distributed among network components to manage and control an SNA network.

Manchester encoding

Digital coding scheme, used by IEEE 802.3 and Ethernet, in which a mid-bit-time transition is used for clocking, and a 1 is denoted by a high level during the first half of the bit time.

Manual handling

Lifting or moving any equipment or other objects.

Map

Manufacturing Automation Protocol. Network architecture created by General Motors to satisfy the specific needs of the factory floor. MAP specifies a token-passing LAN similar to IEEE 802.4.

Mapi

Microsoft Application Programming Interface. A programming library for Windows developers that provides messaging services to their applications.

Mapped drives

1. In the Windows environment, network drives that have been assigned local drive letters and are locally accessible.
2. Under UNIX, disk drives that have been defined to the system and can be made active.

Margin of error

A measurement of the accuracy of the results of a survey. Example: A margin of error of plus or minus 3.5% means that there is a 95% chance that the responses of the target population as a whole would fall somewhere between 3.5% more or 3.5% less than the responses of the sample (a 7% spread). However, for any specific question, the margin of error could be greater or less than plus or minus 3.5%.

Marginal costing

Determination of incremental cost and hence trade-off value of additional material for performance or safety, additional labor for faster progress, and so on. It is used where unit costs are not appropriate because some costs such as rental or overheads are already in place. Some adjustment must be made for reduction in productivity due to work transfer or for divided responsibility, for example, following introduction of a second shift on the same activity.

Mark

An interval during which a signal is present. Also the presence of an RF signal in cw keying. The key-closed condition (presence of data) in communications systems. A high level in an RS232 System[the opposite of a Space].

Markup language

A set of codes in a text file that instruct a computer how to format it on a printer or video display or how to index and link its contents. Examples of markup languages are Hypertext Markup Language (HTML), which is used in Web pages, and Standard Generalized Markup Language (SGML), which is used for typesetting and desktop publishing purposes and in electronic documents. Markup languages of this sort are designed to enable documents and other files to be platform-independent and highly portable between applications.

Marking

How a component or device is marked with a part number, date code, and place of manufacturer [depending on available space]. Same as the term Part Marking, but the government uses Marking.

Marquee

A dashed line, used to define an area in a window to be operated upon. In Excel it defines items placed on the clipboard or to be used in a calculation or chart.

Mask

A binary value used to selectively screen out or let through certain bits in a data value. Masking is performed by using a logical operator (AND, OR, XOR, NOT) to combine the mask and the data value. For example, the mask 00111111, when used with the AND operator, removes (masks off) the two uppermost bits in a data value but does not affect the rest of the value.

XOR Mask

Mask ROM

A Read Only Memory IC that has been pre-programmed at the factor before the device was shipped. A ROM that has had a mask applied to it. .

Masking Circuit

The Masking circuit above uses a predefined mask word to change the incoming Data into an output that depends both on the incoming data and the stored mask. In this case any incoming data bit that is a one is changed to a zero if the mask is also one.

Mass storage

A generic term for disk, tape, or optical disc storage of computer data, so called for the large masses of data that can be stored in comparison with computer memory capacity.

Master oscillator

In a transmitter, the oscillator that establishes the carrier frequency of the output. A highly stable oscillator.

Master oscillator power amplifier

A transmitter in which the oscillator is isolated from the antenna by a power amplifier.

Master-slave flip flop

A circuit formed by two flip flops, the Master flip flop receives incoming data on the leading edge clock pulse and provides the Q output to the Slave flip flop which clocks in the data on the trailing edge of the clock. The output is the Q [or Q-not] from the slave flip flop. Examples include the 4027, CMOS Dual J-K Master-Slave Flip Flop, or TTL devices; 5476, 5473, and 5472.

Master-slave timing

Timing in which one station or node supplies the timing reference for all other interconnected stations or nodes.

Matched load

A device or component used to terminate a transmission line so that all of the incoming energy is absorbed.

Matching transformer

A transformer used to match the impedance between circuits separated by the transformer.

Material

A collection of surface properties for the texture of a 3D model.

MATHML

The Math Mark-up Language is a subset of XML used to represent mathematical formulae and equations. Typically it is found embedded within XHTML documents, although as of this writing not all popular browsers support it.

Mau

Media Access Unit. The component of a network adapter that directly attaches to the Transmission media.

Maximal length sequence

A pseudo-random sequence of length 2^N-1 generated by a shift register of length N.

Maximize button

In Windows 3.x, Windows 95, and Windows NT, a button in the upper right-hand corner of a window that, when clicked, maximizes a window to fill all of the space available within a larger window or on the screen.

Maximum burst

Specifies the largest burst of data above the insured rate that will be allowed temporarily on an ATM PVC but will not be dropped at the edge by the traffic policing function, even if it exceeds the maximum rate. This amount of traffic will be allowed only temporarily; on average, the traffic source needs to be within the maximum rate. Specified in bytes or cells.

Maximum clock frequency

The highest rate at which the clock input of a bistable circuit can be driven through its required sequence and still maintain stable transitions of logic level at the output.

Maximum limit

The highest-magnitude limit of a range of some quantity. For logic levels the Maximum Limit is the most positive (least negative) limit.

Maximum power dissipation

The maximum total power dissipation a component will operate at within specification.

Maximum rate

Maximum total data throughput allowed on a given virtual circuit, equal to the sum of the insured and uninsured traffic from the traffic source. The uninsured data might be dropped if the network becomes congested. The maximum rate, which cannot exceed the media rate, represents the highest data throughput the virtual circuit will ever deliver, measured in bits or cells per second.

Maximum ratings

The maximum operating characteristics a device will operate at with out damage, at some operating temperature.

Maximum safe operating area

Same as Safe Operating Area [SOA] which is the area bounded under a curve such that the combination of maximum current and maximum voltage are not exceeded. The graph to the right shows an example which includes individual lines for current x voltage duration. DC is the lowest blue line, orange is 1000mS, green is 100mS, pink is 10mS and so on. So continuous operation [DC] results in the smallest SOA, while larger voltages or currents may be used as the duration is decreased.

Maximum transfer unit (MTU)

The maximum length of the data field in a packet.

Maximum usable frequency

The maximum frequency that can be used for communications between two locations for a given time of day and a given angle of incidence.

Maxterm

A sum term containing every variable once and only once.

Maxwell

The unit of magnetic flux.

Maxwell bridge

A four-arm [Wheatstone Bridge] ac bridge used to measure inductance in terms of resistance and capacitance.

Maybe call semantics

RPC semantics in which clients cannot tell if remote procedures have been called.

MB

Megabytes. 1,048,576 bytes, often used to mean one million bytes (1,000,000) bytes.

Mbone

Multicast backbone. The multicast backbone of the Internet. MBone is a virtual multicast network composed of multicast LANs and the point-to-point tunnels that interconnect them.

MBPS

A unit of measure used to describe the rate of data transmission equal to one millions bits per second.

MBR

A small program that is executed when a computer boots up. Typically, the MBR resides on the first sector of the hard disk. The program begins the boot process by looking up the partition table to determine which partition to use for booting. It then transfers program control to the boot sector of that partition, which continues the boot process. In DOS and Windows systems, you can create the MBR with the FDISK /MBR command. An MBR virus is a common type of virus that replaces the MBR with its own code. Since the MBR executes every time a computer is started, this type of virus is extremely dangerous. MBR viruses normally enter a system through a floppy disk that is installed in the floppy drive when the computer is started up. Even if the floppy disk is not bootable, it can infect the MBR.

MBYTE

A unit of measure used to describe an amount of information equal to 1,048,576 (220) bytes.

MCA

Micro channel architecture. Bus interface commonly used in PCs and some UNIX workstations and servers.

MCH

Memory Controller Hub is the chipset component that handles communication between the CPU, memory, AGP or PCI Express, and the ICH.

MCI

Multiport Communications Interface. Card on the AGS+ that provides two Ethernet interfaces and up to two synchronous serial interfaces. The MCI processes packets rapidly, without the interframe delays typical of other Ethernet interfaces.

MCR

Minimum cell rate. Parameter defined by the ATM Forum for ATM traffic management. MCR is defined only for ABR transmissions, and specifies the minimum value for the ACR.

MD5

Message Digest 5. Algorithm used for message authentication in SNMP v.2. MD5 verifies the integrity of the communication, authenticates the origin, and checks for timelines.

Media

The environment in which the transmission signal is carried.

Media filter

1. A device used with local area networks (LANs) as an adapter between two different types of media. For example, an RJ-45 connector might be used between coaxial cable and unshielded twisted pair (UTP) cables. Media filters are similar in function to transceivers. As with many components to LANs, manufacturers often choose different names for similar products, so a LAN expert is needed to decide what media filters are required for a particular LAN. See also coaxial cable, connector (definition 1), LAN, transceiver, UTP.
2. A device added to data networks to filter out electronic noise from the environment. For example, a media filter might be added to an Ethernet network based on coaxial cabling to prevent data loss from interference by nearby electronic equipment.

Media rate

Maximum traffic throughput for a particular media type.

Medium

The material used to support the transmission of data. This can be copper wire, coaxial cable, optical fiber, or electromagnetic wave as in microwave.

Megabyte (MEG)

1,048,576 bytes (2^20 bytes).

Megahertz

A million cycles per second, abbreviated MHz. This is often used misleadingly to indicate processor speed, because while one might expect that a higher number would indicate a faster processor, that logic only holds true within a given type of processors as different types of processors are capable of doing different amounts of work within a cycle. For a current example, either a 200 MHz PowerPC or a 270 MHz SPARC will outperform a 300 MHz Pentium.

Memory

A device or medium that serves for temporary storage of programs and data during program execution. The term is synonymous with storage, although it is most frequently used for referring to the internal storage of a computer that can be directly addressed by operating instructions. Your computer's temporary storage capacity, measured in kilobytes (KB) or megabytes (MB) of RAM (random-access memory). Long-term data storage on discs, is also measured in kilobytes or megabytes.

Memory allocation

The amount of memory, usually RAM, that an process reserves for itself.

Memory dialling

The facility to store numbers in memory on the telephone and be able to dial or redial by a code.

Memory object

A contiguous, addressable resource.

Menu

A list of options from which a user can make a selection in order to perform a desired action, such as choosing a command or applying a particular format to part of a document. Many application programs, especially those that offer a graphical interface, use menus as a means of providing the user with an easily learned, easy-to-use alternative to memorizing program commands and their appropriate usage.

Menu bar

A rectangular bar displayed in an application program's on-screen window, often at the top, from which menus can be selected by the user. Names of available menus are displayed in the menu bar; choosing one with the keyboard or with a mouse causes the list of options in that menu to be displayed.

Menu item

A choice on a menu, selectable by either the keyboard or a mouse. In some instances, a menu item that is not available (that is, not appropriate) for a given situation is "grayed" (dimmed in comparison to the valid menu choices).

Menu-driven

Using menus to present choices of commands and available options. Menu-driven programs are usually considered friendlier and easier to learn than programs with a command-line interface.

Mesh

Network topology in which devices are organized in a manageable, segmented manner with many, often redundant, interconnections strategically placed between network nodes.

Message

The unit of information transferred by an e-mail system. It consists of an envelope that identifies the recipients to an MTA; headers containing who the message is from, to, subject, relaying information, etc; and a body that contains the information the sender wishes to communicate.

Message passing

Communication by using the programming primitives *send* and *receive*

Message switching

Switching technique involving transmission of messages from node to node through a network. The message is stored at each node until such time as a forwarding path is available.

Message unit

Unit of data processed by any network layer.

Metaclass

A class describing other classes.

Metadata

Data that describes other data.

Metalanguage

A language that represents another language.

Metasignaling

Process running at the ATM layer that manages signaling types and virtual circuits.

Method

An operation for a specific class; a subroutine that is defined as a member of a class; a capability of an object.

Method signature

a method's name and parameter list, which distinguishes it from other methods. Note that the method's return type is not included in its signature.

Methodology

A methodology is a collection of methods and tools, designed and arranged so as to provide guidance in achieving a specific objective.

MHS

1. Message Handling Service. A synonym of X.400 store and forward messaging.
2. Message Handling System. A Novell protocol for mail handling.

Mhz & megahertz

One megahertz is equivalent to 1000 kilohertz, or 1,000,000 hertz. The clock speed of the main processor of many computers is measured in MHz, and is sometimes (quite misleadingly) used to represent the overall speed of a computer. In fact, a computer's speed is based upon many factors, and since MHz only reveals how many clock cycles the main processor has per second (saying nothing about how much is actually accomplished per cycle), it can really only accurately be used to gauge two computers with the same generation and family of processor plus similar configurations of memory, co-processors, and other peripheral hardware

MIB

Management Information Base. In SNMP, a specification of the data objects and data structures that the Agent is responsible for knowing and reporting to the Console on demand.

MIC

Media interface connector. FDDI de facto standard connector.

Micro

1. A prefix that denotes a one millionth part of a unit of measure, such as a microsecond or microampere.
2. A prefix that denotes something small.
3. A slang term for any personal computer.

Micro ATX

A motherboard form factor where the motherboard size maximum is 9.6x9.6 inches.

Micro channel architecture

The design of the bus in IBM PS/2 computers (except Models 25 and 30). The Micro Channel is electrically and physically incompatible with the IBM PC/AT bus. Unlike the PC/AT bus, the Micro Channel functions as either a 16-bit or a 32-bit bus. The Micro Channel also can be driven independently by multiple bus master processors.

Microcode

Translation layer between machine instructions and the elementary operations of a computer. Microcode is stored in ROM and allows the addition of new machine instructions without requiring that they be designed into electronic circuits when new instructions are needed.

Microcomputer

A category of computer that is generally used for personal computing, for small business computing, and as a workstation attached to large computers or to other small computers on a network.

Microkernel

a kernel that provides the smallest possible set of services and resources on which the remaining services required can be built.

Microprocessor

A central processing unit (CPU) on a single chip. A modern microprocessor can have over 1 million transistors in an integrated-circuit package that is roughly 1 inch square. Microprocessors are at the heart of all personal computers. When memory and power are added to a microprocessor, all the pieces, excluding peripherals, required for a computer are present. The most popular lines of microprocessors today are the 680x0 family from Motorola, which powers the Apple Macintosh line, and the 80x86 family from Intel, which is at the core of all IBM PC-compatible and PS/2 computers. See also 6502, 65816, 6800, 68000, 68020, 68030, 68040, 80286, 80386DX, 80386SX, 8080, 8086, 8088, 88000, DECchip 21064, i486DX, i486DX2, i486SL, i486SX, Pentium, Pentium Pro, PowerPC, SPARC, Z80.

Microsegmentation

Division of a network into smaller segments, usually with the intention of increasing aggregate bandwidth to network devices.

Microwave

1. Any electromagnetic radiation with a wavelength between 1 millimeter and 1 meter.
2. A point-to-point data transmission system employing electro-magnetic radiation using a carrier frequency in the microwave region.

MIDI

Musical Instrument Digital Interface.

Midsplit

Broadband cable system in which the available frequencies are split into two groups: one for transmission and one for reception.

Migration transparency

A type of transparency that allows the movement of information objects. within a system without affecting the operation of programs.

Milli

A prefix denoting a one thousandth part of a unit of measure, such as a millisecond or millimeter.

Milnet

Military Network. Unclassified portion of the DDN. Operated and maintained by the DISA.

Minicomputer

Archaic. A multi-user computer capable of supporting 4 - 16 simultaneous users.

Mini-ITX

A motherboard form factor where the motherboard is typically 6.7x6.7 inches.

Mini-pcie

Also known as PCI Express Mini Card; a form factor developed by PCI-SIG, these cards are typically 30x50.96 mm.

Mini-VGA

Mini-VGA connectors are used on some laptops and other systems in place of the standard VGA connector.

MIP mapping

A graphics term where viewing a distant texture-mapped object in a 3D world, many texels (texture elements) make up each pixel that you see on the screen. The textures often appear aliased or distorted, if point sampling, the most common texture mapping technique, is used. Mip-mapping solves that problem by pre-computing (that is, prefiltering) different levels of detail of your texture image and by accessing the appropriate level according to the object's distance from the camera. For example, a texture image that is 16x16 texels has four more mip-maps at lower resolutions, 8x8, 4x4, 2x2 and 1x1. Bilinear mip-mapping chooses the closest mip-map image to your pixel's level of detail, and then performs a bilinear interpolation upon that texture image to get the color value for the pixel.

MIPS

Millions of instructions per second. Number of instructions executed by a processor per second.

MIS

Management Information System. Used to describe the set of computing resources that hold and allow access to the information owned by an organization.

Mission

Purpose; what you are in business to do.

Mission statement

A brief statement stating the purpose of the organisation.

MLC

Multi-Level Cell; a memory element capable of storing more than a single bit of information.

Mode

1. One particular method or way of accomplishing a goal.
2. In fiber optic transmission, a particular path between a light source and a receiver.
3. In statistics, the result with the highest frequency within the sample group.

Model

An abstraction of something for the purpose of understanding it before building it; a virtual 3D representation of a physical object.

Modem

Short for MOdulation/DEModulation, it is a device that can convert a digital bit stream into an analog signal (modulation) and can convert incoming analog signals back into digital signals (demodulation). The analog communications channel is typically a telephone line and the analog signals are typically sounds.

Modem eliminator

Device allowing connection of two DTE devices without modems.

Modem port

A serial port used for connecting an external modem to a personal computer.

Modem setup

Modem speed or baud rate, parity, data bits, stop bits, and duplex must be set the same at the user's computer as at the network system. Communication software is used to set up the modem.

Modulation

Process by which the characteristics of electrical signals are transformed to represent information. Types of modulation include AM, FM, and PAM.

Module

A logical grouping construct which captures one perspective or view of a situation.

Monitor

An electronic visual display for computers. The monitor comprises the display device, circuitry, and an enclosure.

Monochrome adapter

A video adapter capable of generating

a video signal for one foreground color or sometimes for a range of intensities in a single color, as for a gray-scale monitor.

MOP

Maintenance Operation Protocol. Digital Equipment Corporation protocol that provides a way to perform primitive maintenance operations on DECnet systems.

Mosaic

An Internet-based, global hypermedia browser that provides a unified interface to the various protocols, data formats, and information archives (i.e. gopher) used on the Internet and enables powerful new ways for discovering, using, viewing, and sharing information. It was developed by NCSA as part of the WWW project.

MOSPF

Multicast OSPF. Intradomain multicast routing protocol used in OSPF networks. Extensions are applied to the base OSPF unicast protocol to support IP multicast routing.

Motherboard

The main circuit board containing the primary components of a computer system. This board contains the processor, main memory, support circuitry, and bus controller and connector. Other boards, including expansion memory and input/output boards, may attach to the motherboard via the bus connector.

Motion JPEG

A standard for storing motion video, proposed by the Joint Photographic Experts Group (JPEG), that uses JPEG image compression for each frame.

Mouse

A device that is moved by hand to move a pointer to indicate a precise position on a display screen. The device has one or more buttons on top and a cable connected to a computer; it may use wheels and be friction-driven or it may use light reflected from a special pad.

Mouse potato

Someone who spends a lot of time at the computer, in analogy to a couch potato who spends a lot of time watching TV. Also known as a “Comp Head” in relation to a crack cocaine addict, or “coke head”.

Mouse trails

The creation of a shadowlike trail following the mouse pointer on screen in order to make it easier to see. Mouse trails are useful for laptops and notebooks, particularly ones with passive matrix displays or older models with monochrome screens. The relatively low resolution and contrast of these screens made it easy to lose sight of a small mouse pointer.

Mousekeys

A feature in Microsoft Windows that allows a user to use the numeric keyboard to move the mouse pointer. MouseKeys is primarily intended for people who may have physical limitations that make it difficult to move a conventional mouse.

MOV

Metal Oxide Varister. A device that acts as a surge suppresser by forcing transient high voltages to ground.

Mozilla

A nickname for the Netscape Navigator Web browser, coined by the Netscape Corporation.

MPEG

Stands for Motion Picture Experts Group. A format to make, view, and transfer both digital audio and digital video files.

MQI

Message Queueing Interface. International standard APO that provides functionality similar to that of the RPC interface. In contrast to RPC, MQI is implemented strictly at the application layer.

MSATA

Mini-SATA is a form factor for SATA devices; typically used in netbooks or other small form factor systems.

MSAU

Multistation access unit. Wiring concentrator to which all end stations in a Token Ring network connect. The MSAU provides an interface between these devices and the Token Ring interface.

MS-DOS

The DOS produced by Microsoft. Early versions of it bear striking similarities to the earlier CP/M, but it utilizes simpler commands. It provides only a CLI, but either OS/2, Windows 3.1, Windows '95, Windows '98, Windows ME, or GEOS may be run on top of it to provide a GUI. It only runs on x86 based machines.

MSDS

Material Safety Data Sheets - specifies how to handle certain material and substances.

MSL

Maximum Segment Lifetime.

MSS

Maximum Segment Size.

MTA

Message Transfer Agent. In x.400, a process that is responsible for storing and forwarding messages.

MTBF

Mean Time Between Failures is the average time between system failures.

MTU

Maximum Transfer Unit.

MTU

Maximum Transmission Unit. A specification in a data link protocol that defines the maximum number of bytes that can be carried in any one packet on that link.

MU-LAW

North American companding standard used in conversion between analog and digital signals in PCM systems.

Multiaccess network

Network that allows multiple devices to connect and communicate simultaneously.

Multicast

Single packets copied by the network and sent to a specific subset of network addresses. These addresses are specified in the destination address field.

Multicast group

Dynamically determined group of IP hosts identified by a single IP multicast address.

Multicast router

Router used to send IGMP query messages on their attached local networks. Host members of a multicast group respond to a query by sending IGMP reports noting the multicast groups to which they belong. The multicast router takes responsibility for forwarding multicast datagrams from one multicast group to all other networks that have members in the group.

Multicast server

Establishes a one-to-many connection to each device in a VLAN, thus establishing a broadcast domain for each VLAN segment. The multicast server forwards incoming broadcasts only to the multicast address that maps to the broadcast address

Multicasting

Sending messages to a specified group.

Multidrop line

Communications line having multiple cable access points. Sometimes called a multipoint line.

Multifunction board

A computer add-in board that provides more than one functio Multifunction boards for personal computers frequently offer additional memory, serial/parallel ports, and a clock/ calendar.

Multihomed host

Host attached to multiple physical network segments in an OSI CLNS network.

Multihoming

Addressing scheme in IS-IS routing that supports assignment of multiple area addresses.

Multilayer switch

Switch that filters and forwards packets based on MAC addresses and network addresses. A subset of LAN switch.

Multimedia

This originally indicated a capability to work with and integrate various types of things including audio, still graphics, and especially video. Now it is more of a marketing term and has little real meaning. Historically the Amiga was the first multimedia machine. Today in addition to AmigaOS, IRIX and Solaris are popular choices for high-end multimedia work.

Multimedia mail

Provides the capability to compose, send and read messages that include things such as spreadsheets, line drawings, animated graphics, high-resolution color images, digitized speech, video, and WYSIWYG text that may contain characters in multiple fonts and styles, etc.

Multimode fiber

Optical fiber supporting propagation of multiple frequencies of light.

Multiple domain network

SNA network with multiple SSCPs.

Multiple inheritance

A type of inheritance that permits a class to have more than one superclass and to inherit features from all ancestors.

Multiplexer

1. A hardware circuit for selecting a single output from multiple inputs.
2. A device for funneling several different streams of data over a common communications line. Multiplexers are used to attach many communications lines to a smaller number of communications ports or to attach a large number of communications ports to a smaller number of communications lines.

Multiplexing

Scheme that allows multiple logical signals to be transmitted simultaneously across a single physical channel.

Multiplicity

A specification of how many instances of one class may relate to each instance of an associated class.

Multitasking

A descriptive term for a computing device whose operating system can handle several tasks concurrently. In monoprocessors, each active task is given short periods of time to use the CPU in a rotational fashion.

Multiuser

The capability of some computer systems to provide access to many simultaneous users.

Multivendor network

Network using equipment from more than one vendor.

MVS

Multiple Virtual Storage. The primary operating systems for IBM mainframes.

Nagel's algorithm

Actually two separate congestion control algorithms that can be used in TCP-based networks. One algorithm reduces the sending window; the other limits small datagrams.

Nak

Negative acknowledgment. Response sent from a receiving device to a sending device indicating that the information received contained errors.

Name caching

Method by which remotely discovered host names are stored by a router for use in future packet-forwarding decisions to allow quick access.

Name components

Substrings of a name that are separated by a delimiter.

Name resolution

Looking up a name to obtain the associated attributes.

Name server

Server connected to a network that resolves network names into network addresses.

Name service

In AppleTalk, a computing process that has used Name Binding Protocol to register a process so that it may be located using a network resource management like the Chooser.

Name space

The set of all names recognized by a name service.

Naming context

An abstraction that maps a name to a set of attributes or to another naming context.

Naming domain

A name space with a single authority for assigning names.

NAND

A logic function of A and B that is true if either A or B is false. A 7400 Glue logic function. .

NAND circuit

A combination of a NOT function and an AND function in a binary circuit that has two or more inputs and one output. The output is logic 0 only if ALL inputs are logic 1; it is logic 1 if ANY input is logic 0.

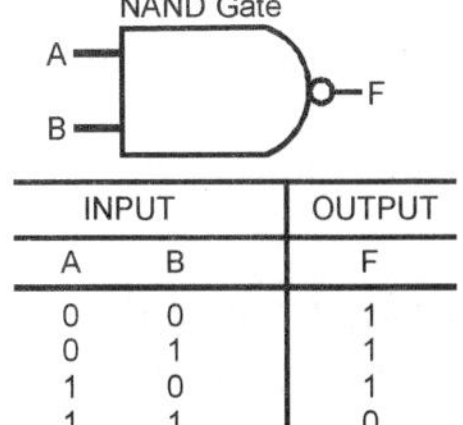

INPUT		OUTPUT
A	B	F
0	0	1
0	1	1
1	0	1
1	1	0

True Table, NAND Gate

Nand flash
A non-volatile computer storage

Nand gate
An integrated circuit that contains one or more gates that performs the NAND operation. An individual NAND gate may have two or more inputs; 2-input [7400], 3-input [7410], 4-input [7420], 8-input [7430].

Nano
One billionth, or 10^{-9} or 0.00 000 0001

Nano
A prefix that denotes a 1 billionth portion of a unit of measure, as in nanosecond or nanometer.

Nanosecond
One billionth of a second. A nanosecond is a time measure used to represent computing speed, particularly the speed at which electrical signals travel through circuits within the computer.

Nap
Network access point. Location for interconnection of internet service providers in the United States for the exchange of packets.

Narrow band amplifier
An amplifier which only functions over a narrow band of frequencies or is optimized for a limited band of frequencies.

Narrow band fm
An FM signal that only uses a small portion of a normal FM channel, used for voice communication. Either NFM, NBFM.

Narrowband signal
Any analog signal or analog representation of a digital signal whose essential spectral content is limited to that which can be contained within a voice channel of nominal 4-kHz bandwidth.

N-ary code
A code that has n significant conditions, where n is a positive integer greater than one.

Native
Something is a standard component of a computer system, such as a native file system or a native protocol.

Natural horizon
The line-of-sight horizon.

NAU
Network addressable unit. SNA term for an addressable entity. Examples include LUs, PUs, and SSCPs. NAUs generally provide upper-level network services.

Naun
Nearest active upstream neighbor. In Token Ring or IEEE 802.5 networks, the closest upstream network device from any given device that is still active.

Navigation
the process of locating data for name resolution from among multiple name servers.

NBMA
Nonbroadcast multiaccess. Term describing a multiaccess network that either does not support broadcasting (such as X.25) or in which broadcasting is not feasible (for example, an SMDS broadcast group or an extended Ethernet that is too large).

NBP
Name Binding Protocol. The AppleTalk protocol that associates

the name, type and zone of a process with its Internet Socket Address.

NC

The term network computer refers to any (usually desktop) computer system that is designed to work as part of a networkrather than as a stand-alone machine. This saves money on hardware, software, and maintenance by taking advantage of facilities already available on the network. The term "Internet appliance" is often used interchangeably with NC.

N-channel fet

A type of Field Effect Transistor, which is voltage controlled.

NCP

Network Control Protocol.

Near end

The originating side of a circuit. The opposite of Far End [terminating side of a circuit].

Near synchronous orbit

An orbit in which the satellite rotates close to but not exactly at the same speed as the earth.

Near-end crosstalk

Crosstalk that is propagated in a disturbed channel in the direction opposite to the direction of propagation of a signal in the disturbing channel.

Nearnet

Regional network in New England (United States) that links Boston University, Harvard University, and MIT.

Negate

The inversion of a function.

Negation

The process of inverting the value of a function or variable.

Negative alteration

That part of a sine wave that is below the reference level.

Negative bias

A voltage applied to an electrode of an electronic device which is negative with respect to ground.

Negative clamper

A circuit that clamps the upper extremity of the output wave shape to a dc potential of 0 volts.

Negative electrode

A terminal or electrode having more electrons than normal. Electrons flow out of the negative terminal of a voltage source.

Negative feedback

Feedback in which a portion of a signal is returned to a previous section of the circuit and is out of phase with the input signal. Also called Degenerative Feedback. Negative feedback reduces the amplitude of the input signal by adding addig to the signal out of phase.

Negative logic

The form of logic in which the more positive voltage level represents a logic 0, FALSE, or LOW and the more negative voltage represents a logic 1, TRUE, or HIGH.

Negative temperature coefficient

The reduction in a components value as temperature is increased; a resistors values decreases with increasing temperature. A characteristic of a semiconductor material, such as silver sulfide, in which resistance to electrical current flow decreases as temperature increases.

Negative-resistance

A component that has a current-voltage characteristic with a negative slope; the current decreases with increasing voltage.

Negative-resistance element

A component having an operating region in which an increase in the applied voltage increases the resistance and produces a proportional decrease in current. Examples include tunnel diodes and silicon unijunction transistors.

Neighboring routers

In OSPF, two routers that have interfaces to a common network. On multiaccess networks, neighbors are dynamically discovered by the OSPF Hello protocol.

Neon

A inert gas used in tubes, bulbs or signs.

Neon bulb

A bulb or lamp filled with the inert gas which lights when an AC or DC voltage potential is applied to the terminals of the bulb. For most applications the LED has replaced the Neon bulb.

Nested if/else

An if/else or if statement appearing as the true portion of another if or if/else statement.

Nesting

Placing documents within other documents. Nesting allows a user to access material in a non-linear fashion - this is the primary factor needed for developing hypertext.

Net

Network entity title. Network addresses, defined by the ISO network architecture, and used in CLNS-based networks.

Netbeui

Netbeui is short for NetBios Enhanced User Interface. It is an enhanced version of the NetBIOS protocol used by network operating systems such as LAN Manager, LAN Server, Windows for Workgroups, Windows 95 and Windows NT. Netbeui was originally designed by IBM for their Lan Manager server and later extended by Microsoft and Novell.

Netbios

Network Basic Input/Output System. API used by applications on an IBM LAN to request services from lower-level network processes. These services might include session establishment and termination, and information transfer.

Netiquette

The etiquette rules of the Internet.

Netscape

One of the most recent developments in browsing technology, it is considered to be faster than the original Mosaic. Oddly enough, it has been designed by the Mosaic Corporation, made up of programmers that authored Mosaic in the first place.

Netview

A network and device management system developed by IBM.

Netware

A trademark of Novell that includes network operating systems and LAN server processes that run on and/or serve many computing platforms, operating systems and protocols.

Network

A collection of two or more computers interconnected by telephone lines, coaxial cables, satellite links, radio, and/or some other communication technique. A computer "network" is a group of computers which are connected together and which communicate with one another for a common purpose. Computer networks support "people and organization" networks, users who also share a common purpose for communicating.

Network adapter

A hardware device that translates electronic signals between a computing device's native network hardware and the transmission media. A network adapter may also include memory or additional hardware or firmware to aid or perform the computing device's network operations.

Network address

Network layer address referring to a logical, rather than a physical, network device. Also called a protocol address.

Network administrator

A person who is charged with the responsibility of caring for a network and the communication abilities of its users.

Network analyzer

Hardware or software device offering various network troubleshooting features, including protocol-specific packet decodes, specific preprogrammed troubleshooting tests, packet filtering, and packet transmission.

Network architecture

The underlying structure of a computer network, including hardware, functional layers, interfaces, and protocols, used to establish communication and ensure the reliable transfer of information. Network architectures are designed to provide both philosophical and physical standards for the complexities of establishing communications links and transferring information without conflict. Various network architectures exist, including the internationally accepted seven-layer ISO Open Systems Interconnection (OSI) model and IBM's Systems Network Architecture (SNA).

Network control program

In a communications network that includes a mainframe computer, a program that usually resides in a communications controller and takes over communications tasks such as routing, error control, line control, and polling (checking terminals for transmissions), leaving the main computer free for other functions.

Network directory

On a local area network, a directory on a disk that is located on a computer other than the one the user is operating. A network directory differs from a network drive in that the user has access to only that directory. Whether the rest of the disk is accessible to the user depends on whether he or she has been granted access rights by the network administrator. On the Apple Macintosh, a network directory is referred to as a shared folder. Also called networked directory, shared directory.

Network drive

On a local area network, a disk drive whose disk is available to other computers on the network. Access to a network drive might not be allowed to all users of the network; many operating systems contain security provisions that enable a network administrator to grant or deny access to part or all of a network drive. Also called networked drive.

Network interface

Boundary between a carrier network and a privately-owned installation.

Network interface card

[NIC] A PC card used to interface between a communication network [Ethernet] and the personal computer.

Network latency

The time it takes for information to be transferred between computers in a network.

Network layer

Layer 3 of the OSI reference model. This layer provides connectivity and path selection between two end systems. The network layer is the layer at which routing occurs. Corresponds roughly with the path control layer of the SNA model.

Network management

A set of activities and duties whose goal is to provide high-quality,reliable communication among a group of networked computerusers. Typical activities may include resource planning, network design, providing user assistance and training, reconfiguration ofthe network due to a change in user requirements, assessing userneeds and designing appropriate solutions and troubleshootingand remedying network problems as they arise.

Network name

Also called a SSID, it identifies your network. It is a unique name and controls access to a given network. The network name can be up to 32 characters and is case sensitive.

Network node server

SNA NN that provides resource location and route selection services for ENs, LEN nodes, and LUs that are in its domain.

Network number

Part of an IP address that specifies the network to which the host belongs.

Network operator

Person who routinely monitors and controls a network, performing tasks such as reviewing and responding to traps, monitoring throughput, configuring new circuits, and resolving problems.

Network peripheral

A hardware device connected to the network allowing users on the network access to that device.

Network printer

A printing device connected to the network; it is accessed through a print server or may be directly connected to the network, without using a server.

Network time protocol

An Internet protocol used to synchronize the clocks in computers connected to the Internet.

Network topologies

A Network is any connection of two or more computers that enables them to communicate. Networks may include transmission devices, servers, cables, routers and satellites. The phone network is the total infrastructure for transmitting phone messages.

Neutral

In a normal condition, hence neither positive nor negative. A neutral object has a normal number of electrons (the same number as protons). A current-carrying conductor normally tied to ground so that the electrical potential is zero. In ac power distribution, the conductor that (a) is intentionally grounded on the supply side of the service disconnect and (b) provides a current return path for ac power currents. At ground potential (0 volts) because of a connection to ground.

Neutralization

The process of counteracting or "neutralizing" the effects of inter-electrode capacitance.

Newsgroup

Discussion group or forum.

Newsreader

A software program designed to read newsgroup articles.

Newton's second law of motion

If an unbalanced outside force acts on a body, the resulting acceleration is directly proportional to the magnitude of the force, is in the direction of the force, and is inversely proportional to the mass of the body.

NFS

Network File System. A file metalanguage and set of procedurecalls to access and manage files that is standard issue on nearlyevery computer that uses TCP/IP protocols as its standard network protocols. Designed by Sun Microsystems, NFS is now astandard feature of nearly all Unix systems.

NHRP

Next Hop Resolution Protocol. Protocol used by routers to dynamically discover the MAC address of other routers and hosts connected to a NBMA network. These systems can then directly communicate without requiring traffic to use an intermediate hop, increasing performance in ATM, Frame Relay, SMDS, and X.25 environments.

Nibble

One-half of a byte, which can be represented by a single hexadecimal digit.

NIC

Network Interface Card is a piece of hardware that allows computers to communicate over a network.

NIC

1. Network Information Center. The group responsible for theassignment of IP addresses.
2. Network Interface Card. A network adapter on a circuit board that plugs into a computerinternal bus architecture.
3. A 16-bit Ethernet chip designed by Texas Instruments.

Nichrome wire

A wire sometimes used in wire wound resistors.

Nickname

A name that can be used in place of an e-mail address. Same as alias.

NIS

Network Information System. Protocol developed by Sun Microsystems for the administration of network-wide databases. the service essentially uses two programs: one for finding a

NIS server and one for accessing the NIS databases.

N-ISDN

Narrowband ISDN. Communication standards developed by the ITU-T for baseband networks. Based on 64-kbps B channels and 16- or 64-kbps D channels.

NIST

National institute of Standards and Technology. Formerly the NBS, this U.S. government organization supports and catalogs a variety of standards.

Nixie tube

A vacuum tube that contained wires in the shape of numbers or wires that would light when powered.

NLM

NetWare Loadable Module. Individual program that can be loaded into memory and function as part of the NetWare NOS.

NLSP

NetWare Link Services Protocol. Link-state routing protocol bases on IS-IS.

NMS

Network management system. System responsible for managing at least part of a network. An NMS is generally a reasonably powerful and well-equipped computer such as an engineering workstation. NMSs communicate with agents to help keep track of network statistics and resources.

NMVT

Network management vector transport. SNA message consisting of a series of vectors conveying network management-specific information. NNNetwork node. SNA intermediate node that provides connectivity, directory services, route selection, intermediate session routing, data transport, and network management services to LEN nodes and ENs. The NN contains a CP that manages the resources of both the NN itself and those of the ENs and LEN nodes in its domain. NNs provide intermediate routing services by implementing the APPN PU 2.1 extensions.

NNI

Network-to-Network Interface. ATM Forum standard that defines the interface between two ATM switches that are both located in a private network or are both located in a public network. The interface between a public switch and private one is defined by the UNI standard. Also, the standard interface between two Frame Relay switches meeting the same criteria.

NOC

Network Operations Center. Organization responsible for maintaining a network.

Node

A networked computing device that takes a protocol address andcan initiate and respond to communication from other networked devices that employ similar protocols.

Noise

Undesirable signals bearing no desired information and frequently capable of introducing errors into the communication process.

Nonseed router

In AppleTalk, a router that must first obtain and then verify its configuration with a seed router before it can begin operation.

Non-stub Area

Resource-intensive OSPF area that carries a default route, static routes, intra-area routes, interarea routes, and external routes. Nonstub areas are the only OSPF areas that can have virtual links configured across them and are the only areas that can contain an ASBR.

Non-verbal

Without talking (words)

Non-volatile

Information that will remain usable by a computer despite loss of power or shutdown.

Non-volatile memory

Nonvolatile memory, NVM or non-volatile storage is computer memory that can retain the stored information even when not powered.

Non-volatile random-access memory

Non-volatile random-access memory (NVRAM) is random-access memory that retains its information when power is turned off (non-volatile). This is in contrast to dynamic random-access memory (DRAM) and static random-access memory (SRAM), which both maintain data only for as long as power is applied.

NOOB

A new or unexperienced person, someone who does not know the rules of a website, or has only recently joined.

Northbridge

Another name for MCH

Northwest net

NSF-funded regional network serving the Northwestern United States, Alaska, Montana, and North Dakota. Northwest Net connects all major universities in the region, as well as many leading industrial concerns.

NOS

Network operating system. Generic term used to refer to what are really distributed file systems.

Notebook

A notebook is a small laptop with similar price, performance, and battery life

NREN

National Research and Education Network. Component of the HPCC program designed to ensure US. technical leadership in computer communications through research and development efforts in state-of-the-art telecommunications and networking technologies.

NRM

Normal response mode. HDLC mode for use on links with one primary station and one or more secondary stations. In this mode, secondary stations can transmit only if they first receive a poll from the primary station.

NRZ

Nonreturn to zero. NRZ signals maintain constant voltage levels with no signal transitions (no return to a zero-voltage level) during a bit interval.

NTFS

Acronym for NT file system. An advanced file system designed for use specifically with the Windows NT operating system. It supports long filenames, full security access control, file system recovery, extremely large storage media, and various features for the Windows NT POSIX subsystem. It also supports object-oriented applications by treating all files as objects with user-defined and system-defined attributes.

NTLDR

Short for NT Loader, a program loaded from the hard drive boot sector that displays the Microsoft Windows NT startup menu and helps Windows NT load.

NTLM

(Stands for NT LanMan) The Windows NT Challenge / Response authentication protocol. This protocol uses encryption to help protect transmission of passwords.

NTP

Network Time Protocol.

Nubus

A high-performance expansion bus used in Apple Macintosh computers, offering high bandwidth and multiple bus controllers. Invented at the Massachusetts Institute of Technology (MIT), NuBus was eventually licensed to Texas Instruments & other companies.

Null RPC

An RPC without parameters.

Object

An entity consisting of attributes (such as color and size) stored as data and behaviors or functions (such as draw and move) that manipulate the attribute data. It is capable of interacting with other objects. As defined by OMG: encapsulation of the attributes, relationships, and methods of software-identifiable program components. Complete and reusable pieces of data or applications. Essentially packets of program code wrapped with data that behave like things in the real world.

Object code

Output from a compiler or assembler that is itself executable machine code or is suitable for processing to produce executable machine code.

Object design

A stage of the development cycle during which the implementation of each class, association, attribute, and operation is determined.

Object manager

The collection of procedures and data values that characterize a class of objects.

Object model

A description of the structure of the objects in a system including their identity, relationships to other objects, attributes, and operations.

Object-based

Supports the concept of the object and the use of messages to communicate between the objects.

Object-oriented

A software development strategy that organizes software as a collection of objects that contain both data structure and behavoir.

Object-oriented analysis

Analysis based on considering the system as a collection of objects (entities, relationships, and attributes).

Object-oriented technology

A collection of languages, tools, environments and methodologies aimed at supporting development of software applications centered around interrelated, interacting objects.

OCL (object constraint language)

A supplement to UML, this formal language allows a software engineer to construct unambiguous statements about the characteristics of various design model elements.

Octal

The base-8 number system consisting of the digits 0 through 7, from the Latin octo, meaning "eight." The octal system is used in programming as a compact means of representing binary numbers.

Octet

Eight bits. In networking, this term is sometimes used instead of "byte," because some systems have bytes that are not 8 bits long.

Odbc

Acronym for open database connectivity. In the Microsoft WOSA structure, an interface providing a common language for Windows applications to gain access to a database on a network.

ODD

Optical disk drive.

ODI

Open Data-link Interface. A Novell specification for network interface card device drivers that allows multiple protocol stacks to use the same card simultaneously.

ODM

Original Device Manufacturer is the company that manufactured a device that is being sold by another company.

OEM

Original Equipment Manufacture. A system of distribution where a company markets equipment purchased from another company under its own label.

Office assistant

In Microsoft Office products, it assists in the use of the software, can give on-screen prompts when necessary or can be used as on-line help.

Offline

Not connected to a network. You can save money on pay-for-use networks by preparing your messages off-line using your word-processing software, and uploading them instead of typing them in while you're connected to (or on-line with) the network.

Offline navigator

Software designed to download e-mail, Web pages, or newsgroup articles or postings from other online forums and save them locally to a disk, where they can be browsed without the user paying the cost of idle time while being connected to the Internet or an online information service. Also called offline reader.

Offload

To assume part of the processing demand from another device. For example, some LAN-attached gateways can offload TCP/IP processing from the host machine, thereby freeing up significant processing capacity in the CPU.

Offset

In relative addressing methods, a number that tells how far from a starting point a particular item is located.

OHCI

Open Host Controller Interface is an interface that allows a USB or FireWire controller to communicate with the operating system.

Ohm

The unit of electrical resistance. That value of electrical resistance through which a constant potential difference of 1 volt across the resistance will maintain a current flow of 1 ampere through the resistance.

Ohm (&!)

A measure of the opposition to the flow of electric current.

Ohmic value

Resistance in ohms. .

Ohmmeter

A meter used to measure resistance. Ohmmeters normally also measure the reciprocal of resistance, in Mhos. An Ohm-meter is called a multimeter when it also measures current and voltage.

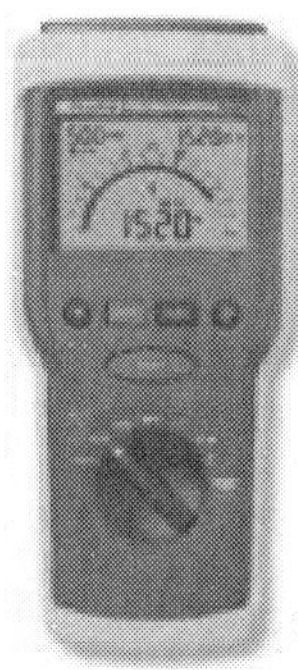

Ohm's law

The current in an electrical circuit is directly proportional to the electromotive force in the circuit. The most common form of the law is E = IR, where E is the electromotive force or voltage across the circuit, I is the current flowing in the circuit, and R is the resistance of the circuit.

Ohms per Square

The resistance of any square area of thin film resistive material as measured between two parallel sides.

OHS committee

A body of workplace employees committed to ensuring a safe work environment; attends regular meetings and carries out regular inspections.

Oilcan tube

A type of planar tube, similar to the lighthouse tube, which has cooling fins. The oilcan tube is designed to handle large amounts of power at uhf frequencies.

OLE

Object Linking and Embedding. A Microsoft approach that allows data from one OLE application to be placed in any document of another OLE application in such a way that you can edit the object using the first application's capabilities without leaving the second application. With OLE2.0 you can move data using drag and drop within and between documents and applications. OLE automation provides a cross-platform infrastructure that allows one application to control another.

Omnidirectional

Not directional, not following any one direction. As in Omnidirectional antenna. Equal sensitivity in all directions, and or equal outputs in all directions.

OMT

Object Modeling Technique; a software development strategy that uses object, dynamic, and functional models throughout the development life cycle.

One time programmable

A semiconductor device, such as a PROM or PLD, that may be user programmable only once, but once programmed the device may not be reprogrammed.

One-copy update semantics

a model for concurrent access to files in which the processes accessing the file see its contents as if only one copy of it existed.

One's complement

An algorithm carried out by inverting all the bits in a binary number.

Ones compliment

A ones compliment number is the compliment of all the binary digits in the binary number.

Online

Active and prepared for operation. Also suggests access to a computer network. Connected to a network or via a network. Examples: Send me a message on-line. In other words, send me an e-mail message.

Online community

1. All users of the Internet and World Wide Web collectively.
2. A local community that places political forums online for the discussion of local government or issues of public concern.
3. Members of a specific newsgroup, mailing list, MUD, BBS, or other online forum or group.

Online documentation

Locally written and commercial documentation that is available by direct access on the computer.

Online help

Can be accessed to explain and help the user with any questions or problems relating to the application being used.

Online service

Commercial online services like America Online, CompuServe, and Prodigy enable their users to send and receive Internet E-Mail, although they don't yet offer access to most other Internet services.

On-the-job training (OJT)

Training by acquiring direct experience in the job environment. Usually implemented by a team or mentor approach.

OO

Object-oriented.

OOPS

Object Oriented Program. A larger program made up of smaller objects.

OOS

Occupational Overuse Syndrome, also know as Repetitive Strain Injury (RSI). Caused by repetitive tasks and/or having poor posture.

Opacity

The quality that defines how much light passes through an object's pixels. If an object is 100 percent opaque, no light passes through it.

Open

Under open systems, unencumbered specifications are freely available, independent branding and certification processes exist, multiple implementations of a single product may be created and competition is enhanced.

Open authentication

Allows any device network access. If encryption is not enabled on the network, any device that knows the Service Set Identifier (SSID) of the access point can gain access to the network.

Open file

A file that can be read from, written to, or both. A program must first open a file before the file's contents can be used, and it must close the file when done.

Open financial connectivity

The Microsoft specification for an interface between electronic banking services and Microsoft Money personal finance software.

Open platform

A national Internet network that would allow citizens the ability to access, create, and publish information.

Open standard

A publicly available set of specifications describing the characteristics of a hardware device or software program. Open standards are published to encourage interoperability and thereby help popularize new technologies.

Open system

A system that implements sufficiently open specifications for interfaces, services and supporting formats to enable properly-engineered applications software to be ported with minimal changes across a wide range of systems, to interoperate with other applications on local and remote systems, and to interact with users in a style that facilitates user portability.

Open systems interconnection (OSI)

A suite of protocols, designed by ISO committees, to be the international standard computer network architecture.

Open URL

The dialog box you use to type the complete URL address for a Web page or other Internet server.

Openbsd

A free variant of Berkeley UNIX available for Alpha, x86, 68xx, PA-RISC, SPARC, and PowerPC based machines. Its emphasis is on security.

Opendoc

An open cross-platform, compound document architecture developed by Apple with help and support from Novell and WordPerfect, among others.

Opengl

Open Graphics Library is a specification that defines an API for writing applications that produce 2D or 3D computer graphics.

Openness

the characteristic of a system that determines whether the system can be extended.

Openview

HP's SNMP console and network management system.

Openwindows

A windowing environment from Sun Microsystems based on X-windows and NeWS.

Operating system

A set of instructions that tell a computer on how to operate when it is turned on. It sets up a filing system to store files and tells the computer how to display information on a video display. Most PC operating systems are DOS (disc ./operated system) systems, meaning the instructions are stored on a disc (as opposed to being originally stored in the microprocessors of the computer). Other well-known operating systems include UNIX, Linux, Macintosh, and Windows.

Operation

An action that may be applied to objects in a class.

Optical disc drive

ODD is a disk drive that uses laser light or electromagnetic waves near the light spectrum as part of the process of reading or writing data to or from optical discs.

Option ROM

Firmware that is called by the system BIOS in order to communicate with a hardware device.

Oral

By way of speaking in words.

Organisation

A group of people working together to accomplish a goal.

Organizer

An organizer is a tiny computer used primarily to store names, addresses, phone numbers, and date book information. They usually have some ability to exchange information with desktop systems. They boast even better battery life than PDAs but are far less capable. They are extremely inexpensive but are typically incapable of running any special purpose applications and are thus of limited use

Origin class

The topmost class that defines an attribute or operation.

Orom

Option ROM.

Os

The operating system is the program that manages a computer's resources. Common OSes include Windows '95, MacOS, Linux, Solaris, AmigaOS, AIX, Windows NT, etc.

Os/2

IBM's operating system for 80x86 based systems.

Oscillate

A condition where a system changes between two or more configurations on a recurring basis.

Oscilloscope

A test and measurement instrument that provides a visual display for an electrical signal. Most commonly, oscilloscopes are used to create a display of voltage over time. Also called cathode-ray oscilloscope.

OSF

Open Software Foundation.

OSI

Open Systems Interconnect. An international standard suite of protocols defined by International Standards Organization, that implements the OSI reference model for network communications between computers.

Osi 7-layer model

A method of describing the relationships between network protocols by grouping them according to the communication functions the protocols provide. The OSI model defines 7 distinct categories (Layers) that act successively on data as it makes its way between the user and the transmission media.

OSPF

Acronym for Open Shortest Path First. A routing protocol for IP networks, such as the Internet, that allows the router to calculate the shortest path to each node for sending messages. The router sends information on the nodes it is linked to, called link-state advertisements, to other routers on the network to accumulate link-state information to make its calculations.

Out of Band

Referring to a transmission system that is separate and auxiliary to the network's transmission system and who's operability is independent of the operability of the network.

Outline font

A font (type design) stored in a computer or printer as a set of outlines for drawing each of the alphabetic and other characters in a character set. Outline fonts are templates rather than actual patterns of dots and are scaled up or down to match a particular type size. Such fonts are most often used for printing, as is the case with most PostScript fonts on a PostScript-compatible laser printer and TrueType fonts.

Output

Information retrieved from a computer, displayed by a computer or produced by a program running on a computer.

Overflow flag (OV)

The sixth bit in the PSW register; a bit that is set when there is an arithmetic overflow — when the result of a signed number operation causes the high-order bit to overflow into the sign bit.

Overload

To define a method with the same name as another method in the same class, but with a different parameter list.

Override

To define a method for an operation that replaces an inherited method for the same operation.

Overtype (OVR)

A word processor feature that can be turned on or off by the Insert Key, which deletes current text as you are typing.

Overwrite

An error condition that occurs when a process stores data in a location that it :

1) has not properly allocated for that purpose or
2) has been allocated by another process.

P

P5

Intel Corporation's internal working name for the Pentium microprocessor. Although it was not intended to be used publicly, the name P5 leaked out to the computer-industry trade press and was commonly used to reference the microprocessor before it was released.

Packed decimal

A method of encoding 2 pieces of information in a single byte. For instance, instead of storing a digit in one byte and a sign in another byte using a traditional character encoding scheme, a packed decimal format might use a binary number to indicate the value of the digit in 4 bits of the byte and a code indicating whether the digit is positive or negative in the other 4 bits. The International Monetary Fund distributes data in Packed Decimal format.

PABX

Private Automatic Branch eXchange - can handle many telephone lines within an organisation.

Packet

Basic component of communication over a network. A group of bits of fixed maximum size and well-defined format that is switched and transmitted as a complete whole through a network. It contains source and destination address, data and control information. Parameter. A variable, or quantity that can assume any of a given set of values, of which there are two kinds: formal and actual.

Packet assembler/ disassembler

An interface between non-packet-switching equipment and a packet-switching network.

Packet format

The structure of data, address, and control information in a packet.

Packet switch

A special-purpose computer that is dedicated to the task of sending and receiving data on the behalf of other computers in a WAN.

Packet switching

The process of routing and transferring data by means of addressed packets so that a channel is occupied during the transmission of the packet only, and upon completion of the transmission the channel is made available for the transfer of other traffic.

Pad layout

The size, shape and spacing of the printed wiring board copper pads required for the mounting of a integrated circuit or component to the board.

Padding

Additional, meaningless data adds to a packet to increase its size.

Page makeup

The assembling of graphics and text on a page in preparation for printing.

Page up key

A standard key (often labeled "PgUp") on most computer keyboards whose specific meaning is different in different programs. In many cases, it moves the cursor up to the top of the previous page or a specific number of lines.

Pager

A small device used to page a person by displaying a message or telephone number.

Paging

A technique for implementing virtual memory. The virtual address space is divided into a number of fixed-size blocks called pages, each of which can be mapped onto any of the physical addresses available on the system. Special memory management hardware (MMU or PMMU) performs the address translation from virtual addresses to physical addresses. See also memory management unit, paged memory management unit, virtual memory.

Paired cable

A term that refers to a cable that contains one or more twisted paired wires. A cable that contains wires that are twisted in pairs, but the wires pairs are not twisted with one another.

Palm

A hand-held computer.

Panel study

A longitudinal study in which a panel of individuals is interviewed at intervals over a period of time. In general usage, the definitions of longitudinal study and panel study overlap. At least one author says that the term "panel study" is sometimes used for studies that are restricted to a short period of time or are limited to two or three interviews and "longitudinal study" is used for studies that last longer or include more interviews; but there are significant examples where this distinction is not accurate. In general, longitudinal studies involve panels of respondents and panel studies are longitudinal studies. Examples of panel studies include the Survey of Income and Program Participation (SIPP) and the Panel Study of Income and Dynamics (PSID).

Pantone matching system

In graphic arts and printing, a standard system of ink color specification consisting of a swatch book in which each of about 500 colors is assigned a number.

Paper capacitor

A fixed capacitor that uses paper as a dielectric. The paper used in the capacitor is impregnated with oil or wax to remove any moisture.

Paper prototype

A paper representation of an application (e.g., story boards that describe the interaction at a human interface).

Paperless office

The idealized office in which information is entirely stored, manipulated, and transferred electronically rather than on paper.

Parabolic reflector

A paraboloid shaped reflector used in both the RF & Microwave frequencies.

Paradigm

An archetypical example or pattern that provides a model for a process or system.

Parallel computing

The use of multiple computers or processors to solve a problem or perform a function.

Parallax error

The error in meter readings that results when you look at a meter from some position other than directly in line with the pointer and meter face. A mirror mounted on the meter face aids in eliminating parallax error [graphic in side-bar].

Parallel ATA

An IDE standard for connecting storage devices like hard drives and optical drives to the motherboard.

Parallel circuit

Two or more electrical devices connected to the same pair of terminals so separate currents flow through each; electrons have more than one path to travel from the negative to the positive terminal.

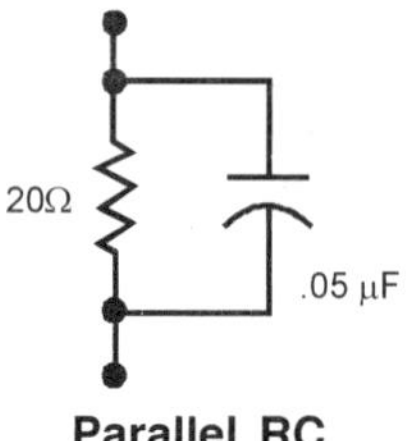

Parallel RC

Parallel data

Some number of bits, such as a byte or word, transmitted over multiple lines at the same time.

Parallel port

A port through which two or more data bits are passed simultaneously, such as all the bits of an 8-bit byte, and that requires as many input channels as the number of bits that are to be handled simultaneously. .

Parallel server

A computer system that implements some form of parallel processing to improve its performance as a server.

Parallel transmission

The simultaneous transmission of a group of bits over separate wires. With microcomputers, parallel transmission refers to the transmission of 1 byte (8 bits). The standard connection for parallel transmission is known as the Centronics interface.

Parallel tuned circuit

A circuit which contains both a capacitor and inductor in parallel with each other [a resistor may or may not be included in the circuit].

Parallel-negative limiter

A resistor and diode, connected in series with the input signal, in which the output is taken across the diode and the negative alternation is eliminated.

Parallel-positive limiter

A resistor and diode connected in series with the input signal, in which the output is taken across the diode and the positive alternation is eliminated.

Parallel-resonant circuit

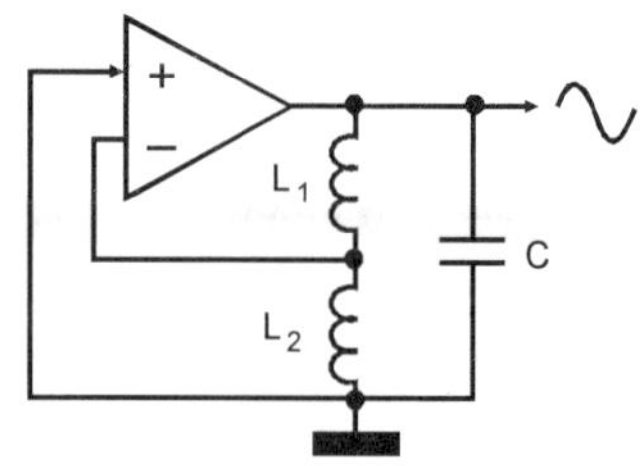

A resonant circuit in which the source voltage is connected across a parallel circuit (formed by a capacitor and an inductor) to furnish a high impedance to the frequency at which the circuit is resonant.

Parallel-to-Serial Converter

A component or circuit that receives parallel data [all bits of a word simultaneous] and outputs serial data [one bit of a word transmitted one after another]. Normally the serial portion needs to operate x times faster [8x faster with an 8 bit word] because only one bit is being transmitted at a time instead of the entire word. An IC example would be a Shift Register.

Parameter

A variable that is declared in the parentheses of a method signature and whose purpose is to store the value of the corresponding argument; naturally, the type of the argument and the parameter must match in some sense.

Parametric amplifier

A microwave amplifier which has its reactance varied with time.

Paraphase amplifier

An amplifier that outputs two out of phase signals based on a single input.

Parasitic capacitance

An unintended capacitance residing between pins of a component or conductors in a circuit. The circuit to the right shows the unwanted parasitic capacitance between the terminals of a transistor amplifier. Older texts may refer to parasitic capacitance as interelectrode capacitance, as the capacitance between electrodes or terminals of a device [used for tubes or transistors]. In general, parasitic capacitance changes the intended characteristics of a device or circuit, which than has to be compensated for. The example shows a few capacitors, but parasitic capacitance could exist between any nearby component or net in that circuit.

Parasitic oscillation

An unwanted and unintended oscillation in a circuit due to stray or parasitic elements [stray capacitance and stray inductance].

Parent, in scheduling

The source from which an activity, i.e. the child, is derived.

PA-RISC

The PA-RISC is a RISC processor developed by Hewlett-Packard. It is currently produced only by HP. At the moment only one OS runs on PA-RISC based machines: HP-UX. There is an effort underway to port Linux to them, though.

Parity

A method of checking the accuracy of binary data. In binary-coded data, a condition that is maintained such that, in any permissible coded expression, the total number of 1s, or 0s, is always odd or always even. A binary digit appended to a group of digits or character so that there are an even number of 1s or 0s in the stream, or an odd number of 1s or 0s in the data field. .

Parity bit

A bit which is automatically set or cleared each machine cycle in order to maintain an even number of 1-bits, such that the count of 1-bits in the accumulator plus the parity bit equals an even number; the eighth bit in the PSW register.

Parity check

The process of checking the accuracy of binary data, by counting the total number of 1s, or 0s, to insure that there is always an odd or always an even amount depending on the parity.

Parity error

A condition that occurs when the received number of 1s, or 0s do not equal the expected value. A signal output from a device that indicates the parity or number of 1s or 0s do not match the expected count. Sometimes abbreviated as PERR.

Park

To position the read/write head over a portion of a disk that stores no data (and therefore can never be damaged) or beyond the surface of the disk, prior to shutting down the drive, especially in preparation for moving it. Parking can be performed manually, automatically, or, most typically, by a disk utility program.

Part

One piece, or two or more pieces joined together, which are not normally subject to disassembly. An item, such as an individual part or assembly, in its final or completed state. An element or component used in the production of electronic equipment or subsystem, such as a microcircuit, diode, transistor, capacitor, resistor, relay switch, or transformer.

Part marking

How a component or device is mark with its part number, or some other identifying mark.

Partition

A subsystem that provides a particular kind of service. A partition may itself be built from lower level subsystems.

Pascal

A concise procedural language designed between 1967 and 1971 by Niklaus Wirth. Pascal, a compiled, structured language built upon ALGOL, simplifies syntax while adding data types and structures such as subranges, enumerated data types, files, records, and sets.

Passband

The frequency range not attenuated by a filter. The portion of spectrum, between limiting frequencies.

Passivation

A chemical reaction that eliminates the detrimental effect of electrically reactive atoms on a semiconductor's surface.

Passive

When you do not clearly communicate what you think or feel.

Passive component

A device that does not require a source of energy for its operation.

Passive filter

A filter that does not use active components.

Passive satellite

A satellite that reflects radio signals back to earth.

Passive serial interface

A term used with programming an FPGA. In the Passive Serial [PS] interface, an external host (configuration device, embedded processor, or host PC) controls configuration of the FPGA. Also called Passive Serial Mode, or Passive Serial Scheme; where Passive Serial may be Abbreviated as PS.

Password

A sequence of alphanumeric characters that, when coupled with a userid provides controlled access to a computer account. It may be either chosen by a user, assigned by a systems administrator,or generated by a key distribution program. Along with a valid login ID, this constitutes the two parts of the authentication process on most systems.

Password protection

The use of passwords as a means of allowing only authorized users access to a computer system or its files.

Paste

To insert text or a graphic that has been cut or copied from one document into a different location in the same or a different document.

PATA

An IDE standard for connecting storage devices like hard drives.

Patch

In programming, to repair a deficiency in the functionality of an existing routine or program, generally in response to an unforeseen need or set of operating circumstances. Patching is a common means of adding a feature or a function to a program until the next version of the software is released.

Patch bay

An arrangement of Patch Panels.

Patch cord

A cable used to connect two pieces of electrical equipment together.

Patch panel

A Panel used to tie different circuitry together by means of Patch Cords, usually of the same or similar type, appearing on jacks for monitoring, interconnecting, and testing purposes. Patch Panels facilitate flexibility in the use, routing or restoration of a variety of circuit types. There are a number of standard patch panels; Bantam, 1/4" Longframe, Mini WECO, XLR Patchbays, Telecom Patchbays. Also called a Patch Bay, Although sometimes a patch panel is referred to as a part of a patch bay. .

Patent defect

Any defect which exists at the time of acceptance and is evident and hence not a Latent Defect.

Path loss

The attenuation undergone by a signal between a transmitter and a receiver.

Path, network

The continuous, linear series of connected activities through a network.

Pattern

An abstraction from a concrete form that recurs in specific non-arbitrary contexts; within software, "pattern" most often refers to the key aspects of a common design structure.

Pattern recognition

1. A broad technology describing the ability of a computer to identify patterns. The term usually refers to computer recognition of visual images or sound patterns that have been converted to arrays of numbers.
2. The recognition of purely mathematical or textual patterns.

PBA

Printed Board Assembly (for Server Boards and Components)

PBX

Acronym for Private Branch Exchange. An automatic telephone switching system that enables users within an organization to place calls to each other without going through the public telephone network. Users can also place calls to outside numbers.

PC

The term personal computer properly refers to any desktop, laptop, or notebook computer system. Its use is inconsistent, though, and some use it to specifically refer to x86 based systems running MS-DOS, MS-Windows, GEOS, or OS/2. This latter use is similar to what is meant by a WinTel system.

PC board

Printed Circuit board. A board printed or etched with a circuit and processors. Power supplies, information storage devices, or changers are attached.

PC-DOS

Acronym for Personal Computer Disk Operating System. The version of MS-DOS sold by IBM. MS-DOS and PC-DOS are virtually identical, although filenames of utility programs sometimes differ in the two versions.

PCH

Platform Controller Hub

PCI

Peripheral Component Interconnect is a computer bus that is used to attach devices to a motherboard.

PCI Express

PCI Express (Peripheral Component Interconnect Express), officially abbreviated as PCIe, is a computer expansion bus standard designed to replace the older PCI, PCI-X, and AGP bus standards.

PCI-X

PCI-X, short for PCI-eXtended, is a computer bus and expansion card standard that enhances the 32-bit PCI Local Bus for higher bandwidth demanded by servers.

PCMCIA

The Personal Computer Memory Card International Association is a standards body that concern themselves with PC Card technology. Often the PC Cards themselves are referred to as “PCMCIA cards”. Frequently flash memory can be found in PC card form.

PCX

A graphical file format that compresses its image data with RLE-type compression, used by early versions of Windows Paintbrush.

PDA

A personal digital assistant is a small battery-powered computer intended to be carried around by the user rather than left on a desk. This means that the processor used ought to be power-efficient as well as fast, and the OS ought to be optimized for hand-held use. PDAs typically have an instant-on feature (they would be useless without it) and most are grayscale rather than color because of battery life issues. Most have a pen interface and come with a detachable stylus. None use mouses. All have some ability to exchange data with desktop systems. In terms of raw capabilities, a PDA is more capable than an organizer and less capable than a laptop (although some high-end PDAs beat out some low-end laptops). By far the most popular PDA is thePilot, but other common types include Newtons, Psions, Zauri, Zoomers, and Windows CE hand-helds. By far the fastest current PDA is the Newton (based around a StrongARM RISC processor). Other PDAs are optimized for other tasks; few computers are as personal as PDAs and care must be taken in their purchase. Feneric's PDA / Handheld Comparison Page is perhaps the most detailed comparison of PDAs and handheld computers to be found anywhere on the web

PDS

Processor Direct Slot. One of a large number of computer bus architecture's used in Macintosh computers.

Peek

A term used to describe the viewing of network data not ordinarily visible to a user.

Peer

In networking, a device to which a computer has a network connection that is relatively symmetrical, i.e. where both devices can initiate or respond to a similar set of requests.

Peer-to-peer architecture

A network of two or more computers that use the same program or type of program to communicate and share data. Each computer, or peer, is considered equal in terms of responsibilities and each acts as a server to the others in the network. Unlike a client/server architecture, a dedicated file server is not required. However, network performance is generally not as good as under client/ server, especially under heavy loads. Also called peer-to-peer network.

Peer-to-peer communications

Interaction between devices that operate on the same communications level on a network based on a layered architecture.

Peer-to-Peer mode

A wireless network structure that allows wireless clients to communicate directly with each other without using an access point.

Pen drive

Another name for a USB flash drive.

Penalties

Sums to be forfeited to which the organization has agreed to be subjected in case of non-fulfillment of requirements. Typically, sums forfeited under contract for late delivery or non-performance or both.

Penalty power

The ability (of a project manager) to gain support because project personnel perceive the project manager as capable of directly or indirectly dispensing penalties that they wish to avoid, i.e. the antithesis of reward power.

Pentium chip

Intel's fifth generation of sophisticated high-speed microprocessors. Pentium means "the fifth element."

Pentium pro

1. Intel's 150-200 MHz family of 32-bit processors, released in November 1995. The Pentium Pro is considered the next generation of processors in the 8086 family, following the Pentium, and is designed for running 32-bit operating systems and applications.
2. A PC that has a Pentium Pro processor.

Performance measurement baseline ("pmb")

The time-phased budget plan against which project performance is measured. It is formed by the budgets assigned to scheduled cost accounts and the applicable indirect budgets. For future effort, not planned to the cost account level, the Performance Measurement Baseline also includes budgets assigned to higher-level CWBS elements. The PMB does not include any management or contingency reserves, which are isolated above the PMB.

Performance measurement system

A project planning and status system that periodically measures variances (usually cost and schedule) and requires documented corrective action to eliminate the variances that exceed predetermined thresholds.

Performance measurement techniques ("pmt")

The methods used to estimate earned value. Different methods are appropriate to different work packages, either due to the nature of the work or to the planned duration of the work package. Another term for Performance Measurement Techniques is Earned Value Methods.

Performance transparency

A type of transparency that allows the system to be reconfigured to improve performance as loads vary.

Peripheral

A device attached to a host computer but not part of it, and is more or less dependent on the host. It expands the host's capabilities, but does not form part of the core computer architecture. Examples of computer peripherals: express card, USB drive, SD card, memory stick, router, external SSD or HDD drive.

Peripheral power supply

An auxiliary source of electricity used by a computer or a device as a backup in case of a power failure.

Personal computer

Any general-purpose computer whose size, capabilities, and original sales price make it useful for individuals, and which is intended to be operated directly by an end user, with no intervening computer operator.

Pert chart

A flowchart that shows all tasks and task dependencies. Tasks are represented by boxes and task dependencies are represented by lines connecting the boxes.

Pessimists

People who always seem to see the negative side of things.

Petabyte

Abbreviated PB. Either 1 quadrillion bytes or 1,125,899,906,842,624 bytes.

PGA

Short for Pin Grid Array, a type of chip package in which the connecting pins are located on the bottom in concentric squares. PGA chips are particularly good for chips that have many pins, such as modern microprocessors. Compare with DIP and SIP.Short for Professional Graphics Adapter, a video standard developed by IBM that supports 640x480 resolution.

Phase

A major period in the life of a project. A Phase may encompass several Stages. A defined segment of work. A logical group of related tasks that completes a major step in a project.

Phase modulation

A method of imposing information onto a waveform signal by shifting the phase of the wave to represent information, such as the binary digits 0 and 1.

Phased planning

A realistic approach to certain types of projects, such as research, where conditional branches are anticipated (i.e. if we get that result we will go in this direction.) It permits the project manager to plan only to the level of detail that is known at the time.

Phishing

The act of attempting to obtain private or sensitive information such as user names, passwords and credit card information through the use of fake emails from trustworthy sites.

Phoenix BIOS

An IBM-compatible ROM BIOS manufactured by Phoenix Technologies, Ltd. A popular ROM BIOS in many so-called PC "clone" computers, the Phoenix BIOS was an early leader in IBM-compatible computers shortly after they began to appear in the marketplace.

Phone connector

An attachment, usually an RJ-11 connector, used to join a telephone line to a device such as a modem.

Photo editor

A graphics application used to manipulate an image, such as a scanned photograph, digitally.

Photorealism

The process of creating images that are as close to photographic or "real-life" quality as possible. In computer graphics, photorealism requires powerful computers and highly sophisticated software and is heavily mathematical.

Photo typesetter

A printer similar to a laser printer but capable of resolutions over 2000 dots per inch. Photo typesetters apply light directly to a photographic film or photosensitive paper.

PHP

PHP Hypertext Preprocessor, the coding language to create interactive web pages and so forth.

Physical address

A synonym for Hardware Address or MAC - layer address.

Physical layer

The first layer of the OSI reference model. It governs hardware connections and byte-stream encoding for transmission.

Pico

A prefix denoting a 1 trillionth portion of a unit of measure, as in picosecond or picofarad.

Pin

A type of electrical contact point for a single conductor.

Ping

1. A network diagnostic utility on Unix systems that sends an ICMP Echo Request to a distant node which must then immediately return an ICMP Echo Reply packet back to the originating node.
2. An ICMP Echo Request packet.

Pixel

A graphics term that is short for PIcture ELement. A pixel is the smallest unit that can be addressed and given a color or intensity. The pixel is represented by some number of bits (usually 8, 16, 24, or 32) in the frame buffer.

Pixel image

The representation of a color graphic in a computer's memory. A pixel image is similar to a bit image, which also describes a screen graphic, but a pixel image has an added dimension, sometimes called depth, that describes the number of bits in memory assigned to each on-screen pixel.

Pixel map

A data structure that describes the pixel image of a graphic, including such features as color, image, resolution, dimensions, storage format, and number of bits used to describe each pixel.

Plasma

Plasma display is a type of flat panel display

Platform

Roughly speaking, a platform represents a computer's family. It is defined by both the processor type on the hardware side and the OS type on the software side. Computers belonging to different platforms cannot typically run each other's programs (unless the programs are written in a language like Java)

Plotter

A plotter is a computer printing device for printing vector graphics. In the past, plotters were widely used in applications such as computer-aided design, though they have generally been replaced with wide-format conventional printers. It is now commonplace to refer to such wide-format printers as "plotters," even though they technically aren't.

Plug

A synonym for male connector.

Plug and play

Computer hardware or peripherals that come set up with necessary software so that when attached to a computer, they are "recognized" by the computer and are ready to use.

Plug-ins

Software applications that expand a browser's basic capabilities by becoming extensions of the browser itself.

PM

Part of the product name for specific mobile Intel chipsets without integrated graphics.

PNP

Plug and Play is a feature of computers that allows a device to be added without reconfiguration or the installation of device drivers.

Poke

A term used to refer to the transmission of a packet on a network for test purposes only.

Polarity

A term used to describe the orientation of a differential voltage.

Policy

The making of context-dependent decisions.

Polling

A means of Media Access Control where a device may only transmit information when it is given permission to transmit by a controller device.

Polymorphic

"Takes on many forms"; the ability of an object to have many identities based on inheritance, interfaces, and overloaded methods; the property that an operation may behave differently on different classes.

Polymorphic virus

Virus which modifies its program code every time it attaches itself to another program file

Polymorphism

A technique for generalizing a single behavior across many kinds of objects. It simplifies software design, since a programmer need only specify an action or behavior (such as draw) and elaborate on how it is implemented.

POP3

Protocol to retrieve email.

Port

That portion of a computer through which a peripheral device may communicate. Often identified with the various plug-in jacks on the back of your computer. On a network hub, it is the connector that receives the wire link from a node.

Portable

In computer usage, a file or program is "portable" if it can be used by a variety of software on a variety of hardware platforms. Numeric data files written as plain character format files are fairly portable.

Portrait

The orientation of the document when printed; longer than it is wide.

Ports

The interface or point of attachment an external device has to the system unit.

POSIX

Portable Operating Systems Interface. An IEEE standard that specifies requirements for portable UNIX operating systems.

Post

The act of placing a message in an on-line conference. The noun "posting" is sometimes used to refer to a conference message.

Postscript

A language defined by Adobe Systems, Inc. for describing how to create an image on a page. The description is independent of the resolution of the device that will actually create the image. It includes a technology for defining the shape of a font and creating a raster image at many different resolutions and sizes.

Power management

A way for a computer to save power by turning off certain components of the computer when not in use.

Powerbook

Any of several computers in the family of portable Macintosh computers made by Apple.

Power-on key

A special key on the Apple ADB and Extended keyboards used for turning on a Macintosh II. The Power-on key is marked with a left-pointing triangle and is used in lieu of the on/off switch. There is no Power-off key; the system is shut down by choosing the Shut Down command from the Special menu.

Power PC

A RISC CPU chip designed by IBM and Apple and manufactured by Motorola. It features a 32/64 bit implementation and full binary compatibility with the IBM RS/6000. Four models are planned: 601, 603, 604,and 620. The 601 borrows its basic architecture from the Model 200 RS/6000. It adopts the internal bus structure of the Motorola 88100 and the construction plans from the 0.5 micron chip fabrication techniques used by the Model 970 RS/6000. The 603 is an entry-level device targeted toward embedded applications and low power consumption uses such as notebooks and low-end workstations. The 604 is a second-generation version of the 601.

Power supply

Converts wall outlet AC power into DC power, which is the type of power required by a computer.

Poweropen

Apple's next-generation operating system co-developed with IBM.

PPC

1. Process-to-Process Communication.
2. Sometimes used as an acronym for PowerPC.

PPP

Point-to-Point Protocol. A specification for synchronous or asynchronous data communication between two routers or between a computer system and a network.

Preamble

A term that is used in telecommunications to describe the introduction to a message or header.

Precision

Referring to the smallest difference in measurement that a test instrument can distinguish.

Preferred network

One of the networks that has been configured. Such networks are listed under Preferred networks on the Wireless Networks tab of the Wireless Network Connection Properties (Windows* XP environment).

Presentation layer

The sixth layer of the OSI reference model. It lets an application interpret the data being transferred.

PRI

Primary Rate Interface. An ISDN service over a T1 link that provides 23 data channels "bearer" or "b" Channels" at 64 KBPS and one 16 KBPS control channel (or "D" channel).

Primary cache

Primary cache is the cache located closest to the CPU. Usually, primary cache is internal to the CPU, and secondary cache is external. Some early-model personal computers have CPU chips that don't contain internal cache. In these cases the external cache, if present, would actually be the primary (L1) cache.

Primary copy model
A replication model in which all front ends communicate with the same primary server when updating a data item.

Primary industry
Industries that are involved in the production of raw materials.

Primary key
One or more fields in a table that uniquely identify a record.

Prime number
An integer whose only factors are 1 and itself.

Principal
An agent accessing the resources held in a distributed system.

Print driver
Software component that translates the printer device driver interface (DDI) into printer specific commands.

Print monitor
Software component that transmits the print job to the printing device.

Print processor
Performs any necessary modifications to the print job before passing the job to the print monitor.

Print router
Directs print jobs to the appropriate print spooler.

Print server
A computer configured to accept print requests from other computers over the network and may send the resulting print jobs over the network to a physical printer.

Print spooler
A software process that accepts a print job from a workstation as if it were a printer and then sends the print job to an actual printer at a later time. There are two styles, a background spooler, where the print spooling process is resident in the same node as the process seeking the print service, and a hardware spooler, where the print spooling process is in a separate node.

Printer
A peripheral which produces a text or graphics of documents stored in electronic form, usually on physical print media such as paper or transparencies.

Printer controller
The processing hardware in a printer, especially in a page printer. It includes the raster image processor, the memory, and any general-purpose microprocessors. A printer controller can also reside in a personal computer, attached via a high-speed cable to a printer that simply carries out its instructions.

Printer driver
In the Macintosh, a System Extension that is intermediate between the CPU and the printer. It accepts the Macintosh's internal representation of an image and translates it into the control codes and image descriptions necessary for the printer to manufacture an image.

Printout
The printed output of a computer.

Private folders
In a shared network environment, those folders on a user's computer that are not currently accessible by other users on the network.

Private key
One of two keys in public key encryptio The user keeps the private key secret

and uses it to encrypt digital signatures and to decrypt received messages.

Private member

a variable or function that can only be accessed from within the same class.

Proc ID

Intel® Processor Identification Utility is a utility developed by Intel Corporation to identify the processor inside a computer system.

Procedure

A portion of a high-level language program that performs a specific task.

Process

A set of instructions, as in a computer program or application that is currently active, i.e. consuming CPU time and memory resources. While an "application" is a process, that term usually refers to a process that a user can launch from the Finder and directly control, where the use of the term "process" often implies that the process has been launched by the system and is not under direct user control.

Process color

A method of handling color in a document in which each block of color is separated into its subtractive primary color components for printing: cyan, magenta, and yellow (as well as black). All other colors are created by blending layers of various sizes of halftone spots printed in cyan, magenta, and yellow to create the image.

Process group

A construct that enables a number of concurrent processes to cooperate by sharing a single communication mechanism.

Processor

The processor (also called central processing unit, or CPU) is the part of the computer that actually works with the data and runsthe programs. There are two main processor types in common usage today: CISC and RISC. Some computers have more than one processor and are thus called "multiprocessor". This is distinct from multitasking. Advertisers often use megahertz numbers as a means of showing a processor's speed. This is often extremely misleading; megahertz numbers are more or less meaningless when compared across different types of processors

Processor pool model

A modification of the workstation-server model in which processors can be dynamically allocated to user tasks for the lifetime of the process.

Product brief

A document that provides product information such as an overview, benefits, features, and system requirements.

Profile

Data and configuration information that is associated with a wireless network.

Program

A program is a series of instructions for a computer, telling it what to do or how to behave. The terms "application" and "app" mean almost the same thing (albeit applications generally have GUIs). It is however different from an applet. Program is also the verb that means to create a program, and a programmer is one who programs.

Program counter

A register in the CPU that serves as a pointer to the next instruction in memory to be executed.

Program status word register (PSW)

The flag register; an 8-bit register which indicates a variety of arithmetic conditions.

Programmer

A person who designs, write and tests computer programs.

Programming

A notation for the precise description of computer programs or algorithms. Programming language languages are artificial languages in which the syntax and semantics are strictly defined.

Programming language

Any artificial language that can be used to define a sequence of instructions that can ultimately be processed and executed by the computer. Defining what is or is not a programming language can be tricky, but general usage implies that the translation process—from the source code expressed using the programming language to the machine code that the computer needs to work with—be automated by means of another program, such as a compiler. Thus, English and other natural languages are ruled out, although some subsets of English are used and understood by some fourth-generation languages.

Prom

Programmable read-only memory (PROM) or field programmable read-only memory (FPROM) or one-time programmable non-volatile memory (OTP NVM) is a form of digital memory where the setting of each bit is locked by a fuse or antifuse. Such PROMs are used to store programs permanently. The key difference from a strict ROM is that the programming is applied after the device is constructed.

Promiscuous

A LAN station that receives and processes all of the packets on its network.

Prompt

A character or message provided by an operating system or program to indicate that it is ready to accept input.

Propagation

The automatic application of an operation to selected objects in a network when the operation is applied to some starting object in the network.

Proper fraction

A fraction in which the numerator is less than the denominator.

Proprietary

Meaning that information concerning the methods or implementation of a technology are owned by an individual or a company. "Proprietary" may mean that the information is secret or that the information must be licensed from the owner before it can be used.

Protected member

a variable or function that can only be accessed by classes in the same package or by subclasses.

Protocol

A protocol is a means of communication used between computers. As long as both computers recognize the same protocol, they can communicate without too much difficulty over the same network or even via a simple direct modem connection regardless whether or not they are themselves of the same type. This means that WinTel boxes, Macs, Amigas, UNIX machines, etc., can all talk with one another provided they agree on a common protocol first.

Protocol layer

A layer of the network software hierarchy.

Protocol stack

A group of protocols, usually specified by a single vendor or organization, that are implemented at more than one Layer of the OSI 7-Layer model that also have Service Access Points defined.

Protocol suite

A complete set of protocol layers.

Proxy server

A firewall component that manages Internet traffic to and from a local area network (LAN) and can provide other features, such as document caching and access control. A proxy server can improve performance by supplying frequently requested data, such as a popular Web page, and can filter and discard requests that the owner does not consider appropriate, such as requests for unauthorized access to proprietary files.

PS/2

A 6-pin mini DIN socket on most computers used for the mouse and keyboard.

PSE

Packet Switching Exchange.

PSN

Acronym for packet-switching network.

PSU

Power Supply Unit. A unit of the computer that converts mains AC to low-voltage regulated DC for the power of all the computer components.

Public directory

A directory on an FTP server that is accessible by anonymous users for the purpose of retrieving or storing files. Often the directory is called /pub.

Public domain

Not protected by copyright; you may freely make copies and distribute them; you may make derivative works.

Public key

One of two keys in public key encryptio The user releases this key to the public, who can use it for encrypting messages to be sent to the user and for decrypting the user's digital signature.

Public member

A variable or function that can be accessed by all objects.

Publish & subscribe

An Apple proprietary method of defining and maintaining a live link between a file and an external piece of data.

Puck

An input device, like a mouse. It has a magnifying glass with crosshairs on the front of it that allows the operator to position it precisely when tracing a drawing for use with CAD-CAM software.

Pull-down menu

A menu window that opens vertically on-screen to display context-related options. Also called drop-down menu or pop-up menu.

Push technology

Internet tool that delivers specific information directly to a user's desktop, eliminating the need to surf for it. PointCast, which delivers news in user-defined categories, is a popular example of this technology.

PVC

Acronym for permanent virtual circuit. A permanent logical connection between two nodes on a packet-switching network. The PVC appears as a dedicated line to the nodes, but the data can be transmitted on a common carrier. VPN.

PXE

Preboot Execution Environment is an environment to boot computers using a network interface independently of data storage devices (like hard disks) or installed operating systems.

Python

Python is an interpreted, object-oriented language popular for Internet applications. It is extremely portable with free versions existing for virtually every platform.

QPSK

Quadrature Phase-Shift Keying. A method of modulating digital signals using four phase states to code two digital bits per phase shift.

Quad

A low-grade implementation of twisted pair wire, where four conductors (two pairs) are all twisted together with no independent twisting between the pairs.

Quad-core

A processor that combines four independent cores in a single package

Quadratic efficiency

a measure of algorithm efficiency in which the run time is proportionate to the number of elements squared; $O(n^2)$.

Qualifier

An attribute of an object that distinguishes among the set of objects at the "many" end of an association.

Quality

It is meeting your own specifications and meeting your customers expectations. It is also concerned with doing the right things and doing things right.

Quality attribute

A feature or characteristic that affects an item's quality. Note: In a hierarchy of quality attributes, higher-level attributes may be called quality factors, and lower level attributes may be called quality attributes.

Quality function deployment (qfd)

A technique that translates the needs of a customer in technical requirements for software by assessing the value of each requirement.

Quality metrics

Measures of quality.

Quality plan

A document setting out the specific quality practices, resources and sequence of activities relevant to a particular product, service, contract or project. A component of the programme definition statement, setting out quality objectives for the programme 's design and execution.

Quantum

The maximum unit of time that a real-time process can occupy the CPU.

Quasi-language

A derogatory term for any programming language that, because of deficiencies, is not suitable for any serious work.

Query

A general term to describe the formation, usually in a prescribed format, that a computer process would use to retrieve specific information from another process as opposed to a wholesale transfer of data.

Query operation

an operation that returns or computes a value without modifying any objects.

Question mark

In some operating systems and applications, a wildcard character often used to represent any other single character. The question mark is one of two wildcard characters supported by the MS-DOS, Windows NT, and OS/2 operating systems.

Queue

A sequence of stored computer data or programs awaiting processing that are processed in the order first-in first-out (FIFO).

Quickdraw

A high-level 3D graphics library with an emphasis on quick development time created by Apple.

Quickdraw 3-D

A version of the Macintosh QuickDraw library that includes routines for doing 3-D graphics calculations.

Quicktime

A multi-media technology developed by Apple.

Quit

Ends the work without writing out a new file or new version of the exiting work file unless there is a save that interrupts before dumping the session.

QWERTY keyboard

A keyboard layout named for the six leftmost characters in the top row of alphabetic characters on most keyboards—the standard layout of most typewriters and computer keyboards.

R2R ladder

A resistor network made by individual resistors or a resistor package. The resistor values are 'R' and 2x 'R' as shown in the graphic. The R2R configuration is also available in resistor SIP or DIP packages.

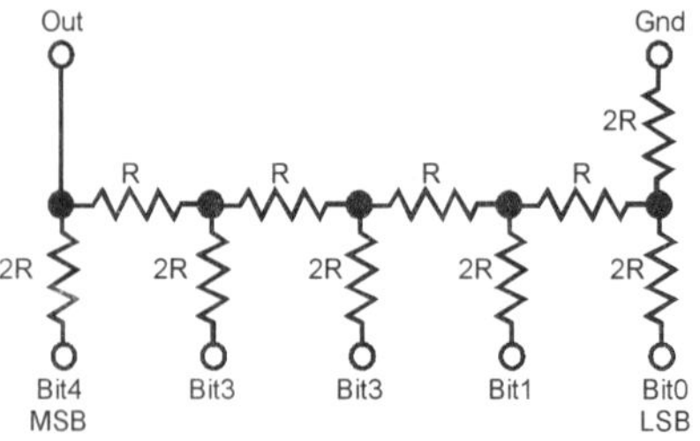

R2r resistor network

Common resistor values are 1K and 2K, 10 and 20K, 25 and 50K and 50K and 100K providing a wide range of resistance depending on the application.

Race condition

defines a condition when a device's output depends on two or more nearly simultaneous events to occur at the input.

Raceway

A channel designed expressly for holding wires, cables, or busbars. Raceways may be of metal or insulating material, and the term includes rigid metal conduit, rigid nonmetallic conduit, intermediate metal conduit, liquid-tight flexible metal conduit, flexible metallic tubing, flexible metal conduit, electrical metallic tubing, under-floor raceways, cellular concrete floor raceways, cellular metal floor raceways, surface raceways, wireways [also Cable Tray], and busways.

Rack

A vertical frame that holds or supports equipment. If the rack uses side panels, than it's called a rack enclosure.A frame upon which one or more units of equipment are mounted.

Rack-mounted

Built for installation in a metal frame or cabinet of standard width (typically 19 inches or 23 inches) and mounting arrangements.

Rack and Panel Connector

Any of a number of connector styles that are designed to attach to an Equipment Rack, Panel or some other component, normally either square or rectangular shape. An example cable-side, connector is shown to the right.

Radar

An acronym for RAdio Detecting And Ranging. A radio detection system that transmits short bursts (pulses) of rf energy and detects their echos from objects (targets) such as aircraft or ships.

Radial lead

A component package that has both leads on the same side of the part, around the central axis. Most components only have two leads on one side, but some four terminal devices have two additional leads on the opposite side of the component. .

Radian

A unit of plane angle measure equal to the angle subtended at the center of a circle by an arc equal in length to the radius of the circle.

Radiant energy

Energy in the form of electromagnetic waves.

Radiation

The emission and propagation of energy by means of electromagnetic waves or particles. .

Radiation hardened

A component that will accept a higher amount of radiation energy either as a Total dose or Single event with out breaking down or failing.

Radiation hardness assurance

The portion of product assurance, used by the department of defense, which insures that parts continue to perform as specified or degrade in a specified manner when subjected to the specified radiation environmental stress.

Radiation losses

The losses that occur when magnetic lines of force about a conductor are projected into space as radiation and are not returned to the conductor as the cycle alternates.

Radiation pattern

The variation of the field intensity of an antenna as an angular function with respect to the axis.

Radiation resistance

The resistance that if inserted in place of the antenna would consume the same amount of power as that radiated by the antenna.

Radiation, space

Radiation from space.

Radio

Telecommunication by modulation and radiation of electromagnetic waves.

Radio communications

The term describing communications over a wireless system.

Radio frequency

Any frequency of electromagnetic energy capable of propagation into space. The frequencies that fall between 3 kilohertz and 300 gigahertz used for radio communications. Any frequency within the electromagnetic spectrum normally associated with radio wave propagation.

Radio frequency carrier shift

The system that uses a keyer to shift a radio frequency signal above or below an assigned frequency. These shifts correspond to marks and spaces.

Radio frequency choke

A choke designed to impede currents in the RF range.

Radio horizon

The boundary beyond the natural horizon in which radio waves cannot be propagated over the surface of the earth. The locus of points at which direct rays from an antenna are tangential to the surface of the Earth.

Radio net

An organization of radio stations that is capable of direct communication on a common frequency.

Radio set control unit

Equipment used to remotely control certain transmitter and receiver functions.

Radio spectrum

A band of frequencies used for radio communication.

Radio waves

A form of radiant energy that can neither be seen nor felt. An electromagnetic wave that is generated by a transmitter. An electromagnetic wave of a frequency arbitrarily lower than 3000 GHz.

Radix

Also called the base. The number of distinct symbols used in a number system. For example, since the decimal number system uses ten symbols (0, 1, 2, 3, 4, 5, 6, 7, 8, 9), the radix is 10. In the binary number system, the radix is 2 because it uses only two symbols (0, 1).

Radix point

Also called Binary Point, Octal Point, Decimal Point and so on, depending on the number system.

Radome

An enclosure designed to protect a radar dish and the measurement equipment used with the dish. In addition to shielding the radar from the weather a radome also conceals the direction the radar is pointing. Refer to the right for a graphic of a radar field.

Raid

Redundant Array of Inexpensive Disks. A way of creating a fault-tolerant storage system. There are 6 levels. Level 0 uses byte-level striping. Level 1 uses mirroring. Level 2 uses bit-level striping. Level 3 stores error correcting information (such as parity) on a separate disk, and uses data striping on the remaining drives. Level 4 is level 3 with block level striping. Level 5 uses block level and parity data striping.

RAM

Random Access Memory. Memory in which each element can be individually addressed and accessed with the same speed as any other element of the memory. The main memory of a computer is usually RAM. One of the earliest forms of RAM was called core, because it consisted of directly addressed doughnuts or cores of ferromagnetic material each of which represented one bit. A faster more recent form of RAM is called Dynamic RAM.

RAM card

An add-in circuit board containing RAM memory and the interface logic necessary to decode memory addresses.

RAM chip

A semiconductor storage device. RAM chips can be either dynamic or static memory.

Random access

Also called “dynamic access” this indicates that data can be selected without having to skip over earlier data first. This is the way that a CD, record, laserdisc, or DVD will behave — it is easy to selectively play a particular track without having to fast forward through earlier tracks. The other common behavior is called sequential access. Range are allowed access to an Internet service. To mask a portion of the IP address, replace it with the asterisk wild card character (*). For example, 192.44.*.* represents every computer on the internet with an IP address beginning with 192.44.

RARP

Reverse Address Resolution Protocol. A method for workstations to ask a server for their IP address during bootstrap operations.

RAS

Short for Remote Access Services, a feature built into Windows NT that enables users to log into an NT-based LAN using a modem, X.25 connection or WAN link. RAS works with several major network protocols, including TCP/IP, IPX, and Netbeui. To use RAS from a remote node, you need a RAS client program, which is built into most versions of Windows, or any PPP client software. For example, most remote control programs work with RAS.

Raster

A rectangular pattern of lines; on a video display, the horizontal scan lines from which the term raster scan is derived.

Rational number

A number that can be written as an integer divided by a non-zero integer.

RCA connector

A connector used for attaching audio and video devices, such as stereo equipment or a composite video monitor, to a computer's video adapter.

Read

The action of transferring data from an input source into a computer's memory or from memory into the central processing unit (CPU).

Read/write

A magnetic mechanism that can read, write and erase data encoded as polarized patterns on magnetic disk or tape.

Real address

An absolute (machine) address specifying a physical location in memory.

Realaudio

This is a method of playing sounds invented by Rob Glasser that creates a buffer between the supplying server and your computer. The file is played without downloading it completely.

Realtime

The processing of transactions as they occur rather than batching them. Pertaining to an application in which response to input is fast enough to affect subsequent inputs and guide the process and in which records are updated immediately. The lag from input time to output time must be sufficiently small for acceptable timeliness. Timeliness is a function of the total system: missile guidance requires output within a few milliseconds of input, scheduling of steamships requires response time in days. Realtime systems are those with response time of milliseconds, interactive system in seconds and batch system in hours or days.

Real-time operating system

An operating system designed or optimized for the needs of a process-control environment.

Real-time system

An interactive system for which time constraints on actions are particularly tight or in which the slightest timing failure cannot be tolerated.

Reboot

A user activity where the user starts a computing device without interrupting its source of electrical power.

Receive

To accept data from an external communications system, such as a local area network (LAN) or a telephone line, and store the data as a file.

Receiver

The node or process for which a packet or other information is intended.

Recode

Often a data analyst or data producer will produce new data values from raw data and include these in a data file; this process is called "recoding." For instance, an age variable might contain a respondent's actual age in years, but this information might be "recoded" to produce a new variable, "eligible voter," with a code of "1" for all those 18 and over and a code of "2" for all those under 18.

Recompile

To compile a program again, usually because of changes that needed to be made in the source code in response to error messages generated by the compiler.

Record

A collection of related data or words, treated as a unit. For example, in stock control, each invoice could constitute one record.

Record length

Depending on the context, the length in bytes (i.e., columns) of a physical record or a logical record . On ICPSR Tape Information Forms and on CDNet, the abbreviation "RecLen" is used for physical record length.

Record type

A record that has a consistent logical structure. In files that include different units of analysis, for instance, different record types are needed to hold the different variables. For example, one record type might have a variable for income in one column and another record type might have a variable for household size in that same column. The codebook will describe these different structures and how to determine which is which so that you can tell your statistical software how to interpret that particular column as income or household size.

Recovery

The process by which data bases are rebuilt after a system fails.

Rectangular file

A physical file structure. A rectangular file is one which contains the same number of card-images or the same physical record length for each respondent or unit of analysis . A Hierarchical file can be stored in a rectangular file structure by storing all units of analysis in a single physical record . For instance, each record might contain one household unit, two family units, and four person units for each family unit. This method of storage of hierarchical files can be very inefficient in terms of storage space, but can make the file easier to describe and work with.

Recursion

The process of using a recursive procedure; the carrying out of a recursive call.

Redditor

A person who scours the Internet for media and posts the findings on the Reddit website. Once posted, other members can upvote or downvote the material based on their evaluation of it.

Redirecting calls

A system whereby you can redirect calls from one place to another if you know where you are going to be eg from an office phone to a mobile.

Reel tape

One-half inch magnetic tape stored on round reels. Also called Round Tape.

Re-engineering

The circular process of going from code to models then back to code that might be in a different language, use a different DBMS or be more structured.

Reflective liquid-crystal display

A liquid crystal display that is not equipped with edge or back lighting to enhance readability but rather depends on reflecting ambient light, making it difficult to read in brightly lit environments such as the outdoors. Also called reflective LCD.

Reflective routing

In wide area networks, the process of using a reflector to distribute data, thereby reducing the load of the network server.

Refresh

Generally, to update something with new data. For example, some Web browsers include a refresh button that updates the currently display Web pages. This feature is also called reload. To recharge a device with power or informatio For example, dynamic RAM needs to be refreshed thousands of times per second or it will lose the data stored in it. Similarly, display monitors must be refreshed many times per second. The refresh rate for a monitor is measured in hertz (Hz) and is also called the vertical frequency, vertical scan rate, frame rate or vertical refresh rate. The old standard for monitor refresh rates was 60Hz, but a new standard developed by VESA sets the refresh rate at 75Hz for monitors displaying resolutions of 640x480 or greater. This means that the monitor redraws the display 75 times per second. The faster the refresh rate, the less the monitor flickers

Region

An area of contiguous virtual memory that is accessible by the threads of the owning process.

Register

A set of bits of high-speed memory within a microprocessor or other electronic device, used to hold data for a particular purpose. Each register in a central processing unit is referred to in assembly language programs by a name such as AX (the register that contains the results of arithmetic operations in an Intel 80x86 processor) or SP (the register that contains the memory address of the top of the stack in various processors).

Registered memory

A type of memory module that has a register between the DRAM modules and the system memory controller. Registered memory, also called buffered memory, is more stable than unbuffered memory, but also more expensive. Registered memory is mainly used in servers and workstations.

Registration
The process of precisely aligning elements or superimposing layers in a document or a graphic so that everything will print in the correct relative position.

Relational database
An organization of data into tables with each column containing the values of a data element and each row representing a record.

Relational operator
An operator that compares two values, producing a boolean expression as the result.

Relational structure
A study that includes different units of analysis, particularly when those units are not arranged in a strict hierarchy as they are in a hierarchical file, has a relational structure. Note that the data could be arranged in several different physical structures to handle such a data structure. For instance, each unit of analysis might be stored in a separate rectangular file with identification numbers linking each case to the other units; or, the different units of analysis might be stored in one large file with a hierarchical file structure; or the different units could be stored in a special database structure used by a relational data base management system such as INGRES. An example of a study with a relational structure is the Survey of Income and Program Participation which has eight or more record types; these record types are related to each other but are not all members of a hierarchy of membership. For instance, there are record types for household, family, person, wage and salary job, and general income amounts.

Relationship
A link made between tables, usually through at least one common field.

Relative reference
A cell or range reference that automatically adjusts to the new location in the worksheet when the formula is copied.

Relative URL
Short for relative Uniform Resource Locator. A form of URL in which the domain and some or all directory names are omitted, leaving only the document name and extension (and perhaps a partial list of directory names). The indicated file is found in a location relative to the pathname of the current document.

Relay
A switch activated by an electrical signal. A relay allows another signal to be controlled without the need for human action to route the other signal to the control point, and it also allows a relatively low-power signal to control a high-power signal.

Remote
Equipment or site that is located out of the way or at a distance from primary equipment or a larger or primary site. Sometimes used as the opposite of local.

Remote access
The ability to access a computer from outside a building in which it is housed. Remote access requires communications hardware, software, and actual physical links, although this can be as simple as common carrier (telephone) lines or as complex as TELNET login to another computer across the Internet.

Remote printer
A printer attached to either another server or workstation on the network.

Remote procedure calling (RPC)
A communication construct that conceals operations behind a procedure-calling abstraction and is implemented in terms of a request-reply protocol.

Remote system
The computer or network that a remote user is accessing via a modem.

Rendering
The creation of an image containing geometric models, using color and shading to give the image a realistic look. Usually part of a geometric modeling package such as a CAD program, rendering uses mathematics to describe the location of a light source in relation to the object and to calculate the way in which the light would create highlights, shading, and variations in color. Realism can range from opaque, shaded polygons to images approximating photographs in their complexity.

Repeater
A Physical Layer device which restores, amplifies, re-clocks or otherwise improves a network signal that it receives on one of its ports and transmits the improved signal without buffering or interpreting it.

Replica manager
A process that holds replicas of data items and performs operations on them directly.

Replication transparency
A type of transparency that enables multiple instances of information objects to be used to increase reliability and performance without knowledge of the replicas by users or programs.

Report
A way of summarising and grouping data which can be formatted as required

Request for proposal (RFP)
A form on which problem details and user requirements are listed. Suppliers use this to submit details of their proposed solution.

Request for Quotation (RFQ)
A form on which hardware and software requirements are listed. The RFQ is forwarded to suppliers and helps to ensure that quotations are based on exactly the same items.

Request protocol
An RPC exchange protocol used when no confirmation or value is required from the executed procedure.

Request-reply protocol
An RPC exchange protocol that uses the server reply message as an acknowledgement of the client request message.

Request-reply-acknowledge protocol
An RPC exchange protocol that uses the a separate acknowledgement message in addition to the request and reply message.

Resedit
A Macintosh utility that allows a user to modify the resource fork of an HFS file.

Reset button
A small button that, when pushed, will restart a Macintosh.

Resistor

A passive electrical device that adds resistance to a circuit.

Resource

An on-line information set or an on-line interactive option. An on-line library catalog or the local school lunch menu are examples of information sets. On-line menus or graphical user interfaces, Internet e-mail, on-line conferences, telnet, FTP, and Gopher are examples of interactive options.

Resource fork

In a Macintosh file, the portion of the file that contains such auxiliary information as the menus, the dialog boxes and sounds that a file may require in addition to its data.

Resource manager

A software module that manages a set of resources of a particular type.

Resource sharing

a situation in which multiple entities within a distributed system use the same set of hardware, software, and/or data.

Response

A message placed in a conference as a follow-up to a topic or to another response; or, a reply to an e-mail message.

Response time

The gap between the time when a user initiates an action and the time that the action displays its results.

Restore

The process where files are returned from a backup to their original condition and location.

Retiming

A function of a repeater or Ethernet hub that receives a signal, cleans and regenerates it, and then sends it.

Return key

The key on a terminal keyboard that, when struck, places the cursor at the left margin one line below its previous horizontal position.

Reuse and reuseability

An approach to software engineering that emphasizes reusing software assets, including designs and code, and building software assets likely to be reuseable in future applications.

Reverse engineering

The process of going from the more concrete level of code to the more abstract level of models for data and processes.

Revisable-form-text dca

A standard within Document Content Architecture (DCA) for storing documents in such a way that the formatting can be changed by the receiver. A related standard is Final-Form-Text DCA.

Rewritable digital video disc

Technology for recording data on disks that have the same storage capacity as digital video discs (DVDs) but can be rewritten like compact disc-rewritable (CD-RW) devices.

Rewrite

To write again, especially in situations where information is not permanently recorded, such as RAM or a video display. Also called refresh, regenerate.

RF interference

Radio Frequency signals that degrade the integrity of a data signal.

RFC

Request For Comment. For the IETF,

the document that specifies a standard after an exhaustive review process.

RFID

Radio-Frequency Identification is an identification method that stores identification data on objects and uses radio waves to retrieve the data.

RFS

Remote File Sharing. The activity of sharing a file among remote computers.

RGB monitor

A color monitor that receives its signals for red, green, and blue levels over separate lines. An RGB monitor generally produces sharper and cleaner images than those produced by a composite monitor, which receives levels for all three colors over a single line.

Right click

To make a selection using the button on the right side of a mouse or other pointing device. Doing so in the Windows 95 environment typically brings up a pop-up menu with options applicable to the object over which the cursor is positioned.

Ring

A type of network topology where the devices are connected to a continuous conductor.

RIP

Routing Information Protocol. A distance vector routing protocol for IP.

RMA

Return Material Authorization is a term used to refer to the process where the recipient of a product arranges to return a defective product to the supplier for repair or replacement or credit.

RMI

Remote Method Invocation — the technology that enables a program to execute a method of an object on a different system.

Roaming

A term used in wireless to refer to the concept of extending service to a geographical location that is outside the geographical coverage area provided by the home network.

Role

One end of an association.

ROM

Stands for Read-Only Memory. A semiconductor-based memory system that stores information permanently and does not lose its contents when power is switched off. ROMs are used for firmware, such as the BIOS used in the PC; and in some portable computers, application programs and even the operating system are being stored in ROM.

Root directory

The directory that contains all other directories.

Router

A device that connects any number of LANs. Routers use headers and a forwarding table to determine where packets go, and they use ICMP to communicate with each other and configure the best route between any two hosts. Very little filtering of data is done through routers. Routers do not care about the type of data they handle.

Routine

Part of a computer program, or a sequence of instructions called by a program, that may have some general or frequent use.

Routing

The process of finding a path over which a packet can travel to reach its destination.

RPC

Remote Procedure Call. A command given by one computer to a second computer over a network to execute a defined system call, such as in an NFS session.

Rs-232

Recommended Standard 232C - now ratified as the EIA-232 standard, which is used by all dial-up modems. The serial port may be either 25-pin or 9-pin D shell.

RTT

Round Trip Time. the time between the transmission of a packet and the receipt of its acknowledgment or reply.

Run

The single, continuous execution of a program by a computer on a given set of data. As a verb, to initiate processing by a program.

Russell's paradox

A logical contradiction in set theory discovered by the British mathematician Bertrand Russell (1872-1970). If R is the set of all sets which don't contain themselves, does R contain itself? If it does then it doesn't and vice versa.

S

S/MIME

Acronym for Secure/Multipurpose Internet Mail Extensions. An Internet e-mail security standard that makes use of public key encryption.

S/PDIF

Sony/Phillips Digital Interface is a standard file format for carrying digital audio signals.

SAA

Systems Application Architecture. IBM's architecture for communications and application development.

SAP

Service Access Point. The interface between one protocol and another in an adjacent layer.

SAPI

Acronym for Speech Application Programming Interface. A feature in Windows 95 and Windows NT that allows applications to include speech recognition or convert text to speech. Also called Speech API.

SATA

Serial ATA, A successor to ATA where the interface between storage devices (hard drives, optical drives, Solid-State drives) and a computer, is a high-speed serial cable.

Satellite

A radio relay station that orbits the earth. A complete satellite communications system also includes earth stations that communicate with each other via the satellite. The satellite receives a signal transmitted by an originating earth station and retransmits that signal to the destination earth station(s).

Satellite eclipse

An eclipse where the rays of the sun do not reach the satellite. This prevents recharging of the solar cells of the satellite and decreases the power to the transmitter.

Satellite-sun conjunction

A period when the satellite and sun are close together and the noise from the sun prevents or hampers communications.

Saturable-core reactor

A coil in which the reactance is controlled by changing the permeability of the core.

Saturation

The condition existing in any circuit in which an increase in the input signal produces no further change in the output. The operating point of a vacuum tube or transistor at which a further increase in grid or base current no longer produces an increase in plate or collector current. The current between the base and collector of a bipolar transistor when an increase in emitter to base voltage causes no further increase in the collector current. The point at which the output of a linear device, such as a linear amplifier, deviates significantly from being a linear function of the input when the input signal is increased. In a magnetic core, the condition in which a magnetic material has reached a maximum flux density and the permeability has decreased to a value of approximately In a communications system, the condition in which a component of the system has reached its maximum traffic handling capacity.

Saw tooth

A waveform that appears like teeth on a saw. A Saw-Tooth waveform has a slow linear rise time and fast fall time.

Saw tooth oscillator

A circuit that generates a saw-tooth waveform. A relaxation oscillator. .

S-band

An obsolete term used to describe a band of frequencies in the microwave range.

Scalability

A quality such that the scale on which a system is used can increase without modification to the system itself.

Scalability

The suitability of a system (particularly a network system to operate properly and efficiently when configured on a large scale.

Scalar processing

A sequential operation in which one instruction produces one result; it starts an instruction, handles one operand or operand pair, and produces one result. Scalar processing complements vector processing by providing solutions to problems not readily adaptable to vector techniques.

Scale

A horizontal or vertical line on a graph that shows minimum, maximum, and interval values for the data plotted.

Scaling factor

The term used to describe the use of unequal resistors in a servos summing network to compensate for differences between input and output signal levels.

Scaling transparency

A type of transparency that allows the system and applications to expand in scale without change to the system structure or the application algorithms.

Scanner

An electronic device that uses light-sensing equipment to scan paper images such as text, photos, and illustrations and translate the images into signals that the computer can then store, modify, or distribute.

Scenario

A sequence of events that occur during one particular execution of a system.

Scheduling

An automated capability to schedule meetings and/or resources (such as meeting rooms, projectors, etc.) by looking at online calendars.

Schematic

A diagram which shows, by means of graphic symbols, the electrical connections and functions of a specific circuit arrangement.

Schematic symbol

A letter, abbreviation, or graphic design used to represent specific characteristics or components on a schematic diagram. Some organizations use different graphics to represent the same thing.

Scheme

Scheme is a typically interpreted computer language. It was created in 1975 in an attempt to make Lisp simpler and more consistent. Scheme is a fairly portable language, but is not particularly fast.

Schering bridge

A four-arm bridge used for measuring an unknown capacitance. Refer to the schematic in the right side-bar.

Schmitt

A Bistable circuit which switches based on the magnitude of the input signal and not the waveform. The output switches high when the input rises above a predetermined level and switches low when the input drops below a predetermined level.

Schmitt trigger

An integrated circuit which has hystersis between an upper voltage limit and lower voltage limit and does not switch until one of those limits are reached.

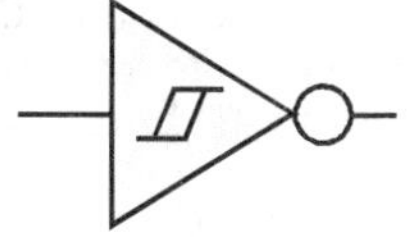

Schottky diode

A junction diode with the device junction formed between the semiconductor and a metal contact rather than between dissimilar semiconductor materials.

Schottky transistor

A type of transistor that utilizes a combination of a transistor and a Schottky diode. The Schottky transistor shown to the right combines a Schottky diode and the transistor formed on the same silicon die [a Schottky diode used to form the transistor]. The circuit in the the right side bar shows individual Schottky diodes and individual Schottky transistors used in the same circuit, also on the same semiconductor die [an input pin to a gate].

SCR

Refer to Silicon Controlled Rectifier. .

Scratch

A memory region or file used by a program or operating system to hold work in progress temporarily. Created and maintained usually without the end user's knowledge, the scratch is needed only until the current session is terminated, at which time the data is saved or discarded. Also called scratch file.

Scratchpad memory

A smaller faster memory section used with [slower] main memory. A memory cache.

Screen
The surface of a monitor on which information can be viewed.

Screen dump
A duplicate of a screen image; essentially, a "snapshot" of the screen that is either sent to a printer or saved as a file.

Screen editor
A program that allows a file to be edited by making changes to the text displayed on the screen. It may also support commands to make changes to the whole file at once. Changes to the portion displayed on the screen are immediately shown.

Screen font
A typeface designed for display on a computer monitor scree Screen fonts often have accompanying PostScript fonts for printing to PostScript-compatible printers.

Screen grid
A grid placed between a control grid and the plate and usually maintained at a fixed positive potential. Used with Vacuum tubes or CRTs.

Screen saver
A background process that monitors system activity such as mouse clicks and key strokes and takes over the system during prolonged periods of idle activity to cover the screen with a display that will prevent damage to its phosphors either by reducing the intensity of electron flow or by displaying an image that changes often enough to avoid screen "burn-in". Some screen savers also offer a security option by requiring a password before a user can regain control of the system.

Screen shot
An image that shows all or part of a computer display. The illustration shown here as well as entries alert box, cell, and menu bar, for example, are screen shots.

Screening
Process of applying nonconductive or semiconductive materials to a substrate to form thick film components. A process of sampling incoming or out going parts for certain parameters to insure the components are acceptable and meet their mechanical or electrical ratings.

Screening calls
Listening to the caller and asking questions to establish the purpose of the call, then make a decision based on this information and the company policy.

Script
A set of instructions that a computer can operate. Unlike a program, script instructions are not compiled into machine language but are interpreted by the system at the time of execution. Scripting languages for the Macintosh include HyperTalk, Frontier and AppleScript.

Scripting language
A simple programming language designed to perform special or limited tasks, sometimes associated with a particular application or functio An example of a scripting language is Perl.

Scroll
To move all or part of the display image vertically or horizontally to view data otherwise excluded. Scrolling can be performed with a mouse in the horizontal/vertical bars on each

window or by using the page up/down - home/end - or arrow keys.

SCSI

Small Computer Systems Interface. A specification (ANSI X3T9.2) for a short distance ((6 meters max.) Local Area Network using bus topology for up to eight devices. The Macintosh uses this network for attaching devices such as external disk drives and scanners.

SCSI bus

A parallel bus that carries data and control signals from SCSI devices to a SCSI controller.

SCSI network

A set of devices on a SCSI bus, which acts like a local area network.

SCSI port

A SCSI host adapter within a computer, which provides a logical connection between the computer and all of the devices on the SCSI bus.

SDLC

Synchronous Data Link Control. IBM's specification for encapsulation of data over synchronous links. Analogous to HDLC.

SDH

Synchronous Digital Hierarchy. A method used for multiplexing many circuits with a low bit rate onto fewer circuits with a higher bit rate, and vice-versa (de-multiplexing). Used primarily in the telecommunications industry to carry telephony traffic. This network can also be used to carry IP traffic.

Sdk

Acronym for software developer's kit.

SDRAM

Synchronous dynamic random access memory is a type of memory that is synchronized with the system bus.

Search engine

1. A program that searches for key words in documents or in a database.
2. On the Internet, a program that searches for keywords in files and documents found on the World Wide Web, newsgroups, Gopher menus, and FTP archives. Some search engines are used for a single Internet site, such as a dedicated search engine for a Web site. Others search across many sites, using such agents as spiders to gather lists of available files and documents and store these lists in databases that users can search by keyword. Examples of the latter type of search engine are Lycos, AliWeb, and Excite. Most search engines reside on a server.

Search key

1. The particular field (or column) of the records to be searched in a database.
2. The value that is to be searched for in a document or any collection of data.

Second detector (demodulator)

The part of the receiver that separates the audio or video component from the modulated intermediate frequency.

Secondary

The output coil of a transformer.

Secondary cache

Short for Level 2 cache, cache memory that is external to the microprocessor.

In general, L2 cache memory, also called the secondary cache, resides on a separate chip from the microprocessor chip. The Pentium Pro, however, has an L2 cache on the same chip as the microprocessor.

Secondary cell

A cell that can be recharged by a current being passed through the cell in a direction opposite to the discharge current.

Secondary emission

The liberation of electrons from an element, other than the cathode, as a result of being struck by other high-velocity electrons.

Secondary industry

Industries that are involved with the manufacture of goods.

Secondary loop

In a cooling system, the loop that transfers the heat from the heat source, such as electronic equipment, to the primary loop; usually distilled water.

Secondary storage

Hardware device used to record and retrieve data and instructions eg floppy disk, tape, CD-ROM

Secondary winding

The output winding of a transformer. The winding that receives electromagnetic induction from the primary winding.

Sector

A predetermined, addressable angular part of a track or band on a magnetic drum or magnetic disk.

Seek time

The time required for the access arm of a direct-access storage device to be positioned on the appropriate track. The movement of a hard disk head in search of the right data track on a platter.

Segment

A section of a program that, when compiled, occupies a contiguous address space and that is usually position independent; that is, it can be loaded anywhere in memory. With Intel-based microcomputers, a native-mode segment is a logical reference to a 64-KB contiguous portion of RAM in which the individual bytes are accessed by means of an offset value. Collectively, the segment:offset values reference a single physical location in RAM.

Segmentation

The act of breaking up a program into several sections, or segments.

Segmented address space

An address space that is logically divided into chunks called segments. To address a given location, a program must specify both a segment and an offset within that segment. (The offset is a value that references a specific point within the segment, based on the beginning of the segment.) Because segments may overlap, addresses are not unique; there are many logical ways to access a given physical locatio The Intel 80x86 real-mode architecture is segmented; most other microprocessor architectures are flat.

Semiconductor

A substance, commonly silicon or germanium, whose ability to conduct electricity falls between that of a conductor and that of a nonconductor (insulator). The term is used loosely to refer to electronic components made from semiconductor materials.

Sequencer
A process to which all messages are sent before being multicast so that the sequencer can assign and identifier to each message before sending.

Sequential
A method of storing and retrieving information that requires data to be written and read sequentially. Accessing any portion of the data requires reading all the preceding data.

Sequential access
This indicates that data cannot be selected without having to skip over earlier data first. This is the way that a cassette or video tape will behave. The other common behavior is called random access.

Sequential consistency
A property where memory operations appear to occur one at at time in the order in which they're expected to happen.

Sequential search
An algorithm for searching an indexed collection checking the elements in the same sequence that they are stored in the collection.

Serial equivalence
A property of some transactions such that concurrent execution has the same effect as serial execution.

Serial port
An input/output location (channel) that sends and receives data to and from a computer's central processing unit or a communications device one bit at a time. Serial ports are used for serial data communication and as interfaces with some peripheral devices, such as mice and printers.

Server
Any combination of hardware or software designed to provide services to clients. When used alone, the term typically refers to a computer which may be running a server operating system, but is also used to refer to any software or dedicated hardware capable of providing services.

Service
An organization that provides access to part of the Internet. You have to arrange for an account with a service to connect your computer to the Internet.

Session
Networking term used to refer to the logical stream of data flowing between two programs and being communicated over a network. There may be many different sessions emanating from any one node on a network.

Session layer
The fifth layer of the OSI reference model, it provides the means for two session service users to organize and synchronize their dialogs and manage data exchange.

Set
In SNMP, the command given by the Console that asks the MIB to change the value of a data object in its MIB.

SFX
A form factor for power supplies.

SGML
Acronym for Standard Generalized Markup Language. An information management standard adopted by the International Organization for Standardization (ISO) in 1986 as a means of providing platform- and application-independent documents

that retain formatting, indexing, and linked informatio SGML provides a grammar-like mechanism for users to define the structure of their documents and the tags they will use to denote the structure in individual documents.

Shared key

An encryption key known only to the receiver and sender of data. This is also referred to as a pre-shared key.

Shared-memory multiprocessor

An architecture that contains several independent processors, each being able to execute a separate program.

Shareware

Protected by copyright; holder allows you to make and distribute copies under the condition that those who adopt the software after preview pay a fee to the holder of the copyright; derivative works are not allowed; you may make an archival copy.

Sharing

Configuration of peripherals attached to a network to allow permitted users to use the peripheral over the network.

Sheet

The mechanism for breaking large objects models into a series of pages.

Shell

A term that usually refers to the user interface of an operating system. A shell is the command processor that is the actual interface between the kernel and the user. The C shell or the Bourne shell are the primary user interfaces on UNIX systems. Contrasts with the kernel, which interacts with the computer at low levels.

Shockwave

A format for multimedia audio and video services within HTML documents, created by Macromedia, which markets a family of Shockwave servers and plug-in programs for Web browsers.

Short

The direct connection of two or more conductors of a circuit with each other.

Signal

The means of conveyance for a communication, typically an electromagnetic wave that is modulated to encode the information communicated.

Signal to Noise Ratio

In an electromagnetic signal, the ratio of the amplitude (strength) of a signal to the amplitude of the ambient radiation and other signal disturbances that are present, usually expressed in decibels (dB).

Significant digits

The digits required to represent the accuracy of an approximate number, beginning with the leftmost non-zero digit and ending with the rightmost digit.

Silicon

A semiconductor used in many devices, especially microchips. Silicon, with atomic number 14 and atomic weight 28, is the second most common element in nature.

Silicon chip

An integrated circuit that uses silicon as its semiconductor material.

SIMM

A SIMM, or single in-line memory module, is a type of memory module containing random access memory used in computers from the early 1980s to the late 1990s.

Simplex

A term applied to data transmission in which data can only sent, and not received.

Simulation

An imitation of the behavior of some existing or intended system, or some aspect of that behavior. Examples of areas where simulation is used include communications network design, weather forecasting and training. Physical systems can also be simulated, for example, chemical or nuclear reactions.

Single sign on

Single Sign On feature set allows the 802.1X credentials to match your Windows log on user name and password credentials for wireless network connections.

Single-channel mode

This mode is used when only one DIMM is installed or the memory capacities are unequal. Also known as asymmetric mode.

Single-sided

A memory module where DRAM chips are found on only one side of the module.

SLC

Single Level Cell; storing one bit of information per cell.

Slewing rate

The maximum rate, usually expressed in volts/second, at which an active device such as a transistor or transformer can change its voltage state.

Slip

Serial Line Internet Protocol. A protocol for carrying IP information over serial links.

Slip chart

A pictorial representation of the predicted completion dates of milestones (also referred to as Trend Chart.

SLIP emulator

Software that mimics a SLIP connection in UNIX shell accounts that do not offer a direct SLIP connectio Many Internet service providers (ISPs) are UNIX based and offer shell accounts to users for Internet access. Like a SLIP connection, the SLIP emulator allows the user to avoid dealing with the ISP's UNIX environment directly when accessing the Internet and to use Internet applications such as graphical Web browsers.

Slotted ring

A LAN in which the computers are linked in a ring structure and data is transmitted in small, fixed-sized packets from node to node around the ring.

SMART

Self-Monitoring, Analysis, and Reporting Technology is a technology for hard drives that monitors various reliability indicators in order to try to anticipate failures.

SMBIOS

System BIOS

SMDS

Switched Multimegabit Data Service. A metropolitan area packet switching data network using T-1 and T-3 lines.

SMI
Structure of Management Information.

Smiley
Character combinations such as :-) to denote whether a message is being made in jest with various modifications thereof ;-) to wink, etc. Also called emoticons, since not all are smiling %-(.

SMTP
Simple Mail Transfer Protocol. The standard protocol for exchanging mail over TCP/IP networks.

SNA
Systems Network Architecture. IBM's communications architecture and strategy.

SNMP
Simple Network Management Protocol. A de facto standard for management of networked devices using a simple request-response data retrieval mechanism.

SNMPV2
Simple Network Management Protocol Version 2. Offers increased performance, better security, greater portability and greater ability to manage non-network resources.

Socket
A communication endpoint-analogous to a telephone-that permits a program to communicate to another program across a network.

Socket address
A communication identifier that consists of a local port number and an Internet address.

SO-DIMM
Small outline dual in-line memory module about half the size of a regular DIMM. This memory is often used in small systems such as notebooks or systems with Mini-ITX motherboards.

Soft copy
An electronic version of a file, usually in computer memory and/or on disk; as opposed to hard copy, the paper printout.

Software
A general term primarily used for digitally stored data such as computer programs and other kinds of information read and written by computers. Today, this includes data that has not traditionally been associated with computers, such as film, tapes and records.

Software design
In software engineering, the process of defining the software architecture (structure), components, modules, interfaces, test approach, and data for a software system to satisfy specified requirements.

Software licence
The terms and conditions under which a piece of software may be used

Software tool
A program that is employed in the development, repair or enhancement of other programs. Tools include editors, compilers and linkers. Also refers to utilities, such as formatters and file utilities.

Solid-state drive
A solid-state drive (SSD), sometimes called a solid-state disk or electronic disk, is a data storage device that uses integrated circuit assemblies as memory to store data persistently.

SONET
Synchronous Optical Network. A standard for a worldwide digital

network using a common transport. SONET can run over copper or fiber.

Sort

To arrange a set of items in sequence according to keys; for example, to arrange the records of a personnel file into alphabetical order by using the employee names as sort keys.

Source

The node or process transmitting information.

Source code

The program in a language prepared by the programmer. This code cannot be directly executed by the computer and must first be translated into object code.

Southbridge

Another name for ICH.

Spamming

the act of sending unsolicited email or posting many useless messages in a forum website. (Possibly derived from a Monty Pythonsketch, in which Vikings repetitively sing about SPAM, annoying the other customers.)

SPARC

Scalable Processor ARChitecture. Trademark of SunMicrosystems 32-bit RISC microprocessor architecture. The architecture is open in the sense that other vendors can obtain the processor chips and documentation sufficient to build computers using it.

Sparcstation

A workstation (usually a Sun Microsystems brand) based on the SPARC chip.

SPD (serial presence detect)

A standardized way to automatically access information about a computer memory module; SPD is a memory hardware feature that makes it possible for the computer to know what memory is present, and what timings to use to access the memory.

Specialization

The creation of subclasses from a superclass by refining the superclass

Specification

A description of the criteria for the construction, appearance or performance of a computer system.

Specular highlighting

A graphics term that adds the effect of a “hot spot” on an object which corresponds to the shininess of its material.

Spellcheck

A process where the words in a document are matched against a list of words in a dictionary. If a word in the document does not match one, it is signalled as a spelling error.

Spike

A sudden and transient increase in the voltage from a power supply.

Sponge

A job that runs in the background on the IBM 3090 mainframe computer in such a way that it uses only those CPU cycles not needed by other work, yet is so computationally intense that it soaks up all unused CPU cycles.

Spool

Simultaneous Peripheral Operations On-Line. A scheme that allows multiple devices to simultaneously write output to the same device such as multiple computers printing to the same printer at the same time. The data are actually written to temporary files while a program called a spooler sends the files to the device one at a time.

Spreadsheet

An program used to perform various calculations. It is especially popular for financial applications. Some common spreadsheets include Lotus 123, Excel, OpenOffice Spreadsheet, Octave, Gnumeric, AppleWorks Spreadsheet, Oleo, and GeoCalc.

SPX

Sequential Packet Exchange. A Transport layer protocol developed by Novell to provide in-sequence data transfer.

SQL

Structured Query Language. ANSI standard data manipulation language used in most relational data base systems. A language for requesting data from a relational database.

Square wave

An electromagnetic wave that oscillates between two voltage states, theoretically requiring no time to accomplish a state transition.

SSID

The service set identification, also known as the network name, identifies your network. It is a unique name and controls access to a given network. The SSID can be up to 32 characters and is case sensitive.

SSPEC

This is the 5 digit alphanumeric number inscribed on the top of the processor. It usually begins with the letter "s".

Standard

1. A synonym for specification.
2. A component or way of accomplishing a task that is so frequently and widely used that is seems to be part of a specification.

Standby monitor

Device placed in standby mode on a Token Ring network in case an active monitor fails.

Star

A network topology that is constructed by connecting computing devices to a common device.

Star topology

LAN topology in which end points on a network are connected to a common central switch by point-to-point links. A ring topology that is organized as a star implements a unidirectional closed-loop star, instead of point-to-point links.

Starlan

CSMA/CD LAN, based on IEEE 802.3, developed by AT&T.

State

The values of the attributes and links of an object at a particular time.

State diagram

A directed graph in which nodes represent system states and arcs represent transitions between states.

Stateless server

A server that can tolerate crashes by not holding information on behalf of particular clients.

Static random-access memory

Static random-access memory (SRAM) is a type of semiconductor memory where the word static indicates that, unlike dynamic RAM (DRAM), it does not need to be periodically refreshed.

Static route

Route that is explicitly configured and entered into the routing table. Static

Routes take precedence over routes chosen by dynamic routing protocols.

Statistical multiplexing

Technique in which information from multiple logical channels can be transmitted across a single physical channel. Statistical multiplexing dynamically allocates bandwidth only to active input channels, making better use of available bandwidth and allowing more devices to be connected than with other multiplexing techniques. Also referred to as statistical time-division multiplexing or stat mux.

Status bar

Located at the bottom of the screen and displays information for the user eg Page no, Section, Total pages, line, column.

STD

Subscriber Trunk Dialling - long distance calls.

Stereotyping

Judging or classifying people into a particular category according to appearance, behaviour, clothes or a belief.

STM-1

Synchronous Transport Module level 1. One of a number of SDH formats that specifies the frame structure for the 155.52-Mbps lines used to carry ATM cells.

Storage

A device or medium that can retain data for subsequent retrieval.

Store and forward packet switching

Packet-switching technique in which frames are completely processed before being forwarded out the appropriate port. This processing includes calculating the CRC and checking the destination address. In addition, frames must be temporarily stored until network resources are available to forward the message.

STP

Shielded twisted-pair. Two-pair wiring medium used in a variety of network implementations. STP cabling has a layer of shielded insulation to reduce EMI.

Strategy

Long-term plan, tactic, or scheme for attaining a vision.

Stream

A source or destination of data that may be associated with a piece of hardware.

Strict two-phase locking

Two-phase locking in which all locks are held until the current transaction commits or aborts.

String

A sequence of characters.

Striping

Disk striping copies blocks, bytes or bits across multiple disks in such a way that if one disk is lost, the data can be created using the blocks or bits on the remaining disks.

STS-1

Synchronous Transport Signal level 1. Basic building block signal of SONET, operating at 51.84 Mbps. Faster SONET rates are defined as STS-n, where n is a multiple of 51.84 Mbps.

STS-3c

Synchronous Transport Signal level 3, concatenated. SONET format that specifies the frame structure for the 155.52-Mbps lines used to carry ATM cells.

Stub area

OSPF area that carries a default route, intra-area routes, and interarea routes, but does not carry external routes. Virtual links cannot be configured across a stub area, and they cannot contain as ASBR.

Stub network

Network that has only a single connection to a router.

Stub procedure

A procedure that converts a local procedure call to a remote procedure call.

Subarea

Portion of an SNA network that consists of a subarea node and any attached links and peripheral nodes.

Subarea node

SNA communication controller or host that handles complete network addresses.

Subchannel

In broadband terminology, a frequency-based subdivision creating a separate communications channel.

Subinterface

One of a number of virtual interfaces on a single physical interface.

Subnet address

Portion of an IP address that is specified as the subnetwork by the subnet mask.

Subnet mask

A representation of a user's Internet address where all of the bit positions corresponding to the user's network and subnetwork id are 1's and the bit corresponding to the user's host id are 0's.

Subnetwork

1. In IP networks, a network sharing a particular subnet address. Subnetworks are networks arbitrarily segmented by a network administrator in order to provide a multilevel, hierarchical routing structure while shielding the subnetwork from the addressing complexity of attached networks. Sometimes called a subnet.
2. In OSI networks, a collection of ESs and ISs under the control of a single administrative domain and using a single network access protocol.

Subsystem

A major component of a system organized around some coherent theme. A system may be divided into subsystems using either partitions or layers.

Subvector

A data segment of a vector in an SNA message. A subvector consists of a length field, a key that describes the subvector type, and subvector specific data.

Sun microsystems

Sun originally stood for Stanford University Network, a name given to a printed circuit board developed in 1981 that was designed to run UNIX.

Sunos

The name of the operating system of the workstation from Sun Microsystems. It is based on Berkeley UNIX and AT&Ts System V UNIX. It is composed of three major parts: the kernel and file system, shells and graphical interfaces, and utility programs.

Suranet
Southeastern Universities Research Association Network. Network connecting universities and other organizations in the Southeastern United States. SURAnet, originally funded by the NSF and a part of the NSFNET, is now part of BBN Planet.

Surfing
Netspeak for wandering, whether one is surfing through cable stations or surfing the Internet.

SVC
Switched virtual circuit. Virtual circuit that is dynamically established on demand and is torn down when transmission is complete. SVCs are used in situations where data transmission is sporadic. Called a switched virtual connection in ATM terminology.

Switch
A switch is a device that forwards packets between nodes based on the packet's destination node address (either hardware or protocol), typically with a buffer time longer than a repeater but shorter than the transmission time of the packet.

Switched 56
A dial-up communication service available from a telephone service provider that offers a fractional portion of a T1 line built from as many as 24 channels of 56 KBPS each. Also called Fractional T1.

Switched LAN
LAN implemented with LAN switches.

Synchronization
Establishment of common timing between sender and receiver.

Synchronous
A communication system where stations may only transmit at prescribed intervals and must provide a timing pulse with their packet.

Synchronous communication
a form of communication in which the sending and receiving processes synchronize at every message.

Synchronous dynamic random-access memory
Synchronous dynamic random access memory (SDRAM) is dynamic random access memory (DRAM) that is synchronized with the system bus.

SYSGEN
System generation. Process of defining network resources in a network.

System
Any computer system that can be controlled by a user consisting of a CPU and optional equipment such as display monitors, disk drives, and other peripherals.

System BIOS
Another term for BIOS

System bus
Another name for front side bus (FSB)

System design
the first stage of design, during which high-level decisions are made about the overall structure of the system, its architecture, and the strategies used to implement the system.

System development life cycle
the process of creating a hardware/ software system from its conception, through analysis, design, implementation, testing, and maintenance.

System error
A software condition that renders the operating system incapable of continuing to function normally. This type of error usually requires rebooting the system.

System file
The Macintosh file that contains system software for the Macintosh OS, including patches or replacements to obsolete code contained in ROM.

System folder
The directory in which the System File resides.

System management
Activities that focus on the care and management of individual computer systems.

System software
Software in a computing system that provides basic functionality like file management, visual display, and keyboard input and is used by application software to accomplish these functions.

T

T-1

A Telecommunications technology for wide area networks (WAN) with a transmission speed of 1.554 MBPS over 24 multiplexed 56 KBPS channels.

T-2

Four multiplexed T-1 lines offering a communication channel at 6.3 MBPS.

T-3

Twenty-eight multiplexed T-1 circuits with a bandwidth of 44.736 MBPS.

Table

A facility, which allows the user to make columns with or without borders, can be used instead of tabulating.

TAC

Thermally Advantaged Chassis

TAC

Terminal Access Controller. Internet host that accepts terminal connections from dial-up lines.

TACACS

Terminal Access Controller Access Control System. Authentication protocol, developed by the DDN community, that provides remote access authentication and related services, such as event logging. User passwords are administered in a central database rather than in individual routers, providing an easilyscalable network security solution.

Tachometer

A small ac or dc generator, sometimes referred to as a rate generator, that converts its shaft speed into an electrical output. The tachometer is frequently used in servo-systems to sense the velocity of a load. An instrument that measures the rate at which a shaft is turning.

Tactile switch

A switch that provides some form of tactile feedback to the operator that the switch has been actuated. Normally a tactile switch is physically small having a very limited mechanical movement, requiring the switch to provide some form of tactile feedback so the user knows that the switch has been actuated or moved. Tactile switches are used for a number of applications, one of the more common applications are for membrane keypads.

Tagged traffic

ATM cells that have their CLP bit set to 1. If the network is congested, tagged traffic can be dropped to ensure deliver of higher-priority traffic. Sometimes called DE (discard eligible) traffic.

Tandem

Pertaining to an arrangement or sequencing of networks, circuits, or links, in which the output terminals of one network, circuit, or link are connected directly to the input terminals of another network, circuit, or link.

Tank circuit

A tuned circuit used to temporarily store energy. Also referred to as a parallel-resonant circuit, or LC circuit [Inductor Capacitor]. The components are placed in parallel in a Tank circuit.

Tantalum capacitor

A capacitor that uses tantalum as a dielectric. .

TAP

A fixed electrical connection point, normally at a location other than the two ends of a line. To draw energy from a circuit.

Tape and Reel

A method of packaging of electronic components in which a component is stored in a cavity of a plastic sheet and held in place by a tape covering the cavity. The plastic sheet and component covered by tape is than wound onto a reel which is than used by pick-and-place equipment. The reel holds some number of components, depending on the size of the component. In some cases a portion of the reel is sold or delivered and known as Cut-tape. .

Tape density

1. A measure of how much data, can fit on a magnetic tape.
2. A device for reading and writing tapes.

Tape drive

A peripheral device that allows only sequential access, typically using magnetic tape.

Taper

How the resistance of a potentiometer or variable resistor varies as the adjustment is changed.

Tapped delay line

A delay line with multiple tapped outputs so the amount of delay may be selected by choosing another tap or point on the delay line. To change the delay on this type of circuit the output needs to be taken from a different output pin. A tapped delay line may be passive, containing only an inductor [sometimes with a capacitor], or active using logic circuits to buffer or drive the signals. The total delay is the sum of all the individual tapped delays.

Tapped resistor

A wire-wound, fixed resistor having one or more additional terminals along its length, generally for voltage-divider applications. .

Tapped winding

A transformers with one or more additional terminals connected to the winding at places other than the extreme ends.

Task

1) Synonym for process.
2) An activity or group of activities necessary to accomplish a goal.

Taskbar

Contains the Start button, the clock and currently running tasks.

Taxi 4b/5b

Transparent Asynchronous Transmitter/Receiver Interface 4-byte/ 5-byte. Encoding scheme used for FDDI LANs, as well as for ATM. Supports speeds of up to 100 Mbps over multimode fiber. TASI is the chipset that generates 4B/5B encoding on multimode fiber.

TB (terabyte)

A unit of memory storage that is equal to 1,024 gigabytes (or 1,099,511,627,776 bytes).

T-carrier

The generic designator for any of several digitally multiplexed telecommunications carrier systems. More detail on the T-carrier hierarchy.

T-coupler

A passive optical coupler having three ports (three fibers). Also called a Splitter.

TCP

Transmission Control Protocol. A reliable Transport Layer Protocol for managing IP that supports re-transmission, sequencing and fragmentation.

TCP/IP

TCP/IP is a protocol for computer networks. The Internet is largely built on top of TCP/IP (it is the more reliable of the two primary Internet Protocols — TCP stands for Transmission Control Protocol).

TCU

Trunk coupling unit. In Token Ring networks, a physical device that enables a station to connect to the trunk cable.

TDM

Time-division multiplexing. Technique in which information from multiple channels can be allocated bandwidth on a single wire based on preassigned time slots. Bandwidth is allocated to each channel regardless of whether the station has data to transmit.

TDP

Thermal Design Power or Thermal Design Point is the maximum amount of power that a computer's cooling system must dissipate

TDR

Time domain reflectometer Device capable of sending signals through a network medium to check cable continuity and other attributes. TDRs are used to find physical layer network problems.

Team

Together Everyone Accomplishes More.

Tech writer

Short for technical writer. One who writes the documentation material for a hardware or software product. Also called technical author.

Technical

Pertaining to the application of specific principles and/or reasoning to the resolution of project management issues or problems. Relating to specified solution performance as opposed to cost and schedule.

Tee connector

A style of connector shaped like a 'T'. The connectors may be any gender in any combination. A BNC style Tee is shown to the right, but a Tee connector could be almost any style.

Telecommunication

The transmission, emission, or reception of signs, signals, writings, images, or sounds. This is done by visual, oral, wire, radio, or other means. The term Telecommunications may also be abbreviated as Telcom.

Telecomputing

Using computers for telecommunication; computer networking.

Telemetry

An electrical system for measuring a quantity, transmitting the result and than indicating the quantity measured.

Telephony

The science and practice of telecommunications.

Telephony device

A mechanism designed to translate sound into electrical signals, transmit them, and then convert them back to sound.

Telex

Teletypewriter service allowing subscribers to send messages over the PSTN.

Telnet

A protocol that enables an Internet user to log on to and enter commands on a remote computer linked to the Internet, as if the user were using a text-based terminal directly attached to that computer. Telnet is part of the TCP/IP suite of protocols.

Temperature coefficient

The ratio of the change in a parameter to the change in temperature. The amount of change of resistance in a material per unit change in temperature.

Temperature compensation

The process of compensating for or nullifying the effects of temperature change on a circuit or device.

Temperature cycling

Component or system testing which includes changing the ambient temperature during the test to exaggerate any faults that may exist. The largest temperature extremes range from -65 to +150 degrees C and may be used with the component powered or un-powered, depending on the test. Temperature cycling is also a form of accelerated test, reducing the testing time by stressing the component. Temperature testing normally also includes some amount of idle time at each increment in temperature.

Temperature inversion

The condition in which warm air is formed above a layer of cool air that is near the earth's surface.

Temperature sensor

A component or device that senses temperature changes and produces a change in its characteristics. A thermometer.

Temperature shock

A rapid change in temperature.

Temperature stabilizer

A circuit, component, or element used to keep the temperature of another device constant. Normally a temperature stabilizer is a heater used to keep a component from becoming to cold when the ambient temperature falls. A resistor or resistive element [contained within a component] could be considered a temperature stabilizer, as current is passed through the resistor.

Temperature, military

-55 to 125 degrees Celsius. The operational temperature range components or equipment is designed for to meet full military operation.

Tempest
A term normally used to describe compromising emanations. These emanations are unintentionally radiated signals that could disclose classified information.

Template
A document that can be used as a pattern for creating other similar documents.

Temporary file
A file created either in memory or on disk, by the operating system or some other program, to be used during a session and then discarded. Also called temp file.

Tensile strength
The greatest stress a substance can withstand along its length without tearing apart.

Tented via
A via with dry film solder mask which completely covers both the via pad and its plated-through hole [PTH]. In the example to the right, the via pad and PTH is yellow while the solder mask is off-set in color.

Tera
A prefix meaning 10^{12}: 1 trillion in the American numbering system, 1 million million in British numbering.

Terabyte
A measurement used for high-capacity data storage. One terabyte equals 240, or 1,099,511,627,776, bytes, although it is commonly interpreted as simply one trillion bytes.

Terena
Trans-European Research and Education Networking Association. Organization that promotes information and telecommunications technologies development in Europe. Formed by the merging of EARN and RARE.

Termid
SNA cluster controller identification. Termid is meaningful only for switched lines. Also called Xid.

Terminal
An electrical connection. That part of the component package used in making an electrical, mechanical, or thermal connection. Examples of terminals are flexible leads, rigid leads, studs, and cases which serve as electrical connections. A number of board mounting terminals are shown in the graphic below. The graphic includes a wire warp terminal, a press-fit, a solder post, a solder cup [which holds solder], and a compression fit connection.

Terminal adapter
Device used to connect ISDN BRI connections to existing interfaces such as EIA/TIA-232. Essentially, an ISDN modem.

Terminal block
An insulating base utilizing one or more terminal connectors. In most cases the Terminal block contains a number of mechanical screw locations so wires may be electrically connected together via the screw connection. Well designed systems use round terminals which the wires are connected to.

Terminal board
Also called a terminal strip. An insulating base or slab equipped with terminals for connecting wiring.

Terminal diagram
A diagram of a switch, relay, terminal board, or other component showing the connections to the equipment.

Terminal emulation

Most communications software packages will permit a personal computer or workstation to communicate with another computer or network as if it were a specific type of hardware terminal.

Terminal impedance

The impedance as measured at the unloaded output terminals of transmission equipment or a line that is otherwise in normal operating condition.

Terminal lug

A device attached to a conductor to permit connection to a terminal.

Terminal server

Communications processor that connects asynchronous devices such as terminals, printers, hosts, and modems to any LAN or WAN that uses TCP/IP, X.25, or LAT protocols. Terminal servers provide the internetwork intelligence that is not available in the connected devices.

Terminal stud

A terminal, generally post-like, having an axial portion of its body designed for projecting through or into a panel for mounting.

Termination

The load connected to a transmission line, circuit, or device. Also refer to the section on Mis-terminating a Transmission Line. An impedance, often resistive, that is connected to a transmission line or piece of equipment as a dummy load, for test purposes.

Terminator

Typically, a resistor placed at the end of a bus to prevent the reflection of signals.

Ternary signal

A signal that can assume, at any given instant, one of three significant conditions, such as power level, phase position, pulse duration, or frequency.

Tertiary winding

A Tertiary winding is a third winding on a transformer, in many cases having the same turns ratio as the second winding. An additional secondary winding on a transformer. An example Transistor Blocking Oscillator using a Tertiary Winding. The word Tertiary means third.

Test case design

A set of techniques for deriving effective test cases.

Text

A string of characters. A text file should contain only characters - as opposed to codes or commands.

Text file

1. In computer usage, any file written in pure character format. Sometimes called a “plain text file.”
2. In a data library situation, “text file” may also refer to a file containing natural language text (e.g., a literary text such as the works of Shakespeare) as opposed to a numeric data file that contains mostly numbers. Such a file could be stored as a character format file but does not necessarily have to be.

TFTP

Trivial File Transfer Protocol. A simplified version of FTP.

TFX

A form factor for a power supply used in a computer case.

TH

Transmission header. SNA header that is appended to the SNA basic information unit (BIU). The TH uses one of a number of available SNA header formats.

The Game

A popular mind game, often referred to on public message boards as a way to irritate other users.

The microsoft network

Microsoft Corporation's feature-rich online service, launched with the introduction of Windows 95 in August 1995.

Thenet

Texas Higher Education Network. Regional network comprising over 60 academic and research institutions in Texas.

Thermal solution

The combination of the heatsink and fan used to cool a processor

Thermally advantaged chassis

An enclosure for computers that can maintain a specific ambient internal temperature with specific Intel® processors

Thesaurus

Provides synonyms (word with similar meanings) and antonyms (words with opposite meanings) for a word or phrase.

Thick ethernet

Also known as 10Base5.

Thinnet

Term used to define a thinner, less expensive version of the cable specified in the IEEE 802.3 10Base2 standard.

Thread

An executable entity consisting of a program counter, a stack, and a set of register values.

Thread of control

A single path of execution through a program, a dynamic model, or some other representation of control flow.

Throughput

Rate of information arriving at, and possibly passing through, a particular point in a network system.

Thumbnail

A small version of an image on a Web page or in a graphics cataloging program, usually containing a hyperlink to a full-size version of the image.

TIA

Telecommunications Industry Association. Organization that develops standards relating to telecommunications technologies. Together, the TIA and the EIA have formalized standards, such as EIA/ TIA-232, for the electrical characteristics of data transmission.

TIC

Token Ring interface coupler. Controller through which an FEP connects to a Token Ring.

Tightly coupled

A term that describes the relationship between two computing processes whose successful completion and individual performance rates are highly inter-dependent.

TIFF

A standard file format commonly used for scanning, storage, and interchange of gray-scale graphic images. TIFF may be the only format available for older programs (such as older versions of MacPaint), but most modern programs are able to save images in a variety of other formats, such as GIF or JPEG.

TIM

Thermal Interface Material is a paste or a pad that is applied between the CPU and heatsink and allows a more complete transfer of heat between the thermal solution and processor.

Time and date

In computing, the timekeeping and datekeeping functions maintained by the computer's operating system, used most visibly as a means of "stamping" files with the date and time of creation or last revision.

Time series

Observations of a variable made over time. Many economic studies such as International Financial Statistics, and Citibase are time series datafiles. Time series, of a sort, can also be constructed from a cross sectional study if the same questions are asked more than once over time.

Timeout

Event that occurs when one network device expects to hear from another network device within a specified period of time, but does not. The resulting time-out usually results in a retransmission of information or the dissolving of the session between the two devices.

Tn3270

Terminal Emulation software that allows a terminal to appear to an IBM host as a 3278 Model 2 terminal.

Tnotify

Time Notify. Specifies how often SMT initiates neighbor notification broadcasts.

Toggle

Using one command or keystroke to change between one mode and its opposite.

Togglekeys

A feature of Windows 95 that sounds high and low beeps when one of the toggle keys (Caps Lock, Num Lock, or Scroll Lock) is turned on or off.

Token

Frame that contains control information. Possession of the token allows a network device to transmit data onto the network.

Token bus

LAN architecture using token passing access over a bus topology. This LAN architecture is the basis for the IEEE 802.4 LAN specification.

Token passing

A MAC method where stations may only transmit when they are in possession of a special bit sequence (token) passed from station to station.

Token ring

A LAN and protocol in which nodes are connected together in a ring and communication is controlled by a special packet called a token that is passed from node to node around the ring. A node can send data only when it receives the token and the token is not in use. Data is sent by attaching it to the token. The receiving node removes the data from the token.

Toner

Also tone generator. In a tone test set, the tone generating device.

Tool

Any device, software program or instrument constructed for the purpose of aiding a human in accomplishing a goal.

Toolbar
A toolbar contain buttons with that can be clicked to provide a shortcut to tasks.

Toolbox
A set of routines stored mostly in the read-only memory of a Macintosh that provide application programmers with the tools needed to support the graphical interface characteristic of the computer. Also called User Interface Toolbox.

Topic
In a conference, a message which is generally written to convey a new idea or a new piece of information, relevant to that conference.

Topology
1. The arrangement of computing devices in a network.
2. A term describing such an arrangement.

Totally-ordered multicast
A multicast of several messages where the messages reach all of the recipients in the same order

Touchpad or trackpad
A pointing device consisting of specialized surface that can translate the motion and position of a user's fingers to a relative position on screen.

TPM
Trusted Platform Module

TPS
Technical Product Specification is a document that specifies the board layout, components, connectors, power, environmental requirements, etc.

Trackball
Input device that controls the position of the cursor on the screen; the unit is mounted near the keyboard, and movement is controlled by moving a ball.

Trailer
The group of bytes that marks the end of a frame and usually contains an error checking mechanism such as a CRC.

Transceiver
1. In Ethernet, an electronic device that transforms signals between a node's internal circuitry and the Ethernet signals and also detects collisions.
2. Any device that can simultaneously transmit and receive.

Transceiver cable
A cable used to connect a host adapter within a computer to a local area network (LAN).

Transfer
To copy or move information from one computer to another.

Transfer rate
The rate at which data is transferred from one device to another, usually expressed in bit per second or in bytes per second.

Transient
A short-lived electrical event.

Transistor
Short for transfer resistor. A solid-state circuit component, usually with three leads, in which a voltage or a current controls the flow of another current. The transistor can serve many functions, including those of amplifier, switch, and oscillator, and is a fundamental component of almost all modern electronics.

Transition
A change of state caused by an event.

Transmission
The activity of sending or conveying information.

Transmit
To send information.

Transparency
Concealment from the user and application programmer of the separation of components in a distributed system.

Transport
Any of the functions carried out by protocols in the Network or Transport Layers.

Transport address
An address for messaging that is composed of a network address and a port number.

Transport layer
The fourth layer of the OSI reference model. It provides transparent, reliable and cost-effective transfer of data.

Transport protocol
The Protocol Layer of the OSI 7-Layer Model that is concerned with management of the data flow between source and destination.

TRAP
In SNMP, a message sent from the Agent to the Console when the Agent detects that condition defined by the network manager has occurred.

Trashers
Someone who searches for information via whatever means needed which would compromise the security of a site. This activity often includes searching trash or refuse disposed in recycle bins of from the facility.

Tree
A way of organizing information with general categories at the top, subcategories below, and narrower subcategories on a further level.

Trim
Allows an operating system to inform a solid-state drive (SSD) of the blocks of data that are no longer in use.

Trojan horse
A maliciously-created computer program or virus that causes significant damage to a system. Trojan Horses are typically given attractive file names and placed on bulletin board systems. Damage usually occurs when the user launches the Trojan horse on his own system. Named after a successful offensive ploy made by the ancient Greek army at the siege of Troy.

Troll
Someone who attempts to gain infamy in chat or on forums by use of but not limited to links to disturbing items, bashing (fighting, put down) with others, copying or mimicking other's real posts into perverted messages.

Troubleshooting
To locate the cause of trouble and removes, fixes or treats it.

Truetype
An outline font technology introduced by Apple Computer, Inc., in 1991 and by Microsoft Corporation in 1992 as a means of including high-grade fonts within the Apple Macintosh and Microsoft Windows operating systems. TrueType is a WYSIWYG font technology, which means that the printed output of TrueType fonts is

identical to what appears on the screen.

Truncate

A method of formatting data by removing characters at the end of the data that do not conform to the format desired.

Trunk

A synonym for bus.

TSO

Time Sharing Option.

Tuple

A set of two related data items.

Twain

Stands for Technology Without An Interesting Name.

Tweak

A minor adjustment.

Tweet

A small message sent by a user of the website Twitter.

Twisted-pair cable

A cable made of two separately insulated strands of wire twisted together. It is used to reduce signal interference introduced by a strong radio source such as a nearby cable. One of the wires in the pair carries the sensitive signal, and the other wire is grounded.

Two-phase locking

A concurrency control technique consisting of two phases: a growing phase, in which new locks are acquired; and a shrinking phase, in which the locks are released.

Two's complement

An algorithm carried out by inverting the bits of a binary number, then adding one to the result.

Type field

A byte or group of bytes that indicates the protocol used by the data that is to follow.

U

UART

Universal Asynchronous Receiver-Transmitter; an integrated-circuit chip designed to facilitate asynchronous (one byte at a time) serial data communication.

UDP

Acronym for User Datagram Protocol. The connectionless protocol within TCP/IP that corresponds to the transport layer in the ISO/OSI model. UDP converts data messages generated by an application into packets to be sent via IP but does not verify that messages have been delivered correctly. Therefore, UDP is more efficient than TCP, so it is used for various purposes, including SNMP; the reliability depends on the application that generates the message.

UDP/IP

UDP/IP is a protocol for computer networks. It is the faster of the two primary Internet Protocols. UDP stands for User Datagram Protocol.

UHCI

Universal Host Controller Interface is an interface that allows USB 1.0 controller to communicate with the operating system.

UI

User Interface is the graphical, textual, and auditory information presented to a user by a computer program and the methods, whether keystrokes, mouse movements, or touchscreen selections that are used by the user to control that program.

Ultra DMA/33

A recently developed data transfer protocol based on direct memory access. Ultra DMA/33 improves ATA/IDE performance, doubles burst transfer rates to 33 megabytes per second, and increases data transfer integrity.

UMA

Acronym for upper memory area. The portion of DOS memory between the first 640K and 1 megabyte.

UMB

Acronym for upper memory block. A block of memory in the UMA (upper memory area) that can be used for device drivers or TSRs. A UMB is allocated and managed by special memory manager programs such as EMM386.EXE.

UML (unified modeling language)

A comprehensive diagrammatic notation for the analysis and design of software.

Unbalanced attenuator

An attenuator which has the resistance elements in one side of the line, with the other line normally used as a ground return.

Unbalanced crystal mixer
A circuit consisting of a section of coaxial transmission line one-half wavelength long that is tuned to the difference (intermediate) frequency between the local oscillator and RF echo signals.

Unbalanced line
A transmission line, such as a coaxial cable, in which the magnitudes of the voltages on the two conductors are not equal with respect to ground.

Unbuffered memory
Memory modules where there is no hardware register between the memory controller and the RAM chips. Unbuffered memory is the opposite of registered or buffered memory, and is usually used in desktop systems.

Uncertainty
An expression of the combined errors in a test measurement process.

UNCL
Universal Naming Convention.

Undelete
1. To restore deleted information, usually the last item deleted.
2. In file storage, to restore a file's storage information so that a deleted file becomes available for access agai Also called unerase.

Underdamped
The attempt at smoothing out oscillations that does not prevent oscillations.

Underflow
In computing, a condition occurring when a machine calculation produces a non-zero result that is smaller than the smallest non-zero quantity that the machines storage unit is capable of storing or representing.

Underground cable
A buried cable used for communication or power distribution; refer to the graphic to the right.

Undernet
An international network of Internet Relay Chat (IRC) servers, created in 1992 as an alternative to the larger and more chaotic main IRC network. For information about connecting to Undernet.

UNDI
Universal Network Device Interface is an API for network cards.

Undo
Allows the user to reverse the last action performed.

Unencased
Having no enclosure. Not residing within an enclosure.

Unfriend
The act of removing someone from a list of friends on social networking profiles of Facebook, MySpace or Bebo. It is also the Oxford dictionary's 2009 Word of the Year.

Unidirectional
In one direction only.

Uniform transmission line
A transmission line that has distributed electrical properties, i.e., resistance, inductance, and capacitance per unit length, that are constant along the line, and in which the voltage-to current ratio does not vary with distance along the line, if the line is terminated in its characteristic impedance.

Unijunction transistor

A three-terminal, semiconductor device with a negative resistance characteristic that is used in switching circuits, oscillators, and wave-shaping circuits. The leads are Anode, Gate, and Cathode.

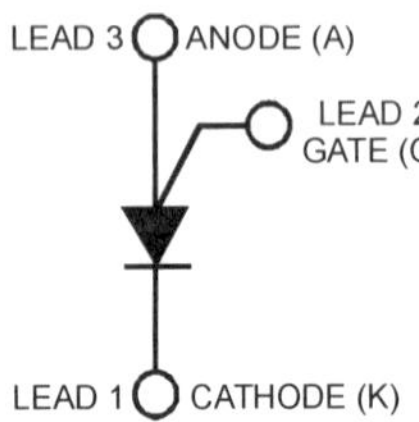

UJT Symbol

Uninterruptible power supply

A device that is inserted between a primary power source, such as a commercial utility, and the primary power input of equipment to be protected, e.g., a computer system, for the purpose of eliminating the effects of transient anomalies or temporary outages.

Union

An association that seeks to defend and improve employee wages and working conditions

Unipolar

An active solid-state device in which only one type of charge carrier, positive or negative, is used to support current flow.

Unipolar signal

A two-state signal where one of the states is represented by voltage or current and the other state is represented by no voltage or current.

Unipolar transistor

A FET. A transistor in which the source to drain current involves only one type of charge carrier.

Unit

An assembly or any combination of parts, subassemblies, and assemblies mounted together. Normally capable of independent operation. A single object or thing.

Unit impulse

A mathematical artifice consisting of an impulse of infinite amplitude and zero width, and having an area of unity.

Unit size

The standards adopted to make comparisons between things of like value (for example, the unit size for conductors is the mil-foot).

Unity coupling

A condition when 100 percent of the magnetic field of an inductor couples energy to another inductor.

Unity gain

A gain of one. An amplifier that appears like a buffer. The graphic shows an Op-Amp configured as a Unity Gain amplifier. Note RL and CL are not required, but are shown to represent the load.

Universal motor

A motor which is designed for operation from either a single phase alternating current or direct current source.

Universal output transformer

A transformer with a large number of taps on both the primary and secondary windings so that a number of different input and output impedances or voltages may be selected or produced.

Universal time constant chart

A chart used to find the time constant of a circuit if the impressed voltage and the values of R and C or R and L are known.

Universal time coordinate

For all practical purposes, the same as Greenwich Mean Time, which is used for the synchronization of computers on the Internet. Also called coordinated universal time format.

Unix

A multiuser, multitasking operating system originally developed by Ken Thompson and Dennis Ritchie at AT&T Bell Laboratories in 1969 for use on minicomputers. UNIX is considered a powerful operating system that, because it is written in the C language, is more portable—that is, less machine-specific—than other operating systems. UNIX is available in several related forms, including AIX (a version of UNIX adapted by IBM to run on RISC-based workstations), A/UX (a graphical version for the Apple Macintosh), and Mach (a rewritten but essentially UNIX-compatible operating system for the NeXT computer).

UNIX shell account

A shell account providing command-line access to a UNIX system.

UNIX shell scripts

Sequences of UNIX commands stored as files that can be run as programs. In MS-DOS, batch (.bat) files provide similar capabilities.

Unix-to-Unix copy (UUCP)

Initially, a program run under the Unix operating system that allowed one Unix system to send files to another UNIX system via dial-up phone lines. Today, the term is more commonly used to describe the large international network that uses the UUCP protocol to pass news and electronic mail.

Unknown host

A response to a request for a connection to a server that indicates that the network is unable to find the specified address.

Unknown recipients

A response to an e-mail message that indicates that the mail server is unable to identify one or more of the destination addresses.

Untapped delay line

A simple fixed circuit delay with out adjustment or programmability.

Untuned line

Another name for the flat or non-resonant line.

UPC

A system of numbering commercial products using bar codes. A UPC consists of 12 digits: a number system character, a five-digit number assigned to the manufacturer, a five-digit product code assigned by the manufacturer, and a modulo 10 check digit.

Update

To change a system or a data file to make it more current.

Up link

The frequency used to transmit a signal from earth to a satellite.

Up-converter

A device that translates frequencies from lower to higher frequencies.

Up-down counter

A counter that can either count up or count down as in a 74192 IC Counter.

Upload

To transfer information from a users system to a remote system. Opposite of download.

Upper frequency cutoff

The highest frequency a circuit can pass.

Upper sideband

All of the sum frequencies above the carrier.

UPS

Acronym for uninterruptible power supply. A device, connected between a computer (or other electronic equipment) and a power source (usually an outlet receptacle), that ensures that electrical flow to the computer is not interrupted because of a blackout and, in most cases, protects the computer against potentially damaging events, such as power surges and brownouts. All UPS units are equipped with a battery and a loss-of-power sensor; if the sensor detects a loss of power, it switches over to the battery so that the user has time to save his or her work and shut off the computer.

Upstream frequency

The frequency used to transmit data from the CM to the CMTS. Normally in the 5-42 MHz range for US systems and 5-65 MHz for European systems.

URL

A uniform resource locator is basically an address for a file that can be given to a browser. It starts with a protocol type (such as http, ftp, or gopher) and is followed by a colon, machine name, and file name in UNIX style. Optionally an octothorpe character "#" and arguments will follow the file name; this can be used to further define position within a page and perform a few other tricks. Similar to but less general than a URI.

Usb

An industry standard for connecting different compatible peripheral devices across multiple platforms. Devices include printers, digital cameras, scanners, game pads, joysticks, keyboards and mice, and storage devices. USB peripherals offer the use of plug-and-play convenience by eliminating the need to turn off or restart the computer when attaching a new peripheral. Users can connect USB peripherals whenever they need them. For example, a user producing a newsletter could easily swap a digital camera for a scanner-without any downtime. Small, simple, inexpensive, and easy to attach, USB supports simultaneous connection of up to 127 devices by attaching peripherals through interconnected external hubs.

USB flash drive

A flash memory data storage device integrated with a USB (Universal Serial Bus) 1.1, 2.0, or 3.0 interface. USB flash drives are typically removable and rewritable, and much smaller than a floppy disc.

USB hub

A multiple-socket USB connecter that allows several USB-compatible devices to be connected to a computer.

Useful life

The second phase of the lifetime of a population of a particular component when only random failures occur.

Usenet

The network of UNIX users, generally perceived as informal and made up of loosely coupled nodes that exchange mail and messages. Started by Duke University and UNC-Chapel Hill. An information cooperative linking around 16,000 computer sites and about 1 million people. Usenet provides a series of "news groups" analogous to on-line conferences.

User

A person who uses a computer system to accomplish a non-computing goal, as compared to a programmer or network manager.

User area

The area where users work and where the computer systems are located.

User interface

The collection of display symbols and other sensory stimuli made by a computer that present information to a human and the collection of physical action that a human can take to present data to a computer.

User package

A library of conventional procedures that can be used in application programs.

User-friendly

A system or program that relatively untrained users can interact with easily.

Userid

A code that uniquely identifies a user and then provides access privileges to a computer system.

Username

Account name or user ID.

Usrt

Acronym for universal synchronous receiver-transmitter. A module, usually composed of a single integrated circuit, that contains both the receiving and transmitting circuits required for synchronous serial communication.

Utility

A specialized program that performs a frequently required everyday task such as sorting, report program generation, or file updating.

Utopia bus

A Bus Standard used as the Test and Operations Physical Interface for ATM standard.

UTP

Acronym for unshielded twisted pair. A cable containing one or more twisted pairs of wires without additional shielding. UTP is more flexible and takes up less space than shielded twisted-pair (STP) cable but has less bandwidth.

UTP ethernet

1) A synonym for 10BaseT.
2) Any of a number of Ethernet technologies in use before the adoption of the 10BaseT Standard that provided a 10 MBPS network system using CSMA/CD.

UUCP

A set of software programs that facilitate transmission of information between UNIX systems using serial data connections, primarily the public switched telephone network.

UV

Ultra-Violet light.

UV erasable

A term which describes how EPROMs or other memory devices might be erased or reset.

UXGA

Ultra Extended Graphics Array. A video resolution of 1600 x 1200 pixels.

V

Vacuum circuit breaker

A vacuum circuit breaker utilizes a vacuum to extinguish arcing when the circuit breaker is opened and to act as a dielectric to insulate the contacts after the arc is interrupted.

Vacuum evaporation

A process of producing thin film components.

Vacuum tube

An electron tube evacuated such that its electrical characteristics are essentially unaffected by the presence of residual gas.

Validation rule

A check that Microsoft Access performs to determine whether entered data meets certain criteria.

Validation text

Text that is displayed when a validation rule is violated.

Vane attenuator

A waveguide component used to provide attenuation.

Vaneaxial fan

A non-positive displacement mechanical device with guide vanes and having an axial fan impeller inclosed within a tubular housing. It is designed primarily for duct installation to move air or gas axially over a wide range of volumes and pressures.

Vaporware

A computer program that has been publicly announced but is not shipping.

Var

Abbreviation for Volt-Amperes Reactive.

Var hour

The reactive power, Volt-Ampere used within an hour; as measured by a VAR Hour meter.

Varactor

A PN junction semiconductor, designed for microwave frequencies, in which the capacitance varies with the applied voltage. 'Varicap' or 'VVC', Voltage [dependent] variable capacitor [varies in picofarads]. A diode operated in reverse bias so that the diode behaves like a voltage dependent diode.

Varactor Diode

Varactor fm modulator

An FM modulator that uses a voltage-variable capacitor.

Variable

1) A situation or aspect that cannot be expressed explicitly because it may have one of several values.
2) In troubleshooting, an aspect of a problem that makes it differ from a normal situation.
3) In a mathematical expression, a symbol that represents a number.

Variable attenuator

An attenuator for reducing the strength of an ac signal either continuously or in steps, without causing signal distortion.

Variable capacitor

An adjustable Capacitor. In this example the dielectric is air, other dielectrics are possible and additional package styles.

Variable resistor

A wire-wound or composition resistor, the value of which may be changed over a designed range.

Variable-mu-tube

Same term as Remote-Cutoff Tube.

Variac

An autotransformer that contains a toroidal winding and a rotating carbon brush so that the output voltage is continuously adjustable from zero to line voltage. A type of transformer used to manually control output voltage.

Varistor

[Variable Resistor] A resistor that changes value with applied voltage. A varistor may also be called a VDR [Voltage Dependent Resistor]. Varistors will have a negative voltage coefficient.

Varmeter

An item which measures the reactive volt-ampere characteristics of an electrical circuit into which it is inserted.

Varnished cambric

Cotton cloth coated with insulation varnish. An insulation used on high-voltage conductors.

Vax

The VAX is a computer platform developed by Digital. Its plural is VAXe VAXen are large expensive machines that were once quite popular in large businesses; today modern UNIX workstations have all the capability of VAXen but take up much less space. Their OS is called VMS.

VBIOS

Video BIOS.

VCOMM

The communications device driver in Windows 95 that provides the interface between Windows-based applications and drivers on one side, and port drivers and modems on the other.

VD

Voltage DMOS. In a power supply circuit, voltage supplied by a MOS circuit, measured next to the MOS device.

VDD

In a power supply circuit supplied to a MOS circuit, the voltage supplied to a MOS device but referenced next to the power supply and not next to the DMOS device.

VDU

Visual Display Unit or screen or monitor.

Vector timestamp

A replica manager's array of update event counts.

Verified by Intel®

A program between Intel, ODMs, and notebook component suppliers to enhance opportunities for customizable build-to-order notebook solutions.

Veronica

Stands for Very Easy Rodent Oriented Net-wide Index to Computerized Archives. A database of menu names from a large number of Gopher servers. A quick and easy way to search Gopher resources for information by keyword.

Version

A variant of some artifact; later versions of an artifact typically expand on earlier versions.

VESA

Having VL bus expansion slots. Also called VLB.

VESA/EISA

Having both EISA and VL bus expansion slots.

VESA/ISA

Having both ISA and VL bus expansion slots.

VGA

A Video Graphics Array (VGA) connector is a three-row 15-pin DE-15 connector. The 15-pin VGA connector is found on many video cards, computer monitors, and some high definition television sets. On laptop computers or other small devices, a mini-VGA port is sometimes used in place of the full-sized VGA connector.

Video BIOS

The BIOS for the graphics hardware

Video clip

A file that contains a short video item, usually an excerpt from a longer recording.

Video compression

Reduction of the size of files containing video images stored in digital form. If no compression were done, 24-bit color video at 640 × 480 pixels would occupy almost one megabyte per frame, or over a gigabyte per minute. Video compression can, however, be lossy without affecting the perceived quality of the image.

Video driver

Software that provides the interface between the video adapter hardware and other programs, including the operating system. The user can access the video driver to specify the resolution and color-bit depth of images on the monitor during the setup process.

Video memory

Memory from which a display image is created, located in the video adapter or video subsystem. If both the video processor and the central processing unit (CPU) have access to video memory, images are produced by the

CPU's modification of video memory. Video circuitry normally has priority over the processor when both attempt to read or write to a video memory location, so updating video memory is often slower than accessing main memory.

Video RAM

A special type of dynamic RAM (DRAM) used in high-speed video applications. Video RAM uses separate pins for the processor and the video circuitry, providing the video circuitry with a "back door" to the video RAM. The video circuitry can access the video RAM serially (bit by bit), which is more appropriate for transferring pixels to the screen than is the parallel access provided by conventional DRAM.

Video teleconferencing

A remote "face-to-face chat," when two or more people using a webcam and an Internet telephone connection chat online. The webcam enables both live voice and video.

Vines

A Network Operating System developed by Banyan.

Virtual

Pertaining to a device or facility that does not physically exist, yet behaves as if it does. For example, a system with 4 megabytes of virtual memory may have only one megabyte of physical memory plus additional (slower and cheaper) auxiliary memory. Yet programs written as if 4 megabytes of physical memory were available will run correctly.

Virtual machine

Software that mimics the performance of a hardware device, such as a program that allows applications written for an Intel processor to be run on a Motorola chip.

Virtual memory

Virtual Memory is the unused memory on the hard disk used when certain applications require more RAM than is available on the machine.

Virtual partition

An abstraction of a real partition that contains a set of replica managers.

Virtual printer

A feature in many operating systems that allows printer output to be saved to a file until a printer becomes available.

Virtual terminal

A program that makes a general purpose computer behave like a terminal.

Virus

A virus is a program that will seek to duplicate itself in memory and on disks, but in a subtle way that will not immediately be noticed. A computer on the same network as an infected computer or that uses an infected disk (even a floppy) or that downloads and runs an infected program can itself become infected. A virus can only spread to computers of the same platform. For example, on a network consisting of a WinTel box, a Mac, and a Linux box, if one machine acquires a virus the other two will probably still be safe.

Vision

A future-oriented statement of where you want to be, of what you want things to be like.

Vision statement

A brief statement on what the organisation sees and wishes for the future.

Visual programming

A method of programming using a programming environment or language in which basic program components can be selected through menu choices, buttons, icons, and other predetermined methods.

Vital

Virtually Integrated Technical Architecture Lifecycle. A conceptual framework, designed by Apple, for designing, building and maintaining enterprise information systems.

VM

Virtual Machine. An operating system for IBM mainframes within which multiple other operating systems can be processing, each with its own applications.

VMS

Virtual Memory System. An operating system for the VAX and Alpha computers of Digital Equipment Corporation.

Voice grade

A classification of communication wiring indicating that the wiring is unsuitable for network data transfer.

Voicemail

A type of answering machine where messages can be recorded.

VOIP

VoIP means "Voice over IP" and it is quite simply a way of utilizing the Internet (or even in some cases intranets) for telephone conversations. The primary motivations for doing so are cost and convenience as VoIP is significantly less expensive than typical telephone long distance packages, plus one high speed Internet connection can serve for multiple phone lines.

Volatile memory

A type of memory that requires power to maintain the stored information. When power is off or interrupted, the stored memory is lost.

Volt

The standard unit of measure for a difference in electric potential.

Volume

A physical unit of a storage medium, such as tape reel or disk pack, that is capable of having data recorded on it and subsequently read. Also refers to a contiguous collection of cylinders or blocks on a disk that are treated as a separate unit.

VRAM

Video RAM is a type of memory that is used to store the frame buffer for some graphics cards. VRAM is also called video memory or graphics memory.

VRML

Stands for Virtual Reality Modeling Language. It's a form of application that gives a 3-D effect to pictures sometimes allowing you to "move" through them.

VSAM

Virtual Storage Access Method. the Primary Mechanism for accessing data on IBM mainframes.

VTAM

Virtual Terminal Access Method. the primary communication control software for SNA.

VTP

Virtual terminal Protocol. OSI's remote terminal protocol.

Wait state

A state in a state machine which holds its value, or doesn't allow the next state to occur until another process or signal is detected. A clock cycle in a clocked process that goes unused as a microprocessor waits for an event to occur.

Wall wart

An AC to DC power adapter which plugs into an AC outlet and contains the power supply within the plug. .

WAN

Wide Area Network. A network that is created between and among devices separated by large distances (typically in excess of 50 miles).

Warm boot

The restarting of a running computer without first turning off the power. Also called soft boot, warm start.

Watchdog Timer

A timer used by a cpu that will cause the cpu to reset if the cpu does not service [signal] the watchdog time at certain intervals. If the WatchDog Timer does not receive a signal within a certain length of time it will cause the processor to reset itself.

Watermark

An image that appears on the background of a page to decorate or identify the page. When used on a Web page, the image does not scroll as the page scrolls. Not all Web browsers support watermarks.

Watertight

An enclosure which prevents leakage when water strikes or covers the enclosure. No ventilation or other openings are permitted in the enclosure.

Watt

The unit of electrical power that is the product of voltage and current. The unit of electric power, or amount of work (J), done in a unit of time. One ampere of current flowing at a potential of one volt produces one watt of power.

Wattage rating

A rating expressing the maximum power that a device can safely handle.

Watt-hour

A practical unit of electrical energy equal to one watt of power for one hour.

Watt-hour meter

A meter used to measure electrical energy.

Wattmeter

A meter used to measure electrical power. An instrument which measures electrical power and is calibrated in watts or any multiple and/or sub-multiple.

Wav

A sound format (pronounced "wave") used to reproduce sounds on a computer.

Wave

The phenomena that occurs when a physical medium is host to a measurable condition that varies in intensity, frequency or velocity with time.

Wave motion

A recurring disturbance advancing through space with or without the use of a physical medium.

Wave train

A continuous series of waves with the same amplitude and wavelength.

Wave winding

An armature winding in which the two ends of each coil are connected to commutator segments separated by the distance between poles.

Waveform

The shape of the wave obtained when instantaneous values of an ac quantity are plotted against time in rectangular coordinates.

Waveform analysis

Observation displays of voltage and current variations with respect to time or by harmonic analysis of complex signals.

Wavefront

A small section of an expanding sphere of electromagnetic radiation that is perpendicular to the direction of travel of the energy.

Waveguide

A rectangular, circular, or elliptical metal pipe designed to transport electromagnetic waves through its interior. A material medium that confines and guides a propagating electromagnetic wave.

Waveguide duplexer

TR and atr tubes housed in a resonant cavity attached to a waveguide system.

Waveguide mode of operation

Any particular field configuration in a waveguide that satisfies the boundary conditions. Usually divided into two broad types: the transverse electric (TE) and the transverse magnetic (TM) modes.

Waveguide post

A rod of conductive material used as impedance changing devices in waveguides.

Waveguide screw

A screw that projects into a waveguide for the purpose of changing the impedance.

Wavelength

The distance, usually expressed in meters, traveled by a wave during the time interval of one complete cycle. Wavelength is equal to the velocity divided by the frequency. The distance between points of corresponding phase of two consecutive cycles of a wave.

Wavemeters

Calibrated resonant circuits that are used to measure frequency. An instrument for measuring the wavelength of an RF wave.

WDDM

Windows* Display Driver Model is a display driver architecture* supported in Microsoft Windows Vista*

Web

A set of interlinked documents in a hypertext system. The user enters the web through a home page.

Web development

The design and coding of World Wide Web pages.

Web directory

A list of Web sites, giving the URL and a description of each.

Web engineering

The application of software engineering principles, concepts, and methods (or adaptations of them) to the development of Web-based applications or systems.

Web index

A Web site intended to enable a user to locate other resources on the Web. The Web index may include a search facility or may merely contain individual hyperlinks to the resources indexed.

Web page

A document on the World Wide Web. A Web page consists of an HTML file, with associated files for graphics and scripts, in a particular directory on a particular machine (and thus identifiable by an URL). Usually a Web page contains links to other Web pages.

Web TV

A system for accessing the World Wide Web and displaying Web pages on a television screen using a set-top box.

Webcam

A webcam is a video camera that feeds its images in real time to a computer or computer network, often via USB, Ethernet, or WI-Fi.

Well behaved

A condition that exhibits expected properties.

WEP

Wired Equivalent Privacy is an optional IEEE 802.11 feature used to provide data security that is equivalent to that of a typical wired LAN. When WEP is enabled, all stations (clients and access points) are required to have the same WEP key. Network access is denied to anyone who does not have the correct key.

White papers

These are documents created to help guide you in the use of a particular piece of hardware or software. Usually some kind of extra or advanced help that is provided that goes beyond the normal manual or set of instructions for that product or item. White Papers can provide special or advanced instructions on special features or setup methods.

Whiteboard

Software that allows multiple users across a network to work together on a document that is simultaneously displayed on all the users' screens as though they are gathered around a physical whiteboard.

WHOIS

The name of the nickname database that contains full name, postal address, telephone number, and network mailbox for registered users. Also the name of the local command to access this database, and the name of the protocol used by this command (RFC-954) that is now an elective draft standard.

WHQL

Windows* Hardware Quality Labs is a testing process* that involves running a set of tests on hardware or software and then submitting the results to Microsoft* for review

Wide area network

A network of computers that are separated by large distances.

Wi-fi

Wireless Fidelity - Otherwise known as Wireless Networking, commonly using the 802.11b protocol. Hardware that displays the WiFi logo claims 802.11b compliance should interconnect seamlessly.

Wildcard character

A keyboard character that can be used to represent one or many characters. The asterisk (*), for example, typically represents one or more characters and the question mark (?) typically represents a single character. Wildcard characters are often used in operating systems as a means of specifying more than one file by name.

Wimax

WiMAX, the Worldwide Interoperability for Microwave Access, is a telecommunications technology aimed at providing wireless data over long distances in a variety of ways, from point-to-point links to full mobile cellular type access.

Win32

The application programming interface in Windows 95 and Windows NT that enables applications to use the 32-bit instructions available on 80386 and higher processors. Although Windows 95 and Windows NT support 16-bit 80x86 instructions as well, Win32 offers greatly improved performance.

Win

Similar to "leet", "win" expresses an ability to perform an otherwise impossible act through pure luck or practice, or an object or statement that constitutes an amusing or amazing element.

Window

A rectangular area on a display screen in which part of an image or file is displayed. The window can be any size up to that of the screen and more than one window can be displayed at once.

Windows 2000

Windows 2000 is the intended replacement for Windows NT but has so far received only lukewarm support. Being based on Windows NT, it inherits some of its driver support problems. Originally it was also supposed to replace Windows '98, but Windows ME has since been made to do that instead, and the merger between Windows NT and Windows '98 has been postponed until Windows XP.

Windows 3.1

Windows 3.1 is the probably currently the fourth most popular variant of MS-Windows. It is lighter weight than either Windows '95 or Windows NT (but not lighter weight than GEOS) but less capable than the other two. It is made to run on top of MS-DOS and will not do much of anything if MS-DOS is not on the system. It is thus not strictly an OS per se, but nor is it a true window manager, either; rather the combination of MS-DOS and Windows 3.1 result in a full OS with GUI. Its driver support is good, but its game selection is limited. Windows 3.1 runs only on x86 based machines. It has some severe Y2K issues that may or may not be fixed.

Windows 7

Windows 7 is the latest release of Microsoft Windows, a series of operating systems produced by Microsoft for use on personal computers, including home and business desktops, laptops, netbooks, tablet PCs, and media center PCs.[5] Windows 7 was released to manufacturing on July 22, 2009, and reached general retail availability on October 22, 2009, less than three years after the release of its predecessor, Windows Vista. Windows 7's server counterpart, Windows Server 2008 R2, was released at the same time.

Windows explorer

The file manager used where you can locate all folders, files and drives available.

Windows vista

Windows Vista is an operating system released in several variations developed by Microsoft for use on personal computers, including home and business desktops, laptops, tablet PCs, and media center PCs. Prior to its announcement on July 22, 2005, Windows Vista was known by its codename "Longhorn."[Development was completed on November 8, 2006; over the following three months it was released in stages to computer hardware and software manufacturers, business customers, and retail channels. On January 30, 2007, it was released worldwide, and was made available for purchase and download from Microsoft's website. The release of Windows Vista came more than five years after the introduction of its predecessor, Windows XP, the longest time span between successive releases of Microsoft Windows desktop operating systems. It was succeeded by Windows 7, which was released to manufacturing on July 22, 2009, and for the general public on October 22, 2009.

Windows XP

Windows XP is an operating system that was produced by Microsoft for use on personal computers, including home and business desktops, laptops, and media centers. It was first released to computer manufacturers on August 24, 2001, and is the most popular version of Windows, based on installed user base. The name "XP" is short for "eXPerience, as it says on the Installation CD.

Wireless

A System that provides communication without the use of wires.

Wireless client

The software that controls a wireless adapter.

Wiring closet

In wiring for telephone or data systems, any location from which the communication wires emanate, usually enclosed.

WLAN

A local area network (LAN) that sends and receives data via radio, infrared optical signaling, or some other technology that does not require a physical connection between individual nodes and the hub. Wireless LANs are often used in office or factory settings where a user must carry a portable computer from place to place.

Word
16 bits; two bytes.

Word processor
A program designed to help with the production of textual documents, like letters and memos. Heavier duty work can be done with a desktop publisher. Some common word processors include MS-Word, OpenOffice Write, WordPerfect, AbiWord, AppleWorks Write, and GeoWrite.

Word wrap
An editor feature that causes a word that will not fit on a line to be moved in its entirety to the next line rather than be split at the right margin.

Work space
Disk space made available to the system to provide temporary storage space for files too large to fit within a users permanent disk storage quota or for files not needed beyond a single run of a program or set of programs.

Workbook
A spreadsheet file containing one or more worksheets.

Workcover
The managing body for NSW Workplace Health and Safety

Worker's compensation
A payment made to any person who is injured or suffers a work-related illness to compensate for the injury or illness.

Workgroup
A group of networked computer users who frequently communicate with each other and share common devices.

Worksheet
A sheet within a spreadsheet workbook; used for displaying rows and columns of figures and labels

Worksheet tab
The tab at the base of a worksheet, default tab names in Excel are Sheet1, Sheet2 etc.

Workstation
A general purpose computer that is small enough and inexpensive enough to reside at a persons work area for his or her exclusive use. It includes microcomputers such as Macintosh, and PCs running DOS, as well as high-performance desktop and deskside computers.

Workstation-server model
a simple architectural model in which processor performance and memory capacity determine the largest task that a user can perform.

WORM
Acronym for "write once, read many." A type of optical disc that can be read and reread but cannot be altered after it has been recorded. WORMs are high-capacity storage devices. Because they cannot be erased and rerecorded, they are suited to storing archives and other large bodies of unchanging information.

WPA
Wi-Fi Protected Access is an optional IEEE 802.11 feature used to provide data security that is equivalent to that of a typical wired LAN. It provides stronger security than WEP through enhanced encryption and user authentication.

Write

To record data in a storage device, a data medium, or an output display. To save information, especially files, to a disk, to replace old data with new and permit later access from within a software package; the complement of read.

WWW

World Wide Web. A wide-area hypermedia information retrieval technology that interconnects information around the world. It allows you to travel through the information by clicking on hyperlinks that can point to any document anywhere on the Internet. Originated at CERN and collaborated upon by a large, informal, and international design and development team, WWW allows links inside and between documents, plus pointers to FTP sites, news, telnet sessions, gopher sites, and WAIS databases.

X window system

A standard for controlling the display on a bitmapped terminal. X-windows normally uses a network connection, and unlike the typical terminal connection, multiple applications possibly on different computers can use the display simultaneously in different windows.

X windows

A way of operating remote systems. The window allows the user to control and application remotely and view the application's output.

X.25

A packet switching network.

X.400

An OSI standard for a group of store and forward message handling services.

X.500

Directory Services for OSI provides consistent data storage, retrieval and management for information about all network objects.

X11

The specifications for X Windows.

X86

An instruction set for one of the most common CPU architectures.

X-axis

The horizontal axis of a chart or graph. The spin axis of the gyro.

X-band

A radio frequency band from 8000MHz to 12,000MHz. Some text use 5.2 to 10.9GHz.

X_c

Symbol Capacitive reactance. The equation is $Xc = 1/[2 \times pi \times f \times C]$. Also refer to the section just covering Capacitor Definitions.

X-cut crystal

A type of crystal cut that leaves the major surface perpendicular to the electrical axis, as shown in the diagram to the right.

XD bit

Execute Disable Bit

XD technology

The Execute Disable Bit capability of Intel processors that is designed to increase overall system security.

Xdr

External Data Representation. The presentation layer protocol used by NFS.

Xenon arc lamp

A high intensity light that excites xenon gas between two electrodes.

X_l

Symbol inductive reactance. The equation is X_L = [2 x pi x f x L].

Xlr connector

A shielded 3-conductor microphone plug and audio connector. .

XMP

Intel® Extreme Memory Profile is a JEDEC SPD extension for DDR3 SDRAM DIMMs to encode performance memory timings.

XNOR

Short for Exclusive-NOR, refer to that term. A logic function and a logic gate [74266 XNOR gate]. An XOR function with an inverter after the gate.

XOFF

An abbreviation for the ASCII transmission-control character meaning; Transmitter off.

XON

An abbreviation for the ASCII transmission-control character meaning; Transmitter on.

XOR

Short for Exclusive-OR. A logic function and a logic gate.

XPDM

Windows XP* Display Driver Model is a display driver architecture supported in Microsoft Windows 2000 and Microsoft Windows* XP (also referred to as XDDM).

X-ray emission

Penetrating radiation similar to light, but with a shorter wavelength, that can penetrate human tissue. .

X-term

An X-windows client that provides a window for terminal emulation.

Yagi antenna

A combination of dipoles to increase the gain. A directional antenna. .

Y-amplifier

The vertical amplifier of an oscilloscope.

Yaw

Side to side motion in a vehicle. The rotation of an object in a plane around a vertical axis.

Y-axis

In a gyro, an axis through the center of gravity and perpendicular to the spin axis. The vertical axis on a chart.

Y-cable

A cable with three ends, with one common end. So that one interface splits in a 'Y' to two different cable ends. A Y-cable could have any type of termination, but a common example is a 3.5mm stereo connector to two RCA connectors [Red, White], or a male 3.5mm connector to two female 3.5mm connectors. A cable splitter, although this usually refers to a component and not a cable.

Y-cut

The manner in which a usable crystal is cut from a quartz crystal.

Yig

Yttrium-Iron-Garnet. A a ferrimagnetic material, or compound.

Yoke

A set of coils placed over the neck of a Cathode Ray Tube to move the electron beam position as it points at the face of the CRT. A ferromagnet placed between two magnetic cores to complete a magnetic field.

Youtuber

A person who produces video content for the video-sharing site Youtube.

Z

Zener effect

A reverse breakdown effect in diodes in which breakdown occurs at reverse voltages below 5 volts. The presence of a high energy field at the junction of a semiconductor produces the breakdown.

Zener voltage

The break-down voltage of a zener diode.

Zero adjustment

The process of Nulling out a circuit or system. Setting a circuit to a zero output condition.

Zero crossing detector

A circuit that detects when an input signal crosses zero volts. A comparator with one input tied to ground. An operational amplifier can also be configured into a Zero Crossing Detector.

Zero insertion force socket

A ZIF socket requires no force to install an IC into the socket. A spring actuated level is used to clamp the device in place once it has been installed. ZIF sockets are used with processors mounted on personal computer mother boards and with EPROM programming devices so the components can be easily inserted and removed with out soldiering.

Zero potential

Earth ground, earth potential.

Zero-bit Insertion

A transmission process when additional zeros are inserted after a fixed number of ones in a transmission sequence to ensure that data will not be misinterpreted as controlling information.

Zero-buffer ddr

A type of Double-Data-Rate [DDR] memory.

Zerofill

To fill unused storage locations with the representation of the character denoting 0.

Zeroing

The process of adjusting a synchro or some other component to its electrical zero position.

Zeroize

To fill a storage location with zeros.

Zig zag package

A component package style that has parallel, alternating terminals which are off-set from one another.

ZIP

ZIP is an acronym for Zone Information Protocol. ZIP application enables transfer of data using compression of files.

Zip drive

A floppy drive system developed by Iomega which had a much larger storage capacity than normal floppy disk drives. This style drive was widely used, along with floppy drives, before the advent of larger memory USB thumb drives.

Zip-cord

A two-fiber cable consisting essentially of two single-fiber cables having their jackets conjoined by a strip of jacket material, so that they may be easily furcated [divided] by slitting or tearing the two jackets apart, permitting the installation of optical connectors.

Zone

In an AppleTalk internet, a reference to a logical group of devices and services.

CAREER & BUSINESS MANAGEMENT

CONCISE DICTIONARIES

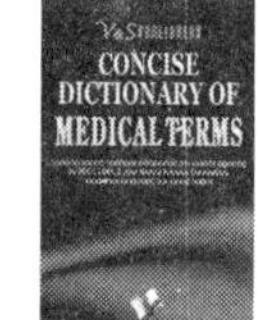

All books available at www.vspublishers.com